ASIANS ON DEMAND

ASIANS ON DEMAND

MEDIATING RACE IN VIDEO ART AND ACTIVISM

Feng-Mei Heberer

University of Minnesota Press
Minneapolis
London

This publication has been supported by a book subvention grant from the NYU Center for the Humanities.

Portions of chapter 1 were previously published in a different form in "The Asianization of Heimat: Ming Wong's Asian German Video Works," in *Asian Video Cultures,* ed. Joshua Neves and Bhaskar Sarkar, 198–213 (Durham, N.C.: Duke University Press, 2017), copyright 2017 Duke University Press, all rights reserved, reprint by permission of the publisher, www.dukeupress.edu. Portions of chapter 1 were previously published in a different form in "How Does It Feel to Be Foreign? Negotiating German Belonging and Transnational Asianness in Experimental Video," in *The Autobiographical Turn in Germanophone Documentary and Experimental Film,* ed. Robin Curtis and Angelica Fenner, 111–36 (Rochester, N.Y.: Camden House, 2014). A different version of chapter 4 was previously published as "Sentimental Activism as Queer-Feminist Documentary Practice; or, How to Make Love in a Room Full of People," *Camera Obscura* 34, no. 2 (2019): 41–69; copyright 2019 *Camera Obscura,* all rights reserved, reprint by permission of the publisher, www.dukeupress.edu.

Copyright 2023 by the Regents of the University of Minnesota

All rights reserved. No part of this publication may be reproduced, stored in a retrieval system, or transmitted, in any form or by any means, electronic, mechanical, photocopying, recording, or otherwise, without the prior written permission of the publisher.

Published by the University of Minnesota Press
111 Third Avenue South, Suite 290
Minneapolis, MN 55401-2520
http://www.upress.umn.edu

ISBN 978-1-5179-1480-6 (hc)
ISBN 978-1-5179-1481-3 (pb)

Library of Congress record available at https://lccn.loc.gov/2023024440.

The University of Minnesota is an equal-opportunity educator and employer.

Contents

Introduction: Asians on Demand and the Refusal to Represent		1
1	Improper *Asiatische Deutsche*: The Video Art of Ming Wong and Hito Steyerl	21
2	Mental Health and Live Fictions: Kristina Wong and *Wong Flew Over the Cuckoo's Nest*	47
3	Stateless Cinema and the Undocument: Miko Revereza, *Distancing*, and *No Data Plan*	69
4	Migrant Erotics: TIWA's *Lesbian Factory* and *Rainbow Popcorn*	99
5	*Me llamo Peng*: Self-Care with a Camcorder	125
Acknowledgments		137
Notes		143
Index		181

Introduction

Asians on Demand and the Refusal to Represent

In the thirty-five-second video *Strike II* (2012), Berlin-based artist Hito Steyerl and her elementary-school-age daughter stand together in the interior of a home.[1] They stare at us as they face the camera. For the entirety of the short video, the frame is out of focus. To the left hangs a painting of a cherry blossom tree, obscured by a lighted, bubbling fish tank. The artist's hand is resting on her daughter's shoulder, "as if preparing for a mother-daughter portrait."[2] Yet this domestic family scenario soon becomes disturbingly off-kilter. Despite its HDV (high-definition video) format, it is as if the video's high-pitched, lo-fi hammering and its grainy, pixelated images are trying to warn us of some imminent technical malfunction or digital crash. Are those hammers or mallets that the mother and daughter are waving? Steyerl appears a bit risqué in her unkempt mane of black hair and tight snake-print dress (her daughter is wearing all pink). Within seconds, the Steyerls swiftly approach the camera and begin to bash it repeatedly with their weapons. The audio cuts out. Silent fuzzy halos of flashing light abruptly end in an apocalyptic blur. "Strike. Refusal to represent," says the accompanying video description.[3]

Asians on Demand: Mediating Race in Video Art and Activism explores an archive of art and activist videos by critically queer, feminist, and rebelliously irreverent Asian filmmakers respectively based in Germany, Taiwan, the United States, and Spain, all economically advanced democracies of the Global North. (Miko Revereza is currently based in Mexico and the Philippines, and filmed the works featured in chapter 3 while living as an undocumented person in the United States.) Inspired by Eve Oishi's work on queer and trans challenges to the status quo and her embrace of candid discussions about sex and desire, this book is dedicated to activist filmmakers who exploit video to challenge oppressive institutional structures of racism, classism, sexism, and homophobia.[4] This book's archive features films that frustrate mainstream institutional demands—by government entities, developed and developing markets, public funding institutions, and even peers and minority advocates—for ethnic Asians to appear on screen in ways that are accessibly and uncomplicatedly available for public education and consumption.

Figure 1. Steyerl and daughter appear to pose for the camera; screenshot from *Strike II*.

Figure 2. The camera records its own destruction; screenshot from *Strike II*.

Invoking the speedy delivery and worldwide currency of today's popular video streaming services, the notion of being *on demand* speaks to an increasingly global culture industry that tends to assign value to minority visibilities insofar as they serve neoliberal wealth and narratives of exceptional minority individualism. The videos featured in this book variously challenge conventional on-screen visibilities of Asian people as poster children of international corporate multiculturalism and institutional diversity. The idea of on-demandness contributes to discussions about the limits of Asianness as a productive visual category on behalf of the neoliberal market, and on behalf of minority advocates and underrepresented groups committed to raising public awareness about immigrant cultures and foreign workers in ways that encourage their political inclusion and civic participation.

Asians on Demand

The concerted promotion of Asians as a group and racial category in the postwar neoliberal era, notes Grace Kyungwon Hong, is paradigmatic of the increasing management of racial and cultural diversity by state and market authorities.[5] Whether within or beyond the United States, such ethnic affirmations leave much to be desired. Scholars like Aihwa Ong, Helen Heran Jun, Homay King, and Colleen Lye have noted how Asians are conventionally understood in ways that promote global stereotypes of the flexibility of Asian labor, for example, or of the special ability of Asian immigrants to assimilate, to succeed professionally, or to get by without drawing much from public resources. Asian people have ostensibly been able to maintain a productive relationship with "capitalist modernity"[6] throughout various nations of the Global North. Examining Asian on-demandness through video allows us to critique neoliberal demands for racial and ethnic visibility that shape a state or territory's law and policy with respect to different minority and immigrant groups. Video's mediating operations are fertile for studying demands for race and Asian representation, especially if we see them as self-invisibilizing media processes that depend upon the inconspicuous web of devices and processes that feature a moving image's "natural" on-screen plenitude—in other words, that relay a sense of seamless availability as if there were no mediators. A seamless visible stream of Asian faces or narratives through increasingly numerous Asian

4 | INTRODUCTION

(diasporic) shows and films and its apparent affirmation of minority inclusion may seem empowering at first. But these "met" demands, such as in the form of more television sitcoms, often presume Asians as easily available to appear on screen in the service of hegemonic market demands, and that is also to remain invisible (or immediately disappear) whenever they appear to disturb, question, or disappoint these demands, or in any other way make them unexpectedly tangible to viewers. The expectation to be readily available for show ultimately operates on a demand for superfluousness: something is always already programmed to go.

The logic of Asians on Demand renders Asian people, and sometimes even Asian states (as in the case of Taiwan), into ready-made exemplars: a seamlessly accessible representational function, an on-demand figure set up to serve. An exemplar, as its Latin etymology reminds us, designates both an image (*exemplum*) and that which is removed (*eximere*), evoking a relational model of virtue and punishment.[7] This framing allows us to understand the Asian on Demand akin to a mediating function that delivers and retracts images readily on demand. Building on critics of Asian media representation who call attention to the perpetual equation of Asianness with visual duplicity, what King describes as a "site of enigmatic indecipherability," I explore how Asian racialization operates itself as a form of mediation, one that renders real-life Asians like media.[8] The Asian on Demand heralds a series of familiar and far-reaching expectations of *readiness on demand,* the expectation that Asians appear seamlessly accessible in ways that please and satisfy their audience—and to remain invisible otherwise. This expectation of on-demandness likens Asians to a mediating function commonly associated with on-demand video streaming. Just as video is expected to instantly transmit high-res audiovisuals, the Asian on Demand is set up to flaunt themself for show. In this sense the idea of the Asian on Demand is not about Asian representation in mainstream media. Rather, I engage the logics of on-demand availability to unpack the everyday representational demands that Asians are expected to navigate and perform to make themselves recognizable to majoritarian publics.

Wendy Chun observes that racialization works in ways similar to media processes, by "linking what is visible to what is invisible."[9] The mediating function of the Asian on Demand determines what we can and cannot see. Its visibility and what it represents thus become the requisite for someone else's invisibility and vice versa. In a similar vein, Hong engages neoliberal race politics as "a structure of disavowal, an epistemological framing, *a way of seeing and not seeing*" that shapes how we apprehend our historical present and perceive (or not) structural violence.[10] Another source of inspiration comes from Kara Keeling's discussion of "cinematic perception," in which they argue that the work of meaning-making inherent in watching film—the cinematic organization of the world—is the same work that produces "social reality and sociality."[11] Keeling writes that "*cinematic perception* . . . is particular not to film spectatorship, but to the reception of images whenever they appear to a sensory-motor schema capable of memory and affect. This includes watching a film, but it also includes, for instance, interacting with one's neighbor," and certainly how we treat, and trade, difference.[12] "Film" and the "cinematic" speak here beyond a specific set of audiovisual technologies, to comprise the ways that social relations and social reality are produced and maintained through particular ways of seeing and not seeing, ones that are rehearsed through our engagement with media technologies but also shaped by the social, economic, and cultural processes through which we apprehend and make sense of our present.[13]

Asians on Demand studies the video work of activist filmmakers and the strategies they use to shape their personas on screen, on video, and into public visibility. I show how these artists mobilize video in ways that conspicuously control their on-screen appearances and disappearances in ways that contest their mandated and on demand visibilities. Like other critics of film and media, I refer to videos as *films,* an umbrella term for fictional and nonfictional stories as told through moving images. A far more affordable and less complicated alternative to capturing moving images on celluloid, most films today are technically *videos*: recorded with a digital video camera, they are shot, produced, and postproduced "on" digital video, or DV. (Alternatively, analog film is now often converted into digital video files for easier sharing and screening purposes, such as the works discussed in chapters 3 and 5.) Unless otherwise noted, *video* and *film* are thus used interchangeably in this book, as are the terms *video artist* and *filmmaker*.[14] I reserve the labels *artist* and *activist* for how these makers self-identify.

The production of video spans various devices, formats, and practices, encompassing both analog and digital modes, from VHS tapes

6 | INTRODUCTION

to computer files. We can distinguish between analog and digital not only by their respective forms of storing information but also by the cultural and representational values and connotations that get attached to these forms. Verisimilitude and objectivity, for example, are often gauged by how the so-called prefilmic reality gets technically translated into an image.[15] I am interested in the rendering of digital video as today's exemplary on-demand technology, a reputation that builds directly on the medium's association with access and people power in its earlier analog days. What characterizes digital video in the twenty-first century is its unparalleled ubiquity in many people's daily lives, as viewers especially in developed countries now take for granted the ability to easily select and watch—as well as record, edit, and share—videos using a personal smartphone, for example. I approach digital video's on-demand rendering as a critical entry into identifying the neoliberal demand for Asians on Demand. I also elaborate how contemporary artists and activists take advantage of video's accessibility, affordability, and globally networked infrastructure to create and circulate their work, and as an activist means to insert themselves into their videos in ways that allow for participation in often elite and exclusive official culture, as the ensuing chapters discuss in more detail.

Video's User-Friendliness and Demand

The ever-evolving versatility of video in recent decades has made the recording and editing of audiovisual material increasingly available to the public. Arguably today's most ubiquitous and flexible media technology, video is notably remarkable for its "plasticity across lo-fi and high tech, on- and offline networks, social groupings, and diverse geographies."[16] Digital video today, like VHS once did with its accessible tape recording system, lends itself to an even faster and user-friendly arena "of streaming, posting, gaming, cloud locations, home editing, and live phone broadcasts and begs the question of where video situates itself in relation to its many practitioners—amateur, professional, and unaligned."[17] With its longstanding reputation as a "medium for the people," video, more than celluloid-based film, is seen as a user-friendly format with which regular and everyday people can share information and representations of themselves and others, which allows ordinary people a creative power apart from the state and corporate worlds.[18] Lucas Hilderbrand observes how during the Cold War, video shifted from its introductory form as a broadcast technology mainly used by the big networks to a popular consumer handheld instrument, providing grassroots U.S. Americans with unprecedented access to consuming, creating, and circulating audiovisual content. "Access" points here first and foremost to the democratic and egalitarian quality of one's ability to participate in cultural creation and public exchange. Video's popularity came of age following the peak of social movements in the 1960s and 1970s, when people power and minority visibility rose to core principles of good governance, which is to say, the promise of a global civil society. Zhen Zhang similarly elaborates how a new generation of urban filmmakers in post-Tiananmen China placed unprecedented control over (self-)documentation into the hands of average citizens. The immediacy of the video camera in capturing and observing oneself, Zhang notes, returns "to ordinary people the right to participate in the production of filmic images about themselves."[19] "And, of course, the utopian promise of media decentralization and democratized production has reappeared with digital video cameras, user-friendly editing software, and video sharing websites."[20]

Activists and artists were the first groups to publicly exploit video's accessibility for progressive ends, spearheading representational practices like live recording and public-access cable broadcasting that today continue to shape how video is used by ordinary people. Alexandra Juhasz and Kate Horsfield observe moments of 1980s AIDS activism in the United States, where artists, queer activists, and AIDS activists—DIVA TV and ACT UP, for example—partnered together "to fight against rising hysteria caused by ignorance, omission, and misinformation presented in mainstream media. Video affinity groups such as Damned Interfering Video Artists Television (DIVA TV) documented ACT-UP demonstrations, and this footage had a leveraging effect that maintained communication, community support, and enthusiasm in the midst of a long and strenuous battle."[21] Due to its wide-ranging accessibility, video uniquely brings together the respective spheres of video art and activism. While video art is commonly associated with emphasis on form and video activism with politics and a serious commitment to social change,[22] their shared genealogical relation to social justice movements highlights video's legacy as the medium of the people. Video works to tighten communal

8 | INTRODUCTION

bonds, bypass mainstream distribution channels, and allow marginalized collectivities to stage themselves as critical participants of an otherwise elite and exclusive public discourse. Today's video artists can use the medium's democratizing power to advocate for the representation of those who are underrepresented. Video's accessibility enables the staging of oneself into public visibility in previously unprecedented ways, allowing them to become managers of their own media image and public persona. And yet, the video artists I examine also critically revise how their public visibility becomes increasingly demanded to serve as official evidence of equity and structural change.

Video's promise of immediacy has largely merged with a "neoliberal, on-demand, personal choice, niche culture" that caters more than ever to individual preference,[23] especially in our new millennium. Here, an endless supply of instantly accessible digital video content provides, if not democratic access, a sense of freedom and choice in consumption. Already in 2018, online video made up 60 percent of all internet traffic, seeing a significant increase during the first year of the Covid-19 pandemic; the market is expected to continuously expand.[24] Media scholars have discussed on-demand culture with focus on industrial and technological developments in the U.S. broadcast industry from the 1980s onward. Video, as television's main medium, has been key to understanding the rise of on demand's "access entitlement": "audiences want access to entertainment on their own terms: what they want, when they want it."[25] As Hilderbrand elaborates, "With the rise of video rentals and later TIVO, on-demand programming, YouTube, and streaming content on the networks' websites (not to mention the World Wide Web generally), technology and the market have moved toward an idea (if not an actuality) of infinite and instant access to specific movies or shows whenever the viewer feels the whim."[26] While video's on-demandness is inseparable from the expansion of digital technologies and media infrastructures, it also bespeaks a novel rendering of access discourses that is not reducible to technological and industrial media developments.

Since the 1980s, the developments in video technology are part of larger global and neoliberal economic shifts that include deregulation, financialization, and the growing need for flexible, low-cost labor and offshoring practices to countries with low labor and production costs—most notably in the Asia Pacific. Rutvica Andrijasevic, Julie

Yujie Chen, Melissa Gregg, and Marc Steinberg offer a more specific origin story, by tracing today's global on-demand market structures to "just-in-time" production in 1950s Japan. First invented in the Toyota auto industry, and known overseas as *lean manufacturing,* "the concept of just-in-time (JIT) refers to a system of temporal contraction and inventory management, wherein a good or service is produced only as it is needed for a subsequent part of the production process."[27] More succinctly, "JIT's model of manufacture and circulation presumes the 'on-demand' delivery of parts to the factory and products to the consumer."[28] This ready access to goods and services depends on a pliable, disposable workforce that is ready to "disassemble and reassemble" as the market demands.[29] The "planned obsolescence" of workers remains central to today's on-demand economy and takes on special meaning in neoliberal race politics.[30]

Asians on Demand transposes the demand for readily accessible and disposable workers outside recognized work environments to study the representational labor that minorities nonstop perform to keep the system running. The Asian on Demand is a worker in disguise. They do the work that media do, which is to provide a steady stream of images, figure an instant representational availability, and disappear otherwise. This labor is hardly acknowledged, instead taken for granted, carefully tucked away behind the curated visibility of Asian exemplarity. Asian dis/appearance looks natural, authentic, labor free. I propose that a closer study of video's on-demand operations can help tease out the ways that Asians are rendered as on-demand workers that readily dis/appear whenever the master feels the whim.

Mediation, Media, Intermediary

Lisa Gitelman explains that "media become transparent when [users] and society at large forget many of the norms and standards they are heeding, and then forget that they are heeding norms and standards at all. Yet transparency is chimerical. As much as people may converse through a telephone and forget the telephone itself, the context of telephoning makes all kinds of difference to the things they say and the way they say them."[31] Like other visual media technologies, video's mediation depends on the transparency of video's mechanics and the inconspicuous process of its own production. From newspapers to projected moving images, the business of media is to relay

10 | INTRODUCTION

information and narrate by making themselves invisible, that is, by encouraging the user to forget what enables their "immediate" delivery, including technical formats, economic investments, social norms, and affective persuasions. In other words, video's success demands its own disavowal, its virtual denial of the existence or interference of the medium itself.[32] This disappearance of the medium relays an easy immediacy, to feature an "unlabored" experience of the world.[33] Sybille Krämer concurs: "The medium disappears in its successful implementation. Its role consists not in being retained, but rather in being made superfluous."[34] The medium is expected to readily appear and disappear in service of transmission. It is both necessary and superfluous.

Sarah Kember and Joanna Zylinska introduce *mediation* as "a term from Marxist theory that refers to 'the reconciliation of two opposing forces . . . by a mediating object.' The way this term is taken up in media studies is as a 'mediating factor of a given culture,'" in the form of communication technologies, or simply put, media.[35] Media mediate. They pass a message from A to B, serving as a connection between two parties. At the same time, media are "designed to make what is mediated appear unmediated."[36] Meaning they have a neutralizing effect, by which the relation between A and B appears immediate or naturally given. Krämer summarizes: "Occupying the middle is precisely what the position of the medium represents. This 'middle' can be understood in three ways: spatially as an intermediate position, then functionally as mediation and finally formally as neutralization."[37] The intermediary denotes the position of Asian entrepreneurs and managers both today and in past colonial societies. Wendy Cheng discusses the positionalities of Asians as historically situated between Western colonial powers, and between whites and other racialized groups; "from Southeast Asia to the Caribbean to the Americas, from 'coolies' and sharecroppers to shopkeepers, merchants, and entrepreneurs," she observes, "it becomes apparent that Asians have more often than not occupied intermediary strata—in many cases consciously constructed and maintained by European imperialist powers—between a white ruling class and other subordinated, nonwhite groups."[38] Kuan-hsing Chen, Jin-kyung Lee, Brian Bernards, Wasana Wongsurawat, and others observe how the role of Asian intermediary has taken shape in international contexts, for example, with the rise of ethnic Chinese entrepreneurial "middlemen" in Southeast Asia's and Africa's postcolonial economies; or in the "subimperial" economies of South Korea and Taiwan, Asian Tigers that are now known as mediators of Western imperial practices in the Global South.[39] The Asian intermediary denotes a socioeconomic position "in the middle"—a buffer between different social strata and types of power. It thus also functions as medium. Situated between two sides, it serves as neutralizer but also as a barrier between them, meaning it naturalizes power discrepancies.[40] The Asian intermediary tends to bear certain privileges, such as greater access to "middle-classness" and upward mobility for certain Asians when compared with other racial minorities.[41] Yet such leverage and status, as Iyko Day observes, remain "highly conditional to the demands of capital."[42] Asians are well tolerated by ruling powers only as long as they promise profitable surplus, most often in the form of cheap labor and disposable workers. This rendering as "human media," in Neferti Tadiar's words,[43] cannot be divorced from imperial fantasies of endlessly compliant and exploitable Asians that inform today's global divisions of labor and outsourcing and offshoring practices.[44] The intermediary position, Krämer confirms, ultimately accommodates the status quo.

Distinguishing the logic of Asians on Demand from traditional codifiers of Asianness are the seemingly unobtrusive mechanisms and benign ways through which this neoliberal racial configuration exploits and renders Asian people and other racialized groups as superfluous. Asians on Demand describes the demand, for instance, for Asians to appear well represented numerically in projects of state multiculturalism, education, and the arts, and in the context of media and other market competitions for new consumer audiences. At the same time, these multicultural displays hinge on the ready figuration of the Asian on Demand, the work of showing up in affirmative ways and covering over anything that does not fit the bill. Building on Hong's notion of neoliberalism as not only "economistic definitions of value" but also "a structure of disavowal, an epistemological framing, a way of seeing and not seeing," I offer the logic of Asians on Demand as a neoliberal rationale that trades in affirmative images in ways that appear devoid of racism and labor demands—to the extent that even its Asian workers cheerfully and proactively participate in making the present look progressive and just.[45] The Asian on Demand is a selfless worker.

Seeing the Messenger

Processes of mediation wield control over what matters, what makes it to the screen, and what need not be visible to the naked eye. "The topos of the 'dying messenger,'" says Krämer, "offers the most radical image of the human becoming a thing, and this extreme example of self-withdrawal reflects the ambiguity and ambivalence embedded in the messenger function."[46] Krämer uses the figure of the dying messenger to describe technological processes of mediation. She maintains that successful communication relies on the messenger's ability "to withdraw or recede, thereby foregrounding [the] message. The embodiment of a foreign voice is only possible by surrendering one's own voice through a form of *selflessness*."[47] The messenger gives themself up and over for their delivery, and in this process self-eliminates. "The medium fulfils its function in the process of its own elimination."[48] Its symbolic function is to deliver and die. While for Krämer the messenger's removal is productive for the successful transmission of the message, let us also remember that the notion of readiness on demand designates a media function that is ascribed to actual people and populations, regulating how and when they become publicly legible and, thus, appreciated, or not. The Asian on Demand is a messenger function that disappears Asians into a ready-made image, becoming full-on transparent. We see through them. Like Tadiar's description of "human media," Asians rendered on demand are envisioned to function as media "rather than full-fledged sovereign (self-determining, self-owning) individual subjects."[49]

The Asian on Demand determines what we can and cannot see. Yet this powerful position comes with a cost. The demand for ready figuration requires a simultaneous disappearance. The Asian on Demand might deliver empowering images, yet their seamless representational availability mirrors the medium's programmed elimination. It is in this sense that affirmative representational images engender a sort of violence, by operating on the demand for the messenger's superfluousness. I am talking first and foremost about symbolic and epistemological violence—what transpires on the level of representation—yet symbolic and epistemological violence extend from and have real-life consequences. We have witnessed this most recently in the hostile anti-Asian hate speech and violence in the wake of the Covid-19 pandemic. Still and again, Asians are presumed to hold no proper self.

Asian Capital in the Neoliberal Age

How do we make sense of Asian superfluousness in an age of "messianic" Asian visibility, where the plenitude or seeming ubiquity of Asian images on screen is celebrated by non-Asian and Asian diasporic viewers and critics alike?[50] If we take the North American media landscape as a gauge for the global currency of Asians, Asianness seems less "on demand" than in demand: from the Oscar successes and box office hits like *Parasite* (2019) and *Everything Everywhere All at Once* (2022), to much-praised arthouse films such as *Nomadland* (2020) by Chloe Zhao, to television favorites including BBC America's *Killing Eve* (2018–2022), Netflix's *Never Have I Ever* (2020–2023), and HBO's *House of Ho* (2020–) and of course the global media phenomenon of BTS. Finally, Asians can feel *seen*.

Coined the "Asian Century" by politicians, economists, and the media, the twenty-first century may be described as one of on-demand Asian capital.[51] It is defined by the ascent of Asian capital markets in the global economy, including the economic poster child of Japan and the Asian Tigers (Singapore, Hong Kong, South Korea, and Taiwan), as well as states that have been largely perceived as unexemplary by the West due to their lagging democratic regimes, including China, India, and Indonesia. Many of these markets have proven resilient in the face of major international crises, most notably the 2008 global recession from which they recovered rather swiftly compared to the United States and the European Union, thus presenting a viable alternative to historical Western hegemony. The recent launch of the Regional Comprehensive Economic Partnership, the world's largest free trade agreement centered in the Asia Pacific, reinforces the impression that Asia (and the world) might not need the West anymore. Rather than being merely conceived as the source of cheap labor and production, Asian economies have given rise to a powerful class of Asians with money, whose buying power and seamless mobility epitomize a new world citizenry. Hong notes that "we might understand [these] bourgeois and elite Asian populations as wielders and beneficiaries of various forms of capital: human, cultural, and literal. [Their] guarantor of security is thus not literal citizenship status but access to cosmopolitanism, flexibility, and neoliberal multiculturalism."[52] Asian value is not merely derived from menial labor anymore, but from access to and ownership of abundant resources.

14 | INTRODUCTION

The century of on-demand Asian capital is also what Jodi Melamed describes as an increasingly "formally antiracist, liberal-capitalist modernity," where *capital* refers not merely to global monetary flows but to an embodied, racialized neoliberal self with social and cultural capital.[53] Neoliberal multiculturalism is about commodifying diversity, as witnessed for example in state-funded public media initiatives spotlighting minority activists and cultural producers in front of the camera to demonstrate progressive politics, discussed in chapters 2 and 4. Rather than repressing or rendering abject racial and other forms of difference, state and market institutions appropriate the language of civil rights and decolonization movements to give the impression of fashionable egalitarianism: "Your dreams are also mine," says the neoliberal mantra.[54] In this process, the worth of populations gets reshuffled along new axes of "privilege and stigma," so that propertied Asians and Asian diasporans assume the status of desirable global citizens.[55]

Media images play a crucial role in branding neoliberal visions of multicultural success. "Diversity work," Sara Ahmed and Nishant Shah remind us, is "image work."[56] Digital video, through its global reach and instant circulation of Asian faces, at times an all-Asian cast, signals a radical change through seamless images—finally, minorities can enjoy the same rights and privileges as the majority (at least in North America). Yet the high-resolution video image has brought about not so much a break with existing representational regimes than what Keeling calls a "transformation" in the ways that onscreen difference is made consumable and commensurate with dominant value economies.[57] On-demand images of Asian superheroes and the superrich do not fundamentally change the terms of inclusion, rendering Asianness instead into a "market identity" that reduces social access to matters of consumption.[58] Sasha Torres writes: "Real political, social, and economic inequalities disappear. In their place, [a set of highly curated media representations] offers up racialized figures as consumers first and last, producing a powerful if misleading alibi both for existing racial formations and for capitalism itself."[59] Sprinkling minority images into the program becomes an effective measure to curb political desire. Here, seeing oneself represented on screen is the end all and be all of liberation.[60]

It thus becomes clear why a sole focus on media images is not enough to understand the perceptual regime through which neoliberal power accumulates and divides. These images are meant to uphold hegemonic ways of seeing and not seeing that see affirmation everywhere and racial violence nowhere. This includes obscuring the mediating labor that Asian people are exacted to perform to affirm neoliberalism's happy "truths," even or especially as Asianness shifts from symbolizing disposable labor to also being recognized as a carrier of fashionable lifestyles and desirable selves. The Asian on Demand is expected to swiftly dis/appear into a globalized "Western-style capitalism."[61] Readily assembled and disassembled, they do not matter otherwise.

Estranging Self-Stagings

Asians on Demand is both a mediating logic and a racial logic that formalizes what we can and cannot see. The filmmakers discussed in this book thwart their on-screen flattenings by casting themselves in their films—and recording their onscreen personas—in ways that estrange and thus draw attention to conventional expectations of Asian and ethnic people on screen and with regard to their public visibility. Like Steyerl in *Strike II,* they sabotage the demand for their compulsory dis/appearance, rendering themselves visible in ways that foil their

Figure 3. Steyerl conspicuously sabotages her on-demand visibility; screenshot from *Strike II.*

ready consumption. In doing so they fashion their personas against the presumption of liberating self-completion that mythically occurs when seeing oneself on screen. Strike. "Refusal to represent."

The Asian on Demand is not merely an external imposition. The archetypical Asian on Demand may best be understood as a neoliberal mode of interpellation into an aspirational subjecthood that promises one's valuable recognition. An artist's self-representation as an on-demand figure or persona involves the labor of self-management and of tailoring oneself in ways most valued by neoliberal hegemony. Rey Chow's discussion of cinematic estrangement allows us to challenge the validity of such recognition by drawing attention to artistic self-management. Estrangement, for Chow, is the feeling of one's distancing or alienation from a contextualizing scene that has become rather "automatized and thus unnoticeable."[62] This distancing allows for the reassessment of a scenario in different, new ways. For Chow, it is the camera's surprising presence in the viewer's frame that, when rendered as a visible object on screen, snaps viewers out of complacency to sharpen their critical awareness with respect to the "cinematic" divisions and demands of framing that shape how we identify, relate, make meaning. Likewise, the filmmakers featured in this book stage themselves as characters in their films, in ways that estrange us from hackneyed and hardly noticeable expectations of seeing and not seeing that render them into a see-through exemplar. Rather than striving for "better" Asian images or, more accurately, biographical narratives, they perform the messenger straying queerly toward the "errant, eccentric, promiscuous, and unexpected."[63] In this sense, the videos featured here create "an opening or horizon" that allude to a future not yet here and to a present not readily knowable in identitarian terms, as José Muñoz and Kara Keeling have described it.[64]

This book reassigns value to sociopolitical change and to international and cross-cultural dialogues about race and racialization as it relates to the increasingly ubiquitous and user-friendly medium of video. Together the following chapters create a cartography of translocal solidarities and queerly unique engagements with video across places within Asia, Europe, and North America, by adding a complexity and relational aspect to single-area, monocultural, and monolingual discussions about the production of Asian visibilities on screen. *Asians on Demand* documents the estranging tactics that activists and artists develop to contest the identitarian registers that demand their ready representational availability. Its video archive investigates how these dynamics play out across different cultures, languages, and geographies. Moving from Germany to the United States, Taiwan, the Philippines, and Spain, I examine the contemporary work of several East and Southeast Asian and Asian diasporic cultural producers that reside in these locales. I draw upon personal interviews with all the filmmakers featured here (except for Hito Steyerl discussed in chapter 1, and Peng, whose video is featured in chapter 5), and upon my participant observation of and TIWA's activist work in Taiwan, as discussed in chapter 4. I also refer to texts written by the filmmakers as sources that question restrictive visual representational politics as they create their own theories about filmmaking and performances. *Asians on Demand*'s visual archive spans commissioned artwork, educational performance, no-budget self-recordings, and activist documentaries. The videos selected here are distributed by the filmmakers themselves, and via television broadcasts, on-demand streaming, film festivals, and gallery exhibits. In chapter 1, I have relied on my native Germanness and fluency in German to account for German-language discussions by nonwhite scholars and activists that interrogate Germany's race politics.

Where media studies tends to focus on racial representation in mainstream mass media and feature films, I discuss tropes of onscreen visibility and concealment as particularly inflected by processes of racialization in works outside of commercial broadcast and theatrical distribution. These processes of racialization are significant because they determine how we position ourselves with others and bolster social orders; they are among topics that have been discussed for some time in ethnic and American studies. *Asians on Demand* places the fields of media studies and ethnic studies into conversation with one another to probe how processes of racialization, like video's mediations, are shaped by structures and relations of visibility and invisibility. This comparative purview allows a more productive understanding of the vitality of perceptual arrangements in visual media and the relationship between racialization and visibility when it comes to perceiving difference. What are the mechanisms by which video artists and activists create and thus manage their visibility and concealment on screen, and specifically in video?

Chapter 1, "Improper *Asiatische Deutsche*: The Video Art of Ming Wong and Hito Steyerl," begins in Germany, where the term *Rasse*

18 | INTRODUCTION

(race) has been considered taboo in formal and casual discussions since World War II, and where open discussions about racism are more often than not avoided and dismissed. East Asians and Southeast Asians have lately been praised by German politicos and national media. This "positive" characterization has been deployed in ways that vilify Germany's Middle Eastern and Muslim communities—communities that have continued to experience racism and discrimination since West Germany's *Gastarbeiter* (guest worker) program that was designed to fortify the country's postwar infrastructure. Recent European film scholarship has made efforts to showcase works by Turkish Germans and other minority filmmakers. Yet especially in Germany, critical discussion about minority aesthetic production continues to be confined by simplistic paradigms of home and host country that rely on expectations of accurately realist, biographical representations of ethnic people on screen. This chapter explores video works of two Berlin-based Asian German media artists, Ming Wong and Hito Steyerl. Where Wong cleverly undermines the sanctity of selected classics of New German Cinema by invoking low-end cultural aesthetics that draw upon themes of drag and piracy, for example, Steyerl withholds the cohesion of her on-screen persona as she casts her presence as fractured and ephemeral. Both artists leverage their positions as acclaimed German artists by featuring themselves as inauthentically Asian and improperly German in their videos, raising questions about the relationship of race to proper European belonging and frustrating mainstream demands for Asian people to appear authentically and realistically on screen.

The scene of interpretation shifts in chapter 2, "Mental Health and Live Fictions: Kristina Wong and *Wong Flew Over the Cuckoo's Nest*," to the dynamic stage of performance art. Here I exploit the eventual translation of live performance to recorded video as a means to highlight the subtler representational demands of Asian representation. The subject is Pulitzer Prize nominee Kristina Wong's brash solo performance, *Wong Flew Over the Cuckoo's Nest* (2006–2013), a satirical quasi-autobiographical show about Asian American women and access to mental health. Rather than offer a precise and realist account of each and every Asian woman who has experienced depression or trauma (as the show's protagonist Kristina sets out to do), *Wong Flew* foils the pressures to represent, bear witness to, and act as a cheery native Asian American informant. This chapter considers how the show's well-marketed and streamable concert video (2013) calls attention to institutional demands for Kristina's Asian American "liveness," and, moreover, to how the artist, however unevenly, resists the "flattening" of her 3-D liveness through her satirical and strategic self-impersonation. Her jarring, comical, and confounding slips between reality and fiction, between embodiment and abstraction, between cynicism and acknowledgement of trauma, sabotage the on-demandness elicited by even the most enlightened of academic institutions and audiences.

Chapter 3, "Stateless Cinema and the Undocument: Miko Revereza, *Distancing,* and *No Data Plan,*" explores Miko Revereza's challenge to U.S. border surveillance and the institutional use of visual documentation with respect to U.S. immigration law. The Philippine-born artist does so in his documentaries *Distancing* (2019) and *No Data Plan* (2019), reflections on his nearly thirty years of having lived as an undocumented person in the United States. Due to their formal qualities that stray from mainstream conventions of documentary storytelling, *Distancing* and *No Data Plan* have been described by critics as experimental and avant-garde, as autobiographical essays, and as slow cinema. Critical discussions about these films tend to focus on the relationship between the filmmaker's choices and his biographical experiences of migrancy and displacement. His own ambivalent description of himself as an "undocumented-documentary filmmaker," helps viewers to take a step back from common expectations of documentary truth. Both films leave no identifying visual trace of Revereza, staging the evasion of his visual capture not only by his own camera but also by U.S. Border Patrol. The filmmaker thus flicks a virtual middle finger to both U.S. immigration law and its system of photographic documentation that has curbed unwanted Asian entry into the United States since the nineteenth century.

Chapter 4, "Migrant Erotics: TIWA's *Lesbian Factory* and *Rainbow Popcorn,*" takes us on a journey to Taiwan and the Philippines. With its curious international status as praiseworthy economic powerhouse and nonsovereign democracy, Taiwan, a.k.a. the Republic of China (ROC), has made concerted efforts to widely showcase its commitments to multiculturalism and ethnic diversity. This chapter investigates the Taiwanese state's promotion of activist documentaries about queer and minority subjects, and the ways in which activist documentaries can exploit the state's rhetoric and embrace of multicultural visibility. Both documentaries created by the Taipei-based Taiwan International Workers' Association, *Lesbian Factory* (2010) and *Rainbow Popcorn* (2012) trace the affective socialities and queer mobilities among its protagonist group of Filipina migrant workers and close friends dedicated to supporting themselves and their families as they work abroad. As both films elicit empathy and emotion from viewers as a form of *sentimental activism*, a tactic intended to garner public recognition with respect to the rights of minorities and foreign migrants in the ROC, I examine how viewers are affectively drawn toward the films' *migrant erotics* as evidenced by affective and sexual relationships among protagonists that neither depend on straightness, patriarchy, nor assignments of value by the state or neoliberal markets. *Lesbian Factory* and *Rainbow Popcorn* enhance Taiwan's embrace of minority and multicultural visibilities, and foreground its cast's queer migrancies and transnational activism in ways that respond to the nonsovereign state's aspirations for global recognition.

In chapter 5, "*Me llamo Peng*: Self-Care with a Camcorder," initially conceived as the book's epilogue, I consider how the intimacy of the camcorder can aid one to care for oneself. The video documentary *Me llamo Peng* (2010) is the distillation of over sixty hours of self-recordings by Chinese migrant worker Peng Ruan. The short film was compiled by directors Jahel Guerra Roa and Victoria Molina de Carranza, who are respectively from Venezuela and Spain. As we follow Peng's creative impulses through the lens of his second-hand camcorder, we are affected by his contagiously aspirational attitude, both of which help us to bear with him through his on-screen hard times. And yet, *Me llamo Peng*'s Asian-Century visual narrative of self-making arguably feeds a cruel optimism that only amplifies Peng's need for solvency and to continue traveling far from home between chronically low-paid temporary jobs. In documenting his difficult precarity, *Me llamo Peng* allows us also to see the camera as a tool that allows Peng to care for himself.

By examining how minority Asian cultural producers play with viewer expectations of instant access to Asian video images, this book therefore does not make a case for a single Asian experience. It mobilizes Asian video productions to unravel and reimagine how contemporary modes of governance, subject-formation, and accumulation deploy the mechanisms of appearance and disappearance in ways that are best exemplified by the rendering of Asianness as on demand.

Improper *Asiatische Deutsche*
The Video Art of Ming Wong and Hito Steyerl

There has, historically, been this pressure to confess or to use confessional discourse among ethnic minorities in Germany. That's more or less the only possible story you're supposed to tell, like relating to your origins or ancestry or stuff like that. But the problem with these stories is that if they do not correspond to the prefabricated stereotypes existing around this specific minority then people will not be satisfied.

—Hito Steyerl in Angelica Fenner and Robin Curtis,
"If People Want to Oppress You, They Make You
Say 'I': Hito Steyerl in Conversation"

In the short video *Lerne Deutsch mit Petra von Kant / Learn German with Petra von Kant* (2007),[1] Berlin-based video artist Ming Wong casts himself as his own leading lady, the lovely Petra von Kant. Subtitled in German and English, the ten-minute *Lerne Deutsch / Learn German* spoofs one of Wong's favorite New German Cinema classics, Rainer Werner Fassbinder's *The Bitter Tears of Petra von Kant (Die Bitteren Tränen der Petra von Kant*, 1972). *Learn German* reenacts key scenes from Fassbinder's original, whose fashionably arrogant Petra falls madly in love with another woman amid postwar Germany's oppressive conservatism. We watch Petra come out, as it were, in a shimmery emerald evening dress and bouncy blond wig—a striking combination that appears to darken Wong's olive complexion on screen. At once she begins to have a nervous breakdown. Relentlessly citing Fassbinder's original 1972 script, Wong's Petra raves and screams in German just like the Petra of *Bitter Tears*. She throws back

| 21

Figure 4. Wong emotes and cusses as his own Petra von Kant; courtesy of the artist.

a glass of gin just like Fassbinder's Petra in the original film, and spins to stop at the very same angle, promptly smashing an entire set of fine china with her shiny high heels. Our Chinese Singaporean Petra dives to the floor, rages, and despairs exactly like the original diva in the German classic. "Crazy? I'm not crazy," she wails. "I love her. I love her as I've never loved before in my life!"

This chapter explores a series of improper video performances by Ming Wong and Hito Steyerl, two established Asian German media artists based in Berlin. By "improper" I refer to how Wong and Steyerl cast themselves in their video works in ways that not only assert their presences and legitimacy as Asian diasporic actors and directors but also wield tactics of filmic estrangement and of frustrating their expected visibilities on screen. I discuss how the artists mobilize low-end cultural practices often associated with grassroots and queer community advocacy, and how these practices comment on recognized mainstream forms (like the essay film or auteur cinema, for example) in ways that draw attention to Germany's aversion to explicit discussions about race and racism, and especially in official German discourse and respected arts institutions. Drawing upon David Theo Goldberg's discussion of political racelessness, Fatima El-Tayeb observes that in Europe, the common claim of "racelessness" is not about a literal "absence of racial thinking." It is rather about "a form of racialization that can be defined as specifically European both in its enforced silence and in its explicit categorization as not European of all those who violate Europe's implicit, but normative whiteness, allowing to forever consider the 'race question' as externally (and by implication temporarily) imposed."[2] My query builds upon El-Tayeb's discussion of European racelessness as part of a distinctly European and certainly German mindset that elides the need for open and explicit discussions about race. In other contexts, like in the United States for example, racelessness might infer that we live in a postracial era where race no longer matters (because "all lives matter"). In Germany, official discourses disappear race altogether as a proper object of formal discussion or critique. In the context of the nation's World War II antihumanisms, and in the name of quieting ongoing racisms and racist violence, it is as if race should not be thought in Germany.

Through their video art, Wong and Hito Steyerl dissect the above logic of Europe's ostensible racelessness. Staging themselves in their video narratives in unanticipated ways, the artists thwart the biographical accuracy that is often demanded of Asians on screen. Their directorial queerings mimic and muddle expectations of valued identitarian and "raceless" categories in ways that center the ostensibly " 'improper,' 'inauthentic' and impossible positionality of racialized Europeans."[3] Knowing that moving-image art is commonly associated with "chi-chi experimentation that goes well with brie and white wine," Wong and Steyerl return us to video's antiestablishment history and roots in radical art and progressive politics.[4] They leverage their positionalities as privileged Asian creatives endorsed by German cultural institutions as well as the international art world to reveal the violent norm of propriety that underwrites the high-end European cultural product and by extension, national identity.

Petra's frenzied reenactments in *Learn German* do not just replicate Margit Carstensen's iconic performance as Petra in *Bitter Tears*.

24 | IMPROPER *ASIATISCHE DEUTSCHE*

They draw attention to Wong's hilarious self-stagings and thus his inability, and lack of desire, to make great European copies. Wong's peculiarities are part of the video's deliberately bad/badass estrangements that render his acts of imitation, homage, and artistic freedom visible.[5] On-screen estrangement, to invoke Rey Chow, is a disturbance to an audience's habituated visual field due to some unanticipated or undesired presence or due to an abrupt change that disturbs a viewer's expectations or unwitting demands.[6] Wong's Petra is a stranger to us, just as much as she is a stranger to Fassbinder's Petra in *Bitter Tears*. Even for a viewer who might be unfamiliar with Fassbinder, *Learn German*'s Chinese Singaporean Petra powerfully elicits our double take—a "Wait . . . wait, what's really happening here?"—as it strays far from the intentions of the original.

Wong created *Learn German* "as part of a personal, self-designed German language and cultural immersion programme" upon relocating to Berlin in 2007.[7] It was a moment marked by political demands for official benchmarks with regard to diversity in Germany and Western Europe, and by debates about multiculturalism and its failures, culminating in the European debt crisis of 2008. Once he had settled in Berlin's posh Kreuzberg district, a neighborhood once dominated by low-income immigrants, Wong was startled by hearing openly racist remarks against Turkish people and those perceived as Muslim more broadly.[8] It was also a time contextualized by the U.S. War on Terror, as European politicians across the ideological spectrum demonized Muslims for failing to assimilate a proper humanist integrity. To add, they did this as they simultaneously and vehemently denied accusations of racism. Political racelessness, El-Tayeb notes, operates on the belief that "you are racist if you 'see' race."[9] Wong's queerings of Fassbinder, whose films are known for their rejection of fascist national ideology and normative gender roles during post–World War II Germany, allow for an interrogation of Germany's ostensibly raceless tenet of assimilation as key to proper national belonging—a notion that also underwrites Europe's claims of raceless inclusivity. I refer in particular to postwar European claims of racelessness as a basis for inclusive cosmopolitanism and the evidently modern European ethos of world openness. The prohibition of explicit discussion about race in Germany is part of a distinctly European mindset that tends to normalize whiteness, to disavow structural racism as systemic to the nation, and to dismiss candid and open discussion about race and racism, especially when it comes to Germany's vital immigrant and nonwhite communities.

Wong has often been presented in a way that underscores the distinction between imitation and original, with his video looming over a tiny feature film. At exhibitions, Wong's *Learn German* is generally installed alongside a smaller screen simultaneously playing Fassbinder's *Bitter Tears*. Without this juxtaposition, however, Wong's video features a Petra whose physical, vulgar, and queer foreignness becomes intensely conspicuous. *Learn German* indeed makes it impossible for the spectator not to see race. To cite Homay King and José Muñoz, Wong's "queer and brown" performance is "a mode of racial performativity, a doing within the social that surpasses limitations of epistemological renderings of race."[10] In her thick masculine voice and Singaporean accent, Petra yells out "Ich bin so im Arsch!" (I'm so fucked!), "Ich will alles kaputt schlagen, alles alles alles!" (I will smash everything, everything everything everything!). The "poor," inappropriately amateurish-looking stage—a nondescript white screen with just a few props—appears to drain away all notably filmic aspects of the original as we fix our eyes upon this unlikely video performance. Petra steals the show as she sticks out like a sore thumb, casting Wong's secondhand production as a poor act of assimilation. Trans-casting himself as Petra illustrates how the Chinese Singaporean Wong, who "grew up in a country with four official languages," writes German critic Birgit Rieger, "likes to approach new cultural milieus by immersing himself into a country's film history— and claims his place in it. Wong cheats his way as an Asian copy, so to speak, into the sacred halls of national identity."[11]

Attending to Asian racialization in post–Cold War neoliberal Germany allows us to understand how the European Union's motto "United in diversity" coincides with the increasing management of difference through an amnesiac rhetoric of inclusion. Although Europe has never been a homogenous cluster of equal members or values, this promoted ideal reaffirms an appropriately democratic and properly dominant West. Germany is a case in point, and I will trace some of the ways in which its raceless pretense operates. The promotion of Asian exemplarity by German politicians and media supports the role of Germany as the poster child of an inclusive European humanist tradition that conceals the violence of its national and cultural foundations. While debates about the continent's race

26 | IMPROPER *ASIATISCHE DEUTSCHE*

and racism often focus upon recognized historical events and colonial formations, Enlightenment ideals, Christian doctrine, and fascism, the rhetoric of endlessly pliable, excellent Asians demonstrates how longstanding practices of "racial Europeanization" persist in seemingly unrelated and contradictory forms,[12] and especially in Germany. The Asian on Demand, or what I describe as a readily available representational function ascribed to Asianness, extends imperial logics of conquest and control that work to guard Europe's borders against its Others.

Starring an Invisible Immigrant History

The promotion of Asian exemplarity in Germany has been going strong since at least 2000, the year of a highly publicized survey organized by the Programme for International Student Assessment (PISA) under the rubric of the intergovernmental Organisation for Economic Co-operation and Development (OECD). Publishing assessments of fifteen-year-old student outcomes from thirty-one countries, the survey indicated that German students ranked below the international OECD average.[13] A national outcry followed, as if the cradle of humanist *Bildung* (self-cultivation) had lost all global credibility. Looking for culprits and a quick fix, many began to celebrate Vietnamese German and Korean German students for their high-ranking educational achievements, and fondly nicknamed them "Asian Prussians" for upholding the Prussian *Bildung* tradition and saving national face.[14] And yet it was under Prussian reign that the rhetoric of "yellow peril" took off and helped to legitimate Germany's annexation of colonial protectorates in East Asia and the Asia Pacific.[15] Toward the end of the nineteenth century, Prussian emperor Wilhelm II deemed Asia a military-economic threat to be forcefully seized and controlled. The recent moniker "Asian Prussians" is now used to approvingly depict the well-performing immigrant guardians of archetypical ur-German values. Media and politicians across the ideological spectrum raved that they "hold up a mirror to Germans. Their virtues once used to be ours."[16]

Unlike their East and Southeast Asian counterparts, students of Turkish heritage and Muslim-identified students were depicted in the German media as the perpetrators of Germany's poor academic performance. Deemed unwilling to adopt and assimilate Western democratic values, Muslims were scapegoated for the nation's poor educational performance and for putting the future of other Germans in jeopardy. As then-chancellor Angela Merkel explained, "It is unacceptable that twice as many of them do not graduate from high school. It is unacceptable that twice as many of them do not have any professional qualification. This will cause social problems for our future."[17] Merkel's infamous statement reflects both Germany's longstanding and entwined anti-Turkish and -Muslim bias and the perceived failure of self-cultivation and assimilation on the part of Muslims and Europe's Others. Certainly not a recent phenomenon, Europe's anti-Muslim sentiment dates back to the "medieval contest between Mediterranean Christianity and Islam" from which the deviant Black Muslim persona was constructed.[18] The fantasy of Black Muslim deviance remains "central to the debates around security and 'core values' in the new Europe" today.[19] Muslim men in particular are still portrayed as regressively patriarchal, overzealously religious, and homophobic, as if living proof of Islam's fundamental incompatibility with Europe.

The polarization of good and bad minority subjects is paradigmatic of Germany's alleged racelessness. It reveals the relational nature of Asian racialization: who counts as "Asian" or exemplary minority subject in the national vernacular is a matter of multiply divided racial maps. More often than not, public perceptions of "Asianness" are limited to persons with East- and Southeast Asian background and explicitly exclude Muslim-identified Middle Eastern diasporans, including Turkish and Arab Germans as the de facto largest Asian German community.[20] Moreover, where anti-Muslim racism has gained new ground through continental anxieties about serial refugee displacements since 2015, the on-demand visibility of Asian exemplarity confirms Europe's nondiscriminating inclusivity. Yet even appreciated Asians remain preempted from veritable Germanhood. Unlike the threat of "yellow peril" to traditional Western hegemony, the Asian on Demand conveys a sense of manageability, that Asia can be dealt with. The more recent term *Asiatisch Deutsch,* literally "Asian German," is still only used in Germany by Asian people among themselves. Indeed, the terms *Asiatisch* and *Deutsch* are understood to be mutually exclusive and thus technically impossible to be used together in formal discussions—unlike "Asian American" in the United States.

28 | IMPROPER *ASIATISCHE DEUTSCHE*

This implicit demand for Asian exemplarity is squarely situated in Germany's migrant history, which begins shortly after the founding of the German Empire in 1871, and the Reich's recruitment of foreign workers from Poland, Italy, and other bordering states to work in the industrial, agricultural, and construction sectors of imperial Germany. It continues on with the Nazis' calculated use of foreign labor, and as part of the large-scale migrant-worker regimes of postwar East and West Germanies, with the latter being partly modelled after the previous Nazi system.[21] In sum, writes Kien Nghi Ha in his book, *Ethnizität und Migration Reloaded,* the German economy has always been organized around the vexed relation between securing cheap labor and prosperity without the costs of long-term care required for citizen workers.[22] Germany's atonement for its fascist past takes on a peculiar role in this context. While it attempts to distance the operations of the state from its history of genocide against Jews, Sinti, Roma, and other ethnic groups, it continues to portray an ethnically exclusive nation bound together by collective guilt.[23] Though the excision of the terms *Rasse* (race) and by extension *Rassismus* (racism) in postwar German public discourse—the former continues to be used in German Basic Law and especially with regard to its prevailing principle of jus sanguinis—documents the nation's transformation from dictatorship to democratic global powerhouse, their explicit absence effectively renders the nation's unceasing antiminority violence unnamable, that is, in the name of maintaining Germany's hard-won image as Europe's poster child, the perfect model of balance between reason and humanitarian spirit.[24]

According to 2020 statistics, out of 10.6 million foreign citizens living in Germany, over 2 million are from Asia—including East Asia (238,000), South and Southeast Asia (881,000), and the Middle East (1.2 million).[25] These numbers exclude residents from Turkey (1.5 million), a perpetual candidate for the European Union. Beyond these numbers, records lag. A consistent German census does not exist, and thus the total number of German-born or naturalized Asians is unknown. The lack of more appropriate or nuanced numbers in part derives from the violent misuse of demographic data collection under fascist rule; no official or national German database is equipped to archive or account for those with migrant background, which also speaks to the lingering institutional reluctance to describe Germany as a country of immigrants. The German government continues to downplay its post–World War II recruitment of approximately 14 million *Gastarbeiter* (guest workers) whose disposability contributed to the rehabilitation and unification of East and West Germany. Postwar migrants to former West Germany were largely recruited from the Mediterranean (especially Turkey), parts of Asia, and Africa. The Democratic German Republic, a.k.a. East Germany, took in approximately 100,000 Allied-nation *Vertragsarbeiter* (contract workers), a large part of them Vietnamese (who faced a great deal of precarity after unification).[26] When "guest" workers attempted to stay, build, or unify their families after years of having lived in a now-familiar Germany, they were framed as foreign invaders by the state. The historical origin of their presence has been effectively expunged from national consciousness, further corroborated by the lack of a state apparatus able to quantify or acknowledge the perpetual violence against those perceived as foreign, including migrant workers, war refugees, students, and naturalized and German-born citizens.[27]

German academia has tended to replicate these official occlusions. In Germany there is no widely accepted equivalent to the field of ethnic studies as it is known in the United States, let alone any sustained interest in Asian European diasporas. A fledgling initiative to study Asian Germans was recently started in American studies in Germany, though it arguably enjoys greater influence among U.S.-based German studies scholars. Guest worker studies do exist, yet tend to overlook the less numerous migrant communities who arrived to Germany after World War II—for example, the twenty thousand South Korean guest worker migrants to West Germany, and the sixty thousand Vietnamese contract workers who migrated to East Germany.[28] Mita Banerjee describes the cause of Asian German studies in Germany as appearing "*demographically* impossible," noting the difficulty in justifying new critical paradigms with which such relatively small yet significant numbers like these could be adequately engaged.[29] Attempts to create greater minority visibility within German academic discourse remain tightly circumscribed. Critics of European film scholarship have made concerted efforts to showcase the work of migrant and diasporic filmmakers, especially that of Turkish Germans. Yet conversations often continue to default to the deep-rooted two-cultures paradigm and home/foreign country dualism through which minority aesthetic productions are taken as realist representations of an artist's life and ethnic heritage, and biographies

30 | IMPROPER *ASIATISCHE DEUTSCHE*

of minority filmmakers are taken as proof of empirically foreign difference.[30] I label Wong and Steyerl as Asian German video artists, a first-time label for the two, not to examine how their work represents an original identity, but to mobilize their conspicuously improper self-stagings to interrogate the claim of German racelessness.

Wong's World Openness: *Angst Essen / Eat Fear* (2008)

Born in Singapore in 1971, a few years after its independence from Malaysia, Wong studied art in Singapore and London. He has lived in Berlin since his artist residency there in 2007. As of 2019 he holds a professorship in performance at the Royal Institute of Art in Stockholm. Wong's video productions have been shown across the globe, among others in France, Hong Kong, Bangladesh, Australia, Senegal, and the United States. Though his engagement with the hybrid performativity of identities resonates with audiences across different political geographies, it has gained equal kudos from major Singaporean art institutions and from critics and connoisseurs of the global art scene. Among other accolades, Wong received a Special Mention at the 2009 Venice Biennale by a jury that included the masterful critic of mimicry, Homi Bhabha. An elite Asian cosmopolitan in high demand, Wong demonstrates in his work his keen awareness of how he and other creatives of color are readily marketed in ways that specifically promote an inoffensive and user-friendly European multiculturalism. Take the following anecdote, a critique of the top-down promotion of cultural diversity during his time in London:

> There was something called the cultural diversity monitoring form that came with every funding application, and applicants had to tick boxes regarding whether their proposals would be relevant to or employ various ethnic groups . . . to the point where you had Black-Afro-Caribbean, Black-African, Asian-Indian, East Asian, Chinese, Irish, Welsh, Eastern European, Jewish and then mixed heritage with White-plus-Black-Afro-Caribbean, White-plus-Black-African, White-plus-Asian and on and on. It was ridiculous and damaging because institutions and individuals seeking funding would respond to these requirements by hiring an obviously "diverse" person to work the front desk without actually changing

their status quo. . . . On my application form I ticked all the boxes and got the funding to do the project.[31]

Internationally pedigreed and publicly gay, Wong flaunts his ability to bend and blend himself and his video personas into a variety of international art environments, as he appears untouched by the policing of national border regimes. A self-described cosmopolitan "guestartworker,"[32] Wong evokes exactly the kind of user-friendly "world openness" that Germany seeks to promote, one gauged by the ability to attract international talent, real estate, and other capital investments.[33]

Wong's serial re-creations of beloved melodramas from different countries—"world cinema," as he describes it—includes video reshufflings of iconic films like *Last Year in Marienbad* (Alain Resnais, 1961), *Persona* (Ingmar Bergman, 1966), *Death in Venice* (Luchino Visconti, 1971), *Chinatown* (Roman Polanski, 1974), and *In the Mood for Love* (Wong Kar-wai, 2000). Wong's *Angst Essen / Eat Fear* (2008) is a twenty-seven-minute video "cover" of Fassbinder's celebrated *Ali: Fear Eats the Soul* (*Angst Essen Seele Auf,* 1974). Fassbinder's original feature narrates a taboo romance between a sixty-year-old West German cleaner named Emmi and the younger Moroccan guest worker El Hedi Ben Salem M'barek Mohammed Mustafa, a.k.a. Ali. In the original film we witness not only Ali's persistent objectification by others as a Black and Arab foreigner in Germany but also Emmi's experiences of discrimination as an older, working-class woman, and as a white German who openly desires Ali. "In *Eat Fear,* Ming plays all the roles," hilariously notes Wong's website. "Speaking an approximate German, he embodies up to five persons at the same time."[34] A one-man drag remix of Fassbinder's treasured work of New German Cinema, *Eat Fear* retains Wong's signature anti-high-art camp aesthetic.[35]

In the opening scene of the original *Ali: Fear Eats the Soul,* Ali befriends Emmi at a bar by asking her to dance. They start to dance, seemingly oblivious to the judgmental stares of other guests. The to-be lovers are soon chatting about their incompatibilities. "Germans with Arabs not good," Ali opines. "Why?" asks Emmi. "Germans and Arabs not the same people," he confirms. An uncanny cut to the nearly hateful gazes of surrounding customers corroborates Ali's observations: "German master. Arab dog," he continues. "Arabs not

32 | IMPROPER *ASIATISCHE DEUTSCHE*

human." Keeping in mind Fassbinder's pessimistic worldview (and perhaps his own exploitative relationship with the actor who plays his Ali, the Moroccan-born El Hedi Ben Salem, after whom he named his film's protagonist), Wong's personal casting transplants Fassbinder's sobering portrait of race in postwar West Germany into today's context of Germany's persistent anti-Muslim sentiment. The artist's outlandish, comedic, and critical rehash casts his own body as abjectly dark and foreign, and virtually renders everyone a stranger. Wong's use of dark makeup to play his Ali, a Black Arab man coded as Muslim in Fassbinder's original, invokes theatrical practices of blackface—a practice that emerged in Germany during the violent Scramble for Africa, and continues today (like yellowface) in the German entertainment industry.[36] Wong's deployment of blackface draws attention to Ali's superfluousness in both the video and original film, as if his face were a screen upon which others can project their racial fantasies. These include the Turkish guest worker—Fassbinder's film was indeed almost called *All the Turks Are Called Ali*—Arab Muslim, and Black African, none of which Ali entirely or conclusively embodies. Wong's switching between blackface and "whiteface" also foregrounds an on-demand pliability that relates to and renarrates Ali's abjection beyond the terms of antagonism and depreciation.

Playing the roles of both Ali and Emmi in his critical-comic knockoff, Wong revises the hostile scene in which the human-and-not-human couple falls in love. "Germans with Arabs not good," says Ali—in Wong's Singaporean accent. "Why?" croons Emmi's also accented and not-so-feminine voice. "Germans and Arabs not the same people," says Ali, in a mimicry of the original. The video then cuts to the cold stares of the bar's other customers—all played by Wong—as the dialogue resumes: "German master. Arab dog." By the end of this truncated, improper, and irreverent knockoff scene, Wong's *Eat Fear* has invoked and undermined the gravity of *Ali: Fear Eats the Soul*. His one-man, multirole performances render these German subjects of ostensibly different human value into close and hilarious intimacy. As he shapeshifts between Ali and Emmi, Wong appears in brown body makeup and dark wig, beard, and suit; later we see him in an old-fashioned patterned dress with whitening makeup, blond wig, and prosthetic breasts and hips. Wong thus remixes Fassbinder's classic (a loose revision of Douglas Sirk's 1955 melodrama *All That Heaven Allows*), into a prismatically personal, quasi-drag, do-it-yourself video that embraces its own amateurishness. Wong's use of prosthetics and extreme makeup, along with some digital editing, turns Fassbinder's original story of stigmatized characters into a carnivalesque in which fear is effectively gobbled up. The conspicuously unprofessional editing renders Ali and Emmi's dancing choppy and their interactions artificial. As each framing fails to maintain appropriate cinematic structures of signification and identification, we witness the flexibility of the video form. What emerges is an overexaggeration and overstylization with political implications. The Black Arab man is no longer the sole object of abjection, and the chorus of "original" Germans, all inauthentic, provoke as much laughter as scrutiny.

In Wong's reenactment of Fassbinder's renowned scene, Emmi introduces Ali, now her husband, to two female colleagues from work. To overcome their hostile attitudes and have them approve of her marriage, she invites the women to come close and examine Ali's body. Not needing to be told twice, they swarm around Ali's masculine, muscular frame like predators circling around their prey. "Terrific!" they exclaim, "the skin is so soft." "Ali is taken to market," writes Anca Parvulescu, "by the German women on the screen, the filmmaker, as well as a viewer fascinated by his sexual versatility."[37] *Ali: Fear Eats the Soul* shows Ali liminally trapped between racial abjection and hypersexualization, exploited by the voyeuristic gaze of his own spouse and her coworkers. In comparison, Wong's conspicuous impersonation of Ali (he is too thin to approximate El Hedi Ben Salem's physique) and of every other character in the scene (he is too flat chested to adequately represent the female coworkers), topples the racial divisions and power relations on which the original's looking relations remain built.

To recover from his humiliation, Wong's Ali seeks comfort from Barbara, a voluptuous white bartender. Just as in the original, *Eat Fear* shows Ali spending the night with her. Yet where Fassbinder ends his film with Barbara and Ali's desperately silent embrace, *Eat Fear* features the couple's loud and unromantic plop upon the mattress, rendering hilarious the original film's melancholic tone. The video's affect relays a masculinity whose "queer and brown" potential performativity is not doomed to misery, but open to silliness, lightness, and flamboyance.[38] Moreover, whereas the original Ali is captured in full nudity as he waits for Barbara, Wong recasts the frontal shot wearing a brown dildo framed in a ridiculous fuzz of pubic hair.

Figure 5. Wong undermines the scene of racial abjection by playing every character in the frame; courtesy of the artist.

His entire body is oddly brown, hairy, and overly thin. Wong's sly impropriety neither renders everyone equal, nor is just about play. It reveals a divide between those who have access to playful masquerade, most often those with majoritarian privilege and a closer proximity to whiteness, and those who have less identitarian flexibility.[39] The artist's promiscuous appearance dismisses the racelessness of white bodies in ways that disengage the Black Muslim figure from its fixed positioning as the outcast Other. We might say that *Eat Fear* intercepts the historical fetishization of Black masculinity as pure sex and casts light on it as an object simultaneously coveted and feared.[40] And yet Wong's practice of blackface also invokes the possibility of his own racist complicity with respect to his privileged mobility not as German, Turkish, or Muslim, but as a Chinese Singaporean "guest-artworker."[41] Wong's racial drag leaves room for productive ambiguity, I suggest: his performance troubles the expected appropriateness of Wong's Asian exemplarity, making the mattering of race awfully conspicuous; it appears rather transgressive, unacceptable, lewd. *Eat Fear*'s suggestive play with male packaging is in fact full of sexual innuendo between and among Germany's historically antagonized masculinities—for example, Black virility, Asian effeminacy, and Muslim regressivism. Indeed, Wong's pliable body copies, borrows,

IMPROPER *ASIATISCHE DEUTSCHE* | 35

and queers in ways that do not promise equal visibility but advance a new repertoire of improper erotics and impossible cross-racial aesthetics as an experiment in envisioning minoritarian affinities.

The Poor Capture of Hito Steyerl

Born in Munich in 1966, Hitomi Steyerl, also known as Hito Steyerl, grew up during the early blossoming of New German Cinema. She studied film in Tokyo and Munich, and later received a doctorate in philosophy from the Academy of Fine Arts in Vienna. Currently a professor of experimental film and video at the University of the Arts in Berlin, Steyerl was ranked in 2017 by *Art Review* as one of the most powerful people in the contemporary art world.[42] Critics have praised her work for its "hybrid" and "deliberately impure" qualities with respect to her combination of different media forms, most notably in her essay videos and lecture performances.[43] Through this exploration of variegated media forms, she tackles topics such as techno-surveillance, military warfare, and the capital-motivated infrastructure of the art industrial complex. Rarely, if ever, does Steyerl discuss her own biracial identity as a Japanese German mixed-race artist or themes of racial identity per se. Her 1998 thesis was a film entitled *Die Leere Mitte* (The empty center) and explores anti-immigrant sentiment in Germany after postunification Berlin. An editor of *Spricht die Subalterne deutsch?* (Does the subaltern speak German?), Steyerl has long promoted the formal study of race and Germany.[44] However, her rise to one of the most powerful figures in the art world has come with a curious forgetfulness, perhaps especially on the part of critics, a notable shift away from the "provincial" realm of German race politics, and toward more "universal" issues. My discussion, by contrast, pays special attention to the artist's racialized appearance in her video work: how she stages herself not as a subject of racial truth, but in ways that reflect on and critique racial capture—the demand that she dis/appear like a readymade image.

Recall the 35-second video *Strike II* with which I opened the introduction to this book. In this video, Steyerl appears as a poorly visible image—grainy, pixelated, hard to observe—before proceeding to bash the recording device altogether. She literally pulls out a mallet, and bam! Similar to the prequel *Strike* (2010), where the artist cracks an LCD television screen using hammer and chisel, *Strike II*

36 | IMPROPER *ASIATISCHE DEUTSCHE*

refuses to deliver serviceable images, exposing instead the taken-for-granted mandate for ubiquitous accessibility. Yet the video does not demonize image delivery per se. *Strike II*'s "freed" digital images, for instance, continue making their rounds on high-definition screens in art galleries and via the popular video-sharing platform YouTube. But they do so as "poor images," what Steyerl also describes as a glitch, valueless visual artifacts outdated in their low resolution:

> The poor image is a copy in motion. Its quality is bad, its resolution substandard. As it accelerates, it deteriorates. It is a ghost of an image, a preview, a thumbnail, an errant idea, an itinerant image distributed for free, squeezed through slow digital connections, compressed, reproduced, ripped, remixed, as well as copied and pasted into other channels of distribution.[45]

The poor image makes the wrong things visible. It "is no longer about the real thing—the originary original." Instead, it draws attention to its own materiality, like a messenger going astray. Media scholars including T. J. Demos, Thomas Elsaesser, and Jihoon Kim have helpfully examined how Steyerl's estranging video aesthetics subvert documentary conventions and indexical truth claims.[46] "In Steyerl's artistic practice," writes Demos, "the documentary genre is still rich in historical reference, but is characterized as well by a heightened consideration of video's formal organization, built on a keen awareness of the uncertain status of truth and meaning."[47] The reflexive nature of Steyerl's work is typically placed in a tradition of leftist radical filmmaking and its political commitment to collective mobilization, including Soviet avant-garde cinema and the oeuvre of European male auteurs like Godard, Marker, and Farocki.[48] Here, I suggest that we situate her image politic also and importantly in relation to Europe's disavowed race politics. I show how the artist tactically deploys the poor image in ways that betray a "raceless" demand for ready Asian accessibility, most strikingly as it pertains to Asian femininity.[49]

The filmmaker's slutty appearance in *Strike II* underlines this point. Suggestively staged against the iconic cherry blossom tree, Steyerl's made-up look recalls the figure of the Asian whore or oriental femme fatale—two staples in Euro-American racial fantasies. While the video evokes the sexual desires associated with the Asian mixed-race woman, the artwork's grainy, choppy, shattered audiovisuals obstruct her easy consumption. *Strike II* appears like a stalled strip show that ends prematurely. The poor image preempts the artist's clean capture and sabotages her ready servitude. Her use of visual poorness indeed exposes and strikes against the patriarchal racializing of, and claim to access, enter, and control, the Asian mixed-race femme. Steyerl's self-staging in *Strike II* affords us an opportunity to dismantle the rendering of Asian femininity as a site of penetration and control, as theorized by feminist race scholars like Celine Parreñas Shimizu, Hoang Tan Nguyen, Lily Wong, Genevieve Yue, Mila Zuo, and Vivian Huang.[50] At the same time, her targeting of visual enframing is specific to the context of European racelessness, where her Asian mixed-race femme-ness (just like Asian femininity)— dangerously beautiful and sexy—is rendered as a token of a "tolerant, free and loving" European ethos.[51]

Strike II has received comparatively little attention among critics, yet the video offers a strikingly effective staging of European race politics. There is an intimate relation, I suggest, between the artist's refusal to readily dis/appear in the video and what she describes as a pervasive expectation to conform to the representational demands placed upon German artists of color. Steyerl details, "There has, historically, been this pressure to confess or use confessional discourse among ethnic minorities in Germany. That's more or less the only possible story you're supposed to tell, like relating to your origins or ancestry or stuff like that. But the problem with these stories is that if they don't correspond to . . . prefabricated stereotypes . . . then people will not be satisfied."[52] I propose that we revisit Steyerl's signature aesthetic of the poor image as also a response to and deeply shaped by the mediating processes of racial knowledge production that is characteristic of contemporary Germany. I now turn to Steyerl's essay video *Lovely Andrea* (2007), where we follow the artist's quest for an image from her past whose accessibility is constantly undermined by improper video form—the poor, the fleeting, the copy image.

Poor, Lovely Andrea

The second part of a video trilogy that includes Steyerl's *November* (2004) and *Abstract* (2012), *Lovely Andrea* (2007) was commissioned by the prominent art exhibition *documenta XII*.[53] Since its debut in 2007, the thirty-minute video has screened at various film festivals,

38 | IMPROPER *ASIATISCHE DEUTSCHE*

museums, and other international art spaces. A video foray into the ostensibly global essay film, *Lovely Andrea* is a commentary on the unruly and unpredictable circulation of images of women. Despite the enabling of bondage images by corporate money, political decision making, military forces, and desires of straight men, the images of women in *Lovely Andrea* forge surprising circuits that are neither readily nor necessarily managed by the original entities that spurred their dissemination.

Lovely Andrea exploits Steyerl's short-lived career as a bondage model in 1980s Japan. At the time, Steyerl was studying film in Tokyo, in the hopes of making a film about rope bondage in Japan's Yakuza-dominated porn industry. As various industry men interviewed in *Lovely Andrea* nostalgically recount, bondage productions in the 1980s were under constant risk of being shut down by police. This only made the industry more edgy and intense, and simultaneously increased demand for the illegal productions. Women were often lured into the business to "model" without being debriefed about the actual job's details; many were forced to pose naked without pay. Steyerl ultimately abandoned the investigative project; it simply became too dangerous. However, her bondage pictures were published, somewhere. Twenty years after her rope shots, *Lovely Andrea* video-documents Steyerl and her small film crew's journey through various Japanese sex-magazine archives to locate the orphaned images of her past. But Steyerl's memory is hazy, and despite thousands of bondage series and even more photos archived every year, the artist and her crew make the unlikely happen. After numerous interviews with industry professionals and studio visits, they finally track down the right magazine in a special library in Tokyo.

As viewers follow along, we learn that the quest to create a properly autobiographical narrative, or "proper" narrative in any sense, is itself an exercise in "self-suspension."[54] The filmmaker herself only appears to us as a subpar media image, an inauthentic iteration, an obvious hoax. Like *Strike II, Lovely Andrea* sets up viewer expectations throughout the video, only to frustrate them ad infinitum. Containing the reflexively documentarian and form-shifting accoutrements of the essay form, *Lovely Andrea* does not present its images as clear vehicles of coherent content. It arranges them in ways that make it seem like we are witnessing multiple streams of consciousness. Footage of Steyerl's travels to Tokyo are blended with archival news footage, music video clips, superhero cartoons, and live self-suspension performances. A great deal of this eclectic audiovisual material is illegally sourced from peer-to-peer networks, raising further questions about consistency, originality, authorship, and ownership.[55] Whose narrative is this? "What is your film *about*?" Steyerl is repeatedly asked. We fail to gather a coherent response. Instead, we watch the artist's story as it unfolds through ellipses and deferrals, mix-ups and occlusions, committed most notably by Asagi Ageha, who is not only Steyerl's assistant director, spokesperson, and translator, but also a former bondage model turned accomplished self-suspension artist whose performances debut in Steyerl's video. Needless to say, Asagi fails to provide a coherent answer to this question; her responses are everywhere, and get us nowhere. They are incoherent, poor, and devoid of any "appropriate" context or coherence.

In lieu of expected outcomes, it is perhaps Steyerl's motif of the rope that best coheres *Lovely Andrea*'s mixed-up repertoire of still and moving images, of bondage models and Guantánamo prisoners, and of female superheroes that save the world with lasso tricks. The

Figure 6. Steyerl refuses to explain what her film is about; screenshot from *Lovely Andrea*.

40 | IMPROPER *ASIATISCHE DEUTSCHE*

rope recalls Celine Parreñas Shimizu's use of the term *bondage* to reference both the harmful subjections and playful freedoms of sex with regard to Asian women's sexualization. Parreñas Shimizu describes as the "bondage" to "perverse hypersexuality" the representational demand that the Asian woman be readily available to audiences, both sexually and epistemologically.[56] Such expectations, the author expands, find their counterpart in U.S. imperial occupations in Asia (and beyond) as if the latter were up for grabs. At the same time, Parreñas Shimizu insists that there is agency and pleasure to be had in performing and playing with " 'bad object' representations such as whorish Asian women."[57] Similarly, *Lovely Andrea* critiques the overt sexualization of Asian women broadly by focusing upon the exploitative nature of the industry; yet Steyerl also delights in seizing the powerful position of the Asian femme to tease, toy with, and torment her audience, and she seeks such freedom in particular in the (allegedly un)restrictive essay form.

The keen reflexivity of images is a key feature of the essay film, a form whose explicit self-referentiality and self-reflectiveness have been lauded as a European invention that is specially equipped to challenge rigid forms of thinking, thanks to its qualities of "hybridity" and "openness."[58] Thomas Elsaesser speaks of "a type of recursiveness, where images are able to comment on themselves, or where voice and image are in a dialogue with each other, in mutual interaction or fruitful tension."[59] In its refusal to make the original photos easily available and monetizable, *Lovely Andrea* can be said to both exploit and parody the essay form. Steyerl describes this form as designed to feed the neoliberal pliability and palatability of Asian women and their power over their representational labor (including their aesthetic productions). As part of the cultural industry, she observes, "the essay as form no longer necessarily meddles with standardized and homogeneous identities. Instead, it runs parallel to the post-Fordist coercion of difference, mobility, extreme flexibilization, and distracted modes of attention, whose ideal subjectivity is hybrid and supple."[60] In other words, the essay form here advances a logic that operates on the demand for a ready pliability that characterizes the Asian on Demand and that informs Steyerl's critique of the immense pressure for artists to base their work upon their putatively original identities, as if readily "confessing" one's original and authentic ancestry could supplant or elide official absences regarding discussions about race, or satisfy the dominant demands and desires of a majoritarian audience.[61] "I always tried to avoid getting caught up in this double bind, so I never made any work which could be understood as fitting into that category."[62] The demand of this double bind is a trap, Steyerl comments: "You are forced to confess, but whatever you say will not be what people expected and will therefore be invalid." The poor image is here more than a technological effect, an intervention into and playful reappropriation of the bondage of gendered race politics. *Lovely Andrea* exploits the reflexive essay form to frustrate—and enjoy the play with—the arrestment of the Asian femme both visually and sexually. "The search is restaged for television," reads a caption as we near the video's climactic event, underscoring our inaccessibility to the purity of a confession, or revelation of Steyerl's "real" bondage pictures. We follow Steyerl and Asagi sifting through a Japanese sex-image archive, followed around by an all-male German public television team that vigorously arranges the women in front of the camera. "I'm shooting"; "I didn't catch that"; and "You should be a little bit forward and she should be a little bit back" are some directives that we can hear. But there is nothing authentic to discover. Instead, we find only clues about the video's arrangement, which include self-referential intertitles and a flashy soundtrack playing Depeche Mode's "Master and Servant" as we find ourselves gazing at the German crew. The video also continues to contest the fetishization of the female bondage model by turning its camera upon those in the porn industry who normally wield its gaze. In lieu of bound and naked women, we are presented with a series of interviews with male Japanese industry leaders discussing how women initiated into bondage modeling were often "told it would be a different kind of job and then talked into it," and "only realized on the set what they were supposed to do," as one photographer says. "Some also cried." We learn that women would be released without pay, that is, "when they became really desperate and said that they just wanted to quit at any price." Taking for granted the women's on-demand servitude, these are the very industry leaders who insist that women's bondage is a pure art.

Finally, the artist renders our long-awaited money shot: the real bondage picture! And it is completely disappointing—an out-of-focus page out of a sex magazine. Is it of Steyerl? The poor image thwarts the claim of visual ownership over the racialized and sexed female

Figure 7. Presented to us: a rather underwhelming money shot of Steyerl in bondage; screenshot from *Lovely Andrea*.

body and obstructs its knowability. Without our bondage to visual access, or a full-on frontal of the photograph, the narrative implodes. What a killjoy.

Lovely Andrea continues to deflate all expectation. The camera is on Asagi as she translates a short text that accompanies Steyerl's coveted but insipid magazine photo. Its title is "Lovely Andrea." The text is announced with the essential—"B: 90; W: 60; H: 98"—before its contents are described in more detail: "Bondage beautiful girl Andrea, this gorgeous body sweats in Roppongi disco clubs every night." Steyerl laughs at hearing about this disco girl, as Asagi reads on, describing this other Andrea who, it turns out, was a businesswoman looking to earn money in Japan, and "by smelling non-Japanese...." Wait... what? Smelling non-Japanese? Asagi laughs at the camera, explaining nothing, except, "this sentence is a bit embarrassing." Steyerl's capture remains poor. Steyerl's "original" bondage pictures insist on remaining unclear, literally and figuratively, suggesting that the act of wanting to know, when framed as a desire for mastery, or as an epistemological and representational pursuit to control what is

IMPROPER *ASIATISCHE DEUTSCHE* | 43

knowable and thus put it in bondage, or as an inquiry wielded "over and above" an Other, always produces a relation of dominance. The act of wanting to know is about control; as Steyerl observes, the ostensible singularity of the European mind has always preempted a readily available Other. "The comparison of as many different cultures as possible was seen as a prerequisite for the acquisition of universalizable knowledge, as overcoming the relativity of knowledge."[63] And indeed, by sabotaging the clarity and value of her photographs as well as proper narrative style, Steyerl foils all demands to capture her ready availability.

The "Real" Andrea

There is more to *Lovely Andrea*'s inception. Steyerl chose the pseudonym "Andrea" to protect her identity in the bondage industry, borrowing the name from her best friend and past creative co-conspirator Andrea Wolf. Asagi explains that Steyerl "was working under the name Andrea. This was her friend's name. But this friend was murdered and it seems as if she was a terrorist. After she was murdered the insurgents put her photo on banners and marched around and . . . she was put on a flag in Turkey, and in Japan she appeared in an SM magazine in bondage." Asagi's cursory statement is the only mention of Wolf in the video. It is accompanied by a similarly dense montage linking Wolf's circulating image in television news and on insurgent posters with a print of Steyerl in bondage. Wolf appears in a poor, low-resolution image that is difficult to see. The montage material in *Lovely Andrea* is taken from the video *November,* with Wolf at the center of its narrative. *November* portrays Wolf as a radical feminist who, after her alleged involvement in German left-wing terrorism in the 1980s, joins the women's army of the Kurdish Liberation Movement in Iraq. Sought after by the German state for her militant activity in the Federal Republic, Wolf is killed by the Turkish army as a Kurdish freedom fighter close to the Iraqi border. Her extrajudicial execution remains unexamined. Steyerl writes: "No official investigation ever took place. No experts went on site . . . not because there were no observers, but because they have not been authorized."[64] Yet this official disappearance spurs unofficial circulations of the image. Following Wolf's death in 1998, her picture appears on Kurdish protest banners across activist networks from Turkey to Berlin. She is

Figure 8. Wolf's traveling portrait, here pictured as an icon of Kurdish liberation; screenshot from *Lovely Andrea*.

celebrated as Martyr Ronahi, her chosen Kurdish name. *November*'s voice-over continues, "I have also seen my friend's picture on demonstrations... as part of a gloriole of martyrs, part of them suicide fighters, surrounding the patriarchal figure of [Kurdish nationalist leader] Abdullah Ocalan." Wolf's multiple renderings and dis/appearances serve to justify the goals of various political parties. Her image does not exist in its own right; it rather dis/appears on demand.

Abstract further investigates Wolf's death. Steyerl visits the site of her friend's murder and records the account of a local witness. The elderly Kurdish man remembers the cruel scenario of Wolf's capture, referring to her as the "German fighter."

> Her code name was Ronahi, she was captured alive. She said she was a journalist. The colonel hit her on the head with a stick. The militia man hit her head with the butt of his weapon. They killed her. Then they cut off her breasts. Whenever I see the perpetrators, I think of this horrible act.

We see no image of Wolf. There are leftover ammunition cases, stained clothes, the rocky landscape of the battle site, and repeated intertitles that liken the camera shot to the firing of a weapon.

This is a shot.
This is a countershot.
This is a 20mm ammunition case fired by Cobra helicopters.
This is where my friend Andrea Wolf was killed in 1998.

"Abstract" refers not to the artist's conceptual distancing from her friend's death. Steyerl rather exploits the medium of video to critique how images are abstractly rendered, how they are arranged in ways that make them appear divorced from reality, to be sold as pure representation. "The image," Steyerl insists, "is the thing in which senses merge with matter."[65] It materializes a perceptual regime that decides who dies. Shortly after the brutal killing of Wolf and dozens of other female insurgents, Turkey was granted candidacy for entry into the European Union. To prove its commitment to European standards of human rights, the Turkish state must conceal its violence. Adherence to human rights becomes a matter of disappearing women's bodies, of merging sense with matter in ways that uphold Turkey's qualification for EU inclusion. Yet Wolf's swift disappearance by the Turkish army alludes to Europe's humanism as a cosmetic farce reliant on the need for human disposability. *Abstract* features shots of Steyerl recording the Berlin office of the U.S. manufacturer, whose weapons the German government sold to the Turkish Army used against the Kurdish insurgents, suggesting once more how abstraction can both conceal and thereby render something, and someone, superfluous.

What I take from *November* and *Abstract* is how the image formalizes a necropolitical framing that decides who disappears, and not only in the symbolic sense. The image is not a representation; its capture is the stuff of life and death. By intersecting Steyerl's search for Andrea with that of Wolf, *Andrea* spotlights the violent ways in which women are readily paraded and removed according to hegemonic demands. The video investigates how women's bodies are rendered as images that serve on demand, living or dead, from the Japanese sex industry and German documentary media to Turkish state nationalism and Kurdish militant activism, and the assertion of Europe's

46 | IMPROPER *ASIATISCHE DEUTSCHE*

democratic core. *Lovely Andrea* traces the racializing, gendered, and sexed dimensions of these renderings through the figure of Steyerl's fleeting femme-ness as she embodies the persona of a great-smelling Western seductress in the Far East, and that of a cosmopolitan intellectual in ostensibly raceless Euro-American art circles. As we witness the real Andrea undergo several identity changes, *Lovely Andrea* suggests that the oppressive demand to deliver and die is exclusive to neither Asian racialization nor Asian femininity. Born a West German citizen, Wolf dies a Kurdish rebel. She is remembered as a Kurdish nationalist and perhaps a Muslim martyr. There is a striking antagonism between Wolf's persona as a menacing Muslim rebel fighter and Steyerl's serviceable Asianness. Steyerl's image politic reimagines such antagonizing mediations by featuring images that move in a haphazard and unwieldy manner. The filmmaker dis/appears into her video, as Lovely Andrea dis/appears, and as Wolf dis/appears, and as Ronahi is sought by a filmmaker—and as that filmmaker is narrated to us by Asagi. These renderings embrace improper and impossible challenges to the demand to deliver and die, and repudiate the original as normal and forever available.

2

Mental Health and Live Fictions

Kristina Wong and *Wong Flew Over the Cuckoo's Nest*

I had no idea. Why are they killing themselves? They seem so beautiful and perfect.

—Kristina Wong, artist's website

In her one-woman show, *Wong Flew Over the Cuckoo's Nest,* Kristina Wong melodramatically and hilariously plays the role of herself—Kristina Wong, a Chinese American female performance artist from the San Francisco Bay Area who just happens to be touring a show about Asian American women and mental health. Due to Kristina's (or perhaps apt in this case, their) ambitious goals and the stresses and demands of her live tour, Kristina experiences a mental breakdown (indeed, both Kristinas do). Prompting an engagement with a more attentive and activist practice of viewing Asian American women on stage and "on scene,"[1] *Cuckoo's Nest* blurs boundaries between reality and fiction in ways that frustrate demands for Kristina's authentic representational availability for both live and streaming audiences. Wong describes her deft use of humor as "subversive" and "endearingly inappropriate";[2] her badass solo performances recall the work of Margaret Cho, Ali Wong, D'Lo, Leilani Chan, and other killjoys in the business of foiling traditional stereotypes about Asian American women with respect to conventional hetero and cisgender womanhood.[3]

The unifying characteristic of my work is employing humor to explore difficult subjects and amplify marginalized experiences, using the premise of "autobiography" as a starting point of exploration.

| 47

48 | MENTAL HEALTH AND LIVE FICTIONS

I criss-cross avant garde performance art, arts and crafts, stand-up comedy and cultural criticism. I am influenced by culture jammers like Banksy, Michael Moore and the Yes Men who subvert the performances of everyday life to make social commentary and change. I am also inspired by a long history of immersive theater and interactive performance art work, artists like Yoko Ono, James Luna, and Guillermo Gómez-Peña who use their bodies as the site of commentary.[4]

Cuckoo's Nest is a spinoff of Miloš Forman's 1975 classic film *One Flew Over the Cuckoo's Nest*, in which con man Randle Patrick McMurphy (played by Jack Nicholson) claims that he is insane to avoid jail, and instead finds himself in a psychiatric institution that silences him. The show enjoyed a live production run of eight years from 2006 to 2013, and has been described by the artist as "a swear-to-god-not-autobiographical, serio-comic portrayal of the high incidence of anxiety, depression and mental illness among Asian American women."[5] A signature Kristinaesque experiment that blends different styles of performance, *Cuckoo's Nest* is also a "take on the high rates of depression and suicide among Asian American women,"[6] whose goal is to promote self-advocacy and awareness with regard to mental health issues and self-care among Asian American women.

Born in 1978, Kristina Wong is a "performer, writer, cultural commentator and 'eco-comedian'" and is best known in the United States for her activist performance art, which brought her a 2022 Pulitzer Prize for Drama nomination and a 2023 artist award from the Doris Duke Foundation, among others.[7] Her form-flitting repertoire includes community theater productions, food-bank-influencer projects, and public commentary in popular venues from the *Huffington Post* and *CNN* to *VICE* and *Playgirl*. Her performance project *Kristina Wong for Public Office* (2020), notes her website, blends together "the aesthetics of campaign rallies, church revivals, and solo theater shows to tell the story of what it means to run for local office, the history of voting, and the impact artists can have on democracy."[8] In 2013 Wong traveled to Uganda with the Volunteer Action Network, an organization that offers microloans to women-run businesses, an experience that led to *The Wong Street Journal*, a "part psychedelic TED lecture, part amateur hip-hop extravaganza, and part nonsense" performance about privilege, economics, and race.[9] Her children's web series *Radical Cram School* (2018–2020) familiarized online kids with social justice and Asian American identity. During the early Covid-19 pandemic in 2020, Wong started up the prolific Auntie Sewing Squad, a women-of-color-led volunteer network that delivered hand-sewn masks to underserved communities.[10] The Squad inspired her Pulitzer Prize–nominated show *Kristina Wong, Sweatshop Overlord* (2021).

In an email to me she details the California-heavy genealogy of her live, loud, and in-your-face style of performance:

> Working under Leilani Chan at TeAda Productions in the 90s, who was doing solo work herself, I was able to meet quite a few Asian Americans doing solo theater work. Among them: Denise Uyehara, Nobuko Miyamoto, Dan Kwong, Alison de la Cruz, Erin O'Brien, and Jude Narita. It felt quite normal for me to see Asian American women making and touring their own theater work. And there were Asian American theater companies like Club O' Noodles, Lodestone, 18 Mighty Mountain Warriors, and Here and Now. I think if I went to college on the East Coast, it would have been a whole different reality where maybe I would have still been starved to just see an Asian face. Let alone seeing Asian Americans working in subversive ways.[11]

I saw Wong perform *Cuckoo's Nest* live in 2007 at the Los Angeles REDCAT Theater, before it was recorded and distributed as a concert video in 2011.[12] Her performative labor draws attention to the demand that her performances provide readily available and authentic knowledge about an entire minority.[13] In this context, I attend to the ways in which *Cuckoo's Nest*'s translation from live performance to video format gets at the subtler representational and affective but by no means less taxing demands of Asian exemplarity that Wong faces—and that I summarize below as her mandated "liveness." *Liveness* signifies here not merely a physical bond between performer and audience but rather exacted forms of public visibility that keep the minoritized subject trapped in servitude.

On stage the artist introduces herself (as herself), Kristina Wong, a Chinese American artist determined to achieve social justice by

50 | MENTAL HEALTH AND LIVE FICTIONS

attempting to tell "*every* story of our community."[14] By the end of the eighty-minute show, Kristina claims, she will have found the cure for each and every Asian American woman who is suffering. The artist performs the role of Nancy, a thirty-three-year-old Korean American woman with postpartum depression. Then she plays a sixty-three-year-old Cambodian refugee struggling with PTSD, and an anxiety-ridden twenty-year-old pre-med student from Taiwan, promptly followed by her portrayal of a thirty-year-old Japanese American woman experiencing sexual abuse and a twenty-five-year-old suicidal Korean Japanese woman. As we feel overwhelmed by the ambitious scope of Kristina's performance, she too senses that she is unable to narrate so many endless stories. She calls each lost story a "dropped stitch," to highlight Asian American women's relatively invisible status in popular consciousness. Each story is represented by a hank of yarn. (Central to the pandemic mutual aid work of the Auntie Sewing Squad, sewing and knitting hold a special place in *Cuckoo's Nest* as a soothing and meditative craft for a silent minority and a troubled mind.[15]) Kristina moves increasingly faster—there are so many women's stories to tell, and so little time. First dropping lines, she apparently skips an entire character monologue, then ends up merely shouting out single names: "Rebecca, Flora, Gwen, Carolyn, Amy." The scene closes with her slumped over and out of breath, with unraveled yarn all over the stage.

In *Cuckoo's Nest,* Kristina's vigorous attempts to shoulder the "overwhelming pressure" of representing every single Asian American woman out there are destined to fail. It is indeed a unique burden for the activist artist "to try and tell the whole story" of the underrepresented "all at once," as Kobena Mercer observes.[16] When word got out that Kristina was working on her on-stage production of *Cuckoo's Nest,* she told me, she was contacted by strangers asking that their personal stories be included into the show. " 'Do something about post-partum!' 'Do something about Lao refugees!' 'Somatic blindness!' It was like I was this miracle worker suddenly to people and I couldn't handle the pressure."[17] It's as if each dropped stitch revisits the inevitable failure to represent an uncontainable diversity—and retraumatizes Kristina all over again. The show hunkers on as Kristina attempts to perform the story of "each and every depressed, mentally ill, suicidal Asian American woman," and yet account for the "specific

Figure 9. Kristina tries hard to represent every story on stage. Production photo of *Wong Flew Over the Cuckoo's Nest* concert video by Vince Tanzilli; courtesy of Kristina Wong.

experience of Asian American/Pacific Islander gays, lesbians, bisexuals, transgender, genderqueer, genderfluid, allied, curious, closeted, questioning, transitioning, and leather people." Disclaimer: while Wong engages the compound "Asian American/Pacific Islander" several times, her show is focused on Asian American women, and I focus my discussion accordingly.[18] Kristina's ambitions also strive to appease the "white people in the audience" by ensuring that they don't feel excluded or part of the problem ("Some of my best friends are white people," she assures). Her interaction with men in the audience gestures toward more all-inclusivity. Holding up her mic, she walks over to a few. She tries hard to pronounce their names ("Jim-my"), learn about their origins and culture ("Ireland" and "Leprechauns"), and express her excitement about their intriguing physicalities ("I've been dying to touch your hair"). Wong amusingly reverses the liberal fetishization of Asian American women as exotic cuties. She also points to the power of many a white patron—"Jimmy, thank you so much for patronizing me ... you know, [for] being an arts patron." Lest the white man not feel offended.

Cheering on, Saying Yes

As a vocal antiracist feminist who contradicts the image of submissive Asian femininity, the artist has since the beginning of her career faced attacks, from death threats before stage shows to organized harassment in the form of online alt-right vitriol directed at her in the form of hate mail and rape threats. "Even before I open my mouth or step on stage," Wong states, "my female Asian American body already performs narratives of *immigrant, quiet, submissive, compliant, invisible, over-achieving academic robot, interchangeable, and sexually consumable.* Much of the humor in my performances comes from me leaning into how absurd these narratives are as I satirize myself playing them out."[19] Feminist critics have elaborated on conventional expectations and popular representations of Asian Americans as quiet, deferential, and unobtrusive promoters of "security, contentment, and comfort"—not really for themselves, but for others.[20] This cheery "Asian uplift," as Helen Heran Jun has observed, tends to cast Asian Americans as "idealized subjects of a neoliberal world order, which not only pathologizes the racialized black poor but also reproduces a neoliberal episteme that has devastated the global South since decolonization."[21] With Kristina's cheerful but increasingly desperate determination to keep at it and make every element of the show a success, *Cuckoo's Nest* recalls Hyoejin Yoon's observation of Asian exemplarity as reliant upon the readiness of female cheer, noting the expectation of Asian American women "to cheer and please regardless of her own condition."[22] Preeti Sharma explains that immigrants and women of color have traditionally been assigned the role of service providers in the United States "from manicurist to nanny," providing notable amounts of their labor to health care, textile, leisure, and hospitality industries.[23] Vivian Huang notes that the mandate of staying happy for the sake of others tends to reaffirm popular representations of Asian Americans as emotional caretakers; "regardless of gender identifications," Huang adds, they "are expected to perform model minority emotionology that, implicitly or explicitly, propagate white heteronormative happiness."[24] At the same time, characterizations of hospitality that do not "acknowledg[e] the historic power differentials that accompany their circulation," Huang writes, generally place yet another burden upon women of color: that of often being expected to say yes.[25]

Cuckoo's Nest invokes expectations for Asian American film and video productions to fill in representational absences and gaps with respect to nonwhite people on screen.[26] I elaborate this demand as the demand for *live* rendering beyond the stage of the theater. More than a demand for immediacy and authenticity, the demand for Kristina's *liveness* denotes the demand for her authentic minority self-presentation, which requires her readiness to show up, perform, and be done according to the demands of the audience. *Cuckoo's Nest* thus acts out what happens when the on-demand Asian woman is unavailable or says no to the demand for liveness.

Kristina's desire to embody a whole community of women backfires and disrupts the cogency of the narratives that she attempts to perform. After a "grueling eight-year run" of her show, writes *The Guardian,* "she felt more like a therapist or social worker than a performer. She became known as 'the depression girl' and started to 'lose track' of her identity as a live artist."[27] On stage and off, the experience of performing the show is emotionally and mentally taxing. Kristina's self-impersonations create apt opportunities for comic relief, and provide a counterpoint to *Cuckoo's Nest*'s other explorations. Witty humor is a "self-preservation mechanism" that protects Kristina from the utter depletion of her energy.[28] The show "was not funny when it first started touring, and I found myself adding more and more self-deprecating jokes to just get me through the hour and a half. And then people were like, it's a comedy!" Humor enables a distance between performer and performed, and often "comes from me leaning into how absurd these narratives are as I satirize myself playing them out."[29] Humor helps us to become attuned to the real and imagined pressures of the show's predominantly liberal audience, of its extrapolated Asian American community, of performance critics and funding institutions, and of fellow artists. These inform the dilemma of performance for Asian American roles and for Asian American actors where the "public" category of Asian Americans, like *Asiatische Deutsche,* is presumed to be exempt from available infrastructures of support. According to Tina Chen,

> If we assume Asian American impersonation to be a specific act that involves the assumption of a public identity that does not necessarily belong to "someone else" but that has been assigned to and subsequently adopted by the performer in question in order to

54 | MENTAL HEALTH AND LIVE FICTIONS

articulate an identity comprehensible to the public, the manifest possibilities of how impersonation and identity are not only related but in some sense mutually constitutive become key sites for thinking through the complicated process of performing into being Asian Americanness.[30]

Kristina's loud obnoxiousness at times draws attention to her acts of impersonation.[31] Indeed, "the very nature of Asian American identity," adds Chen, "might be thought of as *one that requires one to impersonate fundamentally oneself.*"[32] A viewer will eventually realize that it is impossible to tell Kristina the on-stage persona apart from the ostensibly "real" Kristina. Access to offstage Kristina—insofar as a spectator can tell—is constantly foiled by her over-the-top accumulations of stories about other women, in a "semiotic excess" that obfuscates everyone's clear legibility.[33] She is always and already saddled with expectations for her work to properly educate viewers about race and culture, that is, from her presumed positionality as an Asian American native informant. Along these lines, Wong's artistic work is often presumed to have been funded due to her minority status ("She's Asian, so they had to give her money"[34]) and/or dismissed as opportunistic "identity work" created on behalf of an ostensibly homogenous and exemplary community that needs no assistance or support.

Kristina's Nonfictional Arc of Fiction

Playing the exemplary subject of *Cuckoo's Nest,* Kristina tries to do everything humanly possible to help each and every Asian American woman who might need psychological support. Kristina insists the show is fictional, and that it has nothing to do with actual life. Urging the crowd to shout out "Fiction!" with her a number of times, she emphatically denies any association with mental illness: "There [is] no depression, mental illness, or suicide in the Wong family. In fact, there is no mental illness in China." Her use of the first-person "I" is pure "dramatic device." Kristina's concern for suffering Asian American women seems to be part of her naturally empathetic drive to bring "truth" and "light" to "the victims." Her lines are intentionally preposterous as she pokes fun at any and all white liberal saviors in the audience: "So brave, I know. You're welcome." (The audience

MENTAL HEALTH AND LIVE FICTIONS | 55

laughs.) Coaching us through the productively confusing distinction between fiction and authentic truths, Kristina checks in to measure our tolerance for confusion. "Hi guys, my name is Kristina Wong, and I have a dragon that lives in my apartment building." (She cues the crowd and it shouts "Fiction!") She goes on to discuss her experiences touring colleges, a story that begins with her decision to quit her day job during Asian Pacific Heritage month—"the month where we really get to work!"—and fully dedicate herself to her work and to minority empowerment. The audience's initial waves of energy subside, as we start to sense how draining her work can be.

I didn't realize actually how hard it would be on my body to be in and out of airports and kind of living from dorm floor to dorm floor each month. "EMPOWERMENT! YOU CAN DO IT!" It's kind of hard on my body. I actually have my period twice in one week. [Loud audience laughter.] "EMPOWERMENT! YOU CAN DO IT!" I actually have to go on WebMD every night to figure out if I have cancer. [Loud audience laughter.] "EMPOWERMENT! YOU CAN DO IT!" I'm being kind of lowballed for my time. I'm not being paid what I should be paid. But that's not what matters. What matters is, "EMPOWERMENT! YOU CAN DO IT! You're the best!"

On stage, Kristina describes the challenges of traveling and living out of a bag for long stretches of time. She tells us how the stress even manifests in painful bouts of vaginal bleeding. We also learn that she is insufficiently compensated for the unique performance work. (She privately told me that she takes a one-week vacation every year for "self-care."[35]) What matters most is her political cause—"Empowerment!" she cheers herself on. "You can do it! You're the best!"

Increasingly, the activist call for minority representation begins to resemble the disciplinary rhetoric of Asian exemplarity. "You're the best"—if you persevere and excel. Wong's repeated and aggressive cheering-on begins to lose meaning. What remains is the empty ideal of excellence, and its continued chase by the artist herself.

We are watching a drama unfold. Kristina displays her drawing of Freytag's Pyramid for us on the overhead projector, as she starts to explain the five-act form of her theatrical performance and its "dramatic arc of fiction": exposition, rising action, climax, denouement,

Figure 10. Why are Asian American women so depressed, and how can Kristina save them all? Production photo of *Wong Flew Over the Cuckoo's Nest* concert video by Vince Tanzilli; courtesy of Kristina Wong.

and resolution. She pulls up a transparency with a large heading with the words *CRISIS*. She reads on. "Why are APIA women so depressed and killing themselves? And how is Kristina Wong going to save them all before you, before anyone else?" Laughter acknowledges her next comment about the scarcity of opportunities for Asian American artists: "Stay off my topic. . . . I found it first." For the remainder of the show, Kristina repeatedly returns to the dramatic arc of fiction to gauge the success of her great mission, each time realizing she is still at the crisis, in fact, she is just as much in crisis as the women for whom she advocates. None of her methods show any resolution—practicing mindfulness, seeking out role models and the support of friends and family—leaving Wong increasingly distressed. She comments: "Essentially, what the show is in the first few acts, is me going through every attempt to make the show that other people wanted me to make . . . until what really needs to be confronted is my insistence that the show follow a neat 'arc of fiction.' This 'fiction' motif is what really runs my show. I think it echoes the issue of depression in Asian communities on so many levels."[36] What echoes the issue of depression is not Kristina's personal story, but the pressure that she readily perform a certain way, and only this way—a pressure she clearly also puts on herself. *Cuckoo's Nest* indeed illustrates how the logic of Asians on Demand operates through minorities' internalized repetition of normative racial gender scripts, that is, to be exactly "this miracle worker" who speaks authentically for an entire minority group, enlightens a white liberal audience, and installs racial justice—through perfectly fictional form.

Fictions and Facts of Asian American Mental Health

The idea for *Cuckoo's Nest* came into being after Wong's campus visit to Wellesley College, where she learned about the disturbing frequency of student suicides. As she worked on *Cuckoo's Nest* and further grappled with issues related to mental health among Asian American women, she encountered numerous stereotypes about Asian Americans as quietly and perfectly functioning, self-sufficient, and need-free. These presumptions are an example of what Sianne Ngai terms Asian racialization's "noticeable contrast to what we might call the exaggeratedly emotional, hyperexpressive, and even 'overscrutable' image of most racially or ethnically marked subjects in American culture."[37] Asian Americans are more often than not perceived as even tempered or rather unthreateningly flat, "a sleeping race," Mel Chen adds.[38] As with the increasingly visible category of Germany's *Asiatische Deutsche,* the idealized model minority stereotype of Asians in the United States has tended to elide the divisiveness of state violence and its promotion of the exceptional qualities that are ostensibly necessary to achieve "the American Dream."

Health, Jonathan Metzl reminds us, is "a term replete with value judgments, hierarchies, and blind assumptions that speak as much about power and privilege as they do about well-being."[39] There are experts who discount the claim that Asian American women are particularly vulnerable to mental health problems with respect to other communities,[40] although existing statistics show that Asian American women struggle disproportionately with anxiety, depression, and suicide. "U.S.-born Asian American women have reported a higher lifetime rate of suicidal thoughts (15.9%) than that of the general U.S. population (13.5%),"[41] and Asian American women over 65 have been said to have the highest female suicide mortality rate among women across all racial groups.[42] Asian American teenage girls, summarizes another report, are "20 percent more likely to attempt suicide compared to their non-Hispanic white peers."[43] At a population of more than 22 million, Asian Americans are better known as one of "the highest-income, best-educated and fastest-growing racial group in the U.S."[44] Asian Americans showed the fastest population growth of any racial and ethnic group between 2000 and 2019, increasing 81 percent during this span, and they are expected to become the "largest immigrant group by the middle of the century."[45] Despite more nuanced studies that pay attention to intracommunal differences, including those related to legal status and poverty rates, the predominant image of Asian Americans remains that of a homogenous model minority defined by upward mobility, buying power, and the absence of so-called cognitive and emotional disturbances. "Asian Americans must exemplify success, in the classroom and the workplace," writes James Lee, and "by extension, they must also inhabit indefinitely healthy bodies that serve this success frame."[46]

Pure "facts" about Asian American women's mental health are murky at best. The American Psychological Association, the largest organization of psychologists worldwide, dedicates an entire website to dispelling "Myths about Suicides among Asian-Americans." According to the APA, the overall rate of Asian American suicides is only half that of the national rate of suicide incidents.[47] The organization rejects the claim that "Asian-American women aged 15–24 have the highest suicide rates of all racial/ethnic groups," and rather promotes the "fact" that "American-Indian/Alaskan Native women aged 15–24 have the highest suicide rate compared to all racial/ethnic groups." Other studies claim that suicide risk is higher among Native and Pacific Islander groups and suggest that the Pacific Islander category tends to inflate Asian American numbers regarding data aggregations and statistical analyses of depression and suicide, making Native and Pacific Islander statistics even more difficult to scrutinize.[48]

The assumption across the board with regard to shame and stigma about mental illness is that Asian people do not talk about feelings, let alone seek professional help.[49] Another "fact," according to Wong, is that "so many people refuse to believe there is a problem inside such a 'perfect' package. . . . perhaps [this is] one of the main reasons why the problem continues to persist."[50] Kristina's struggle to perfectly represent "every story of our community" foregrounds the precariousness of generalizing about Asian Americans as a singular, as homogenous,

MENTAL HEALTH AND LIVE FICTIONS | 59

a beautiful and perfect readymade. In this context, "Individuals who have disabilities, especially cognitive and neurological disabilities, pose a unique challenge to Asian Americans' understanding of their identity."[51]

Liveness and the Concert Video

It is often thought that audiovisual recordings badly mimic what it really feels like to be a spectator watching the stage with others and sharing the same space together. As the performance artist Denise Uyehara says, "I'm not a damn VHS tape. Each time I perform will be different, and I expect that the viewers will enter the conversation with me."[52] Wong was equally skeptical about offering *Cuckoo's Nest* as a concert recording. "As a theater artist who works so interactively, I didn't feel that even the best recording of this show would do it justice. In the show I throw things at the audience, I pet them, I have them hold hands and sing—how can this be captured on camera? . . . Live theater is best when it is live theater, bottom line."[53] Indeed, stage performance has always been a pivotal site for exploring the "human-to-human connectedness."[54] And yet there is nothing intrinsically "live" about the stage; the presence associated with the stage is distinctly mediated. As critics like Philip Auslander, Suk-Young Kim, and Michelle Cho have elaborated, the sense of being intimately connected with others is contingent upon history and its available technologies of mediation, from the space of the theater to television to mobile online streaming.[55]

Wong conscientiously opted for *Cuckoo's Nest*'s reproduction as a concert video, a format that has historically allowed wider access and exposure for minority productions. The video edition of *Cuckoo's Nest,* Wong's only concert film, offers an unaltered ninety-minute recording of Wong's performance that features an opening soundtrack, animated credits, and live-show reaction shots and laugh tracks that smooth out the editing.[56] The turn to video is a vital strategy for *Cuckoo's Nest*'s increased marketing and sales. But Wong produced the concert video with director Michael Closson, to "get [it] out to audiences who wouldn't catch my show live otherwise."[57] Its accessibility has increased since 2013, when the film became available for online streaming and both individual and educational purchase on DVD; the distributor's website indicates prices ranging from roughly

60 | MENTAL HEALTH AND LIVE FICTIONS

$12 for private use, to $200 for an educational license.[58] To optimize learning outcomes, *Cuckoo's Nest*'s website provides a comprehensive discussion guide, and highly recommends postscreening Q&A sessions with mental health professionals.[59] This recommendation is a good reminder that *Cuckoo's Nest* is a work of creative fiction, not a solution for mental health problems. Yet at times it is seen as a stand-in for a solution. In the aftermath of student suicides and other tragic events in the United States, like the 2007 shooting at Virginia Tech by a South Korean student, Wong began to receive invitation after invitation to college and university campuses to perform and help educate young audiences about mental health issues, and to perform a species of exorcist cleansing throughout various halls of academia. Repeated and persistent requests for her to perform live on campus after the tragic events suggest that the demand for her on-stage liveness is more than a demand for her physical presence. It is also a demand that she readily "say yes" to serve institutional needs and figure the institution's commitment for inclusion and diversity.[60]

The work of José Muñoz and Sasha Torres is helpful in framing liveness as a representational arrestment of sorts. Muñoz considers liveness as a demand for ready and available visibility that translates into a "hegemonic mandate that calls the minoritarian subject to 'be live' for the purpose of entertaining elites."[61] The occasion for liveness, he maintains, is framed as the public opportunity to be acknowledged as easily consumable object, with "difference" emerging as a lucrative neoliberal commodity. Torres discusses how the pressure for minorities to be visible to "the public" is necessarily tied to institutional demands for racial authenticity from minority groups. For Torres, the supreme authenticity of liveness and the pretense of its unfiltered access to actual life is corroborated by its mode of televisual representation that elides the puppet strings of its own creative technology. This mode is thus often understood as a properly ethical framing of racial minorities. Torres observes that this association between liveness and authenticity is the main reason that live broadcast has come to denote "good" minority representation. At the same time she develops how televisual liveness has pivoted on the spectacle of anti-Black violence to establish television as *the* representational authority: "In the first sense, liveness describes both certain technical aspects of the televisual apparatus and the extrapolation of those as-

MENTAL HEALTH AND LIVE FICTIONS | 61

pects into an 'ideology' of television emphasizing the putative immediacy, transparency, and presence of the medium's representation. In the second sense, liveness describes a specific racial imperative, one in which persons of color represented on television act as bearers of liveness on the medium's behalf."[62] In this view, the live framing of minorities in video is first and foremost a staging of progressive politics that (via the claim of ready access) continue to sanction exploitative forms of racial visibility.

Wong's concert video was later marketed to educational establishments that wanted to encourage discussion about topics like race and mental health. Hailed for its pedagogical value, the video recording has been especially popular with higher education institutions. Identifying opportunities to further distribute the video to colleges and universities also informs Wong's decisions about *Cuckoo's Nest* ("What is it that colleges are talking about, where is their need, and how do you fill that need?"[63]). The popularity of *Cuckoo's Nest* as a concert video in schools and the higher education sector also shows how the Asian American artist's representational service, which includes the labor to help feel, help educate, and help others work through historical injustice, makes possible and renders alive liberal advocacy. In digital (and streamable) format, *Cuckoo's Nest* is even more readily available for avid curricular study, and circumvents bureaucratic hurdles to often pricey and potentially controversial "live" invitations of experts of color (who might end up calling out the host). With respect to the logic of assimilation of minority difference into the academy, Wong's repackaged and resaleable performance might appear to be part of what Roderick Ferguson calls liberalism's "will to institutionality."[64]

While the artist's educational emphasis distinguishes her work from entertainment-oriented productions like the concert films of Margaret Cho and the Netflix standup specials of Ali Wong, *Cuckoo's Nest*'s concert video is a return to the pedagogical origin of Asian American film and video. The category of Asian American film and video, Jun Okada notes, emerged in the 1970s as a strategy for disseminating programs promoting racial tolerance, and as part of U.S. public service initiatives whose goal was to increase on-screen diversity and to educate public viewers about different cultures and minority issues. "Without public media and its stance on diversity," Okada writes, "the institution of Asian American film and video—films, film festivals, discourse—would not exist."[65] If Asian American media production was driven by grassroots activist efforts to promote Asian visibility "in the face of the institutional racism and invisibility within Hollywood and dominant media," its origin story also bears traces of being tied to institutional demands that Asians represent and stand in for a pluralistic public whole.[66] "Once filmmakers were theoretically free from institutional obligations," says Okada, "they had proven the market potential of Asian American film and video, the legacy and residue of public media remained as ghostly traces within the text."[67]

Kristina's arcs of fictionalization allow the artist a certain protection, for example, from nosy presumptions about both her private life and performances as obviously autobiographical. By breaking with anticipated narrative form, *Cuckoo's Nest* sabotages the expectation that she deliver her authentic self on demand and be readily legible to audiences. "I was really confused as to who I was supposed to be in the making and performance of this show—a savior? A brochure? A comedian? Myself?" Regarding her early-career gigs, she recalls that

> the first Q&As were some of the most assaulting and horrific experiences ever. . . . the audience would just start asking very invasive questions about me, my mental health and my family. Even though the character I play is a fictitious version of me, people were asking me questions as if all these things had happened to me. It was completely uncomfortable and very upsetting. . . . I thought that maybe it was my duty to put myself out there like that.[68]

After putting the show to rest in 2014, Wong claimed "I was losing my mind after eight years of working and touring. . . . Eight years is a long fucking time to tour a show about depression and suicide."[69] The video's (re)production relieved the artist from the stressful demands for her liveness, and for her to perform the show "over and over and over again."[70] To add, it alleviated the stresses of traveling cross-country, of being underpaid, and of serially having to perform intense scenes of minority crisis. "I was performing the show so much I was becoming the character on stage in real life. . . . Holding onto that show in your body is so much different than when it's a film and you can just go and show up at the screening."

Being the Crisis

Wong's aggressive repetition of the mantra—"Empowerment! You can do it! You're the best!"—becomes droning. Revealed is the emotional and physical labor that Asian Americans and other people of color are expected to perform to keep the system running (and everyone happy). Despite its heavy use of humor, the show indeed fails at being funny. A surprising image of the protagonist's excessively bleeding vagina short-circuits any fantasy of cheery female affect. To paraphrase Rachel Lee, the Asian pussy refuses to provide gratification.[71] Kristina appears "monstrous," unattractive, and sexually repulsive.[72] Even more, contained Asian cheer suddenly moves outward and aggresses, recalling John Limon's description of standup as what "makes vertical (or ventral) what should be horizontal (or dorsal)."[73] While *Cuckoo's Nest*'s abject rendering of the female body provokes laughter, it retains an unresolved tension between comedy and pain, drive and exhaustion, and shows how the cruel demand for cheer renders the Asian woman disposable.[74] *Cuckoo's Nest* thus engages cheer as also a melancholic affect that in its attachment to the "perfect package" engenders certain kinds of loss: it overrides the lived experience of exhaustion, anxiety, and depression that sustain the myth of postracial happiness.[75]

Kristina's frantic physical movements, and of darting all over the stage, draw attention to the artist's bodily work. They reveal her dramatic staging as a fictional act of nonfiction: we are always aware of our confusion between Kristina on stage, and Kristina the artist-worker. With Karen Shimakawa, we can describe Wong's enactment as an abject performance, that is, a performance that lingers in ambivalence or in the liminal space between incorporation and exclusion. The abject, Shimakawa maintains, describes the place of Asian Americanness in hegemonic imaginations of Americanness, as neither fully inside nor outside. Shimakawa describes "national abjection" as the process that keeps Asian Americans simultaneously tethered to and outside of "the (literal and symbolic) 'American' body."[76] In other words, Asian Americans are simultaneously treated as the exemplar of the good U.S. nation-state and the "radical other."[77] *Cuckoo's Nest*'s ambivalent lingering rehearses this abject position of Asian Americanness and stages a willful refusal to come clear. The performer's refusal to deliver clean fictional form engenders a productive stalling, what Fred Moten calls "a

64 | MENTAL HEALTH AND LIVE FICTIONS

queer kind of loitering, a kind of cruising, a kind of calculated drifting in and lingering with perception," one that refuses to provide cathartic resolution.[78] Instead, Wong playing Kristina in abject manner links the work of disappearing actress into role with the representational labor of the Asian on Demand—and effectively intercepts the happy sensorium that the Asian woman is exacted to uphold.[79] What links together the two Kristinas is not a true and single self, but the multiple demands for her ready dis/appearance. The conviction that it was her "duty to put myself out there like that" escalates the artist's real intimacy with feeling like falling off a mental cliff.

We follow Kristina on stage back to her parents' home in San Francisco, where things quickly spiral out of control. A newspaper profile on the popular journalist and historian Iris Chang triggers Kristina into a depressive funk. Known for her work on histories of anti-Chinese violence, Chang committed suicide in her late thirties. Kristina finds it all too close for comfort. "I can totally identify with her. I mean we're these two independent women working on really political issues with very little support to the point that it's not fun anymore." The burden of representation is real, and it is further exacerbated by the pressure she puts on herself to be "this miracle worker." Yet to speak on behalf of one's community also means having to solicit traumatic narratives from others without any support structures in place. "I didn't like the idea of interviewing depressed people and then enacting them on stage," says Kristina, "it felt dirty to me. It felt unethical to interview people about their depression, make them talk about things that could make them more depressed, possibly risk leaving them in a situation where they felt poached, then run off and do a show about their lives."[80] Under these demands, how can an exemplary Asian stay happy? *Cuckoo's Nest* suggests that something has to give. What ensues before our eyes is the experience of Kristina's nervous breakdown as she tries to meet the demand for her liveness.

Kristina recounts her spinning thoughts and feeling alienated at family dinner. "Wow, these people have no clue who I am. I mean, if I were to die tomorrow, what would they say at my funeral?" The protagonist remembers leaving the dinner table and finding herself walking to the beach. "Cause that is what people do in an indie movie moment like this, right, you walk toward the beach?" Her comment indicates her controlled distance, that we are at arm's length from the event. It suggests that she is narrating the (fictional) story of her past from the safety of the present. Yet over the course of her next few lines, she finds herself increasingly pulled into the position of the performed and, in relating the onset of a (fictional) panic attack, takes over her past self's agitation. As she replays disjointed scenes yelling to strangers, freezing by the water, and seeking refuge in a nearby supermarket, the speed of her lines picks up, her voice gets shrill, her body on stage moves without sense of direction. By the time the story reaches the point where parents and police arrive, narrator Kristina appears fully immersed in the (fictional) past. Overwhelmed by the specter of presences that surround her (crying parents, bureaucratic police), she falls into loud anxious babbling before screaming out the words "nervous breakdown." Abrupt silence follows. Kristina stands motionless on stage, grimacing in pain. A moment passes. The artist's face suddenly relaxes, and she resumes her cheerful lesson: "What would that story be, folks? Say the word that I told you?" "Fiction," viewers dutifully respond. "Fiction, yeah." Kristina smiles, satisfied, her eyes still glazed from crying.

We have just witnessed the protagonist's "live" breakdown before our very eyes. And yet, Kristina's switch to the didactic present frames it as fiction, or rather carefully curated from the beginning. The audience feels unsure about its faith in this course of direction. They laugh, but the laughter sounds thinner, less boisterous. Or is it just a laugh track indicating that it's OK to be amused? Is Kristina now safe despite the crisis? Was there ever a crisis at all? Her breakdown leaves its nonfictional traces in her actual teary eyes, trembling voice, and unraveled cardigan. The physicality of her performance is palpable, as we can nearly sense the dwindling space of her visibility, its thickening enclosure. Her glassy eyes and shaky voice move us beyond Kristina's persona and toward her emoting body on stage. "Now, instead of solving the crisis and saving them all, Kristina IS the crisis!"[81] To resume, *Cuckoo's Nest* proposes a more nuanced understanding of liveness, as something that does not simply pass before our eyes, but that operates on the "hegemonic mandate" that the Asian American female artist always say yes to her ready dis/appearance.[82]

Advocacy and Self Care

Kristina is still in a critical mental state. None of her methods offers any resolution, not mindfulness exercises, uplifting songs, role models,

66 | MENTAL HEALTH AND LIVE FICTIONS

nor asking friends and family for help. She becomes increasingly distressed from her aspirations of meeting each and every demand as an exemplary Asian American "miracle worker" who does it all. She finally admits that she needs help . . . and does something about it. She goes online and finds a possible solution—contacting free mental health referrals. As a self-employed artist fighting for social justice, low cost is key. Kristina makes a phone call. When a female voice responds, she is full of readiness to pour out her soul—the pressure she felt growing up in a Chinese American household. The experience of sexual assault and other forms of physical violence throughout her teenage and college years. Her hasty bundle of unraveling confessions ends in tears. "I wonder if you can help me, please can you help me!?" she cries. The woman on the other end of the line seems compassionate enough, but she's only the weekend receptionist. She encourages the protagonist to call back in a couple days.

Days pass. Kristina calls again, and again attempts to share her uncomfortably suppressed memories. But budget cuts have just terminated free referrals. Our protagonist is given a new number to call, and another one. And another. With each call she restages her different traumas, with each call she has less energy, and with each call her self-introduction gets messier and less coherent. Despite starting to feel like she is losing it, Kristina somehow makes it onto a list of candidates for free counseling, but there are more hoops to jump through. She stages the process as a competitive audition, where she is expected to make the most convincing case, and be the best at it. At her audition Kristina wears an oversized bra and garishly smeared red lipstick. She draws on the lexicon of tragedy and melodrama to present herself as a Chinese American "victim" in dire need of (therapeutic) salvation. "Please help me before I hurt myself or someone else." A long pause. "End scene," announces Kristina, again drawing attention to the thespian nature of her self-presentation. She bows to a clapping audience.

Cuckoo's Nest draws attention to the limited scripts through which the Asian American woman is able to engage with public services and institutional support, and the limiting characters in which she can appear in the entertainment industry. Her overblown performance also gestures to the representational demands of Asian American film and video to speak to and move a general audience. Not only must Kristina play a specific recognizable role that could be described as "a sanctioned Asian American identity, which ultimately becomes one of articulation of grievances, injury, and ressentiment";[83] she must do so outstandingly, so that she can receive proper attention and care. *Cuckoo's Nest* exposes this representational demand by taking it to a new level of ridiculousness. "As a fetus I've been molested. I've been raped by chickens." Tragicomic self-victimization gets her the part, and she is ecstatic about her success. "Thank you so much for this opportunity. . . . I'm not going to let you down," she promises. Still, the struggle does not end. There is yet another hurdle—a three-hour-long standardized personality test, before getting the gift of free help. This should be easy? The test "consists of over 560 questions, was first developed in the twenties, edited once like in the eighties. There are two possible answers to the questions of this test, there is 'true' and then there is 'false.'" Filled with anxiety just trying to fill out the questionnaire, Kristina has another breakdown. She fails the test and is disqualified for treatment. "So much power & violence works through exhaustion," Sara Ahmed reminds us, "the exhaustion of having to navigate systems that are designed to make it harder to get what you need."[84] Trying her best to "plow past the crisis," Kristina

Figure 11. Dressed in dictator gown, Kristina tries once again to plow past the crisis. Production photo of *Wong Flew Over the Cuckoo's Nest* concert video by Vince Tanzilli; courtesy of Kristina Wong.

stops her performance, and starts over.[85] She introduces herself again as "Kristina Wong," then swiftly shifts gears, suddenly donned in a service cap and dressed in a judge's robe made of USPS envelopes. Kristina decrees that the audience be gerrymandered into different neighborhoods with varying access to social services. As she arbitrarily presides over the people's well-being, the act of distributing uneven life chances makes her feel great, and even makes her feel sexually aroused.

In a waking moment of clairvoyance, Kristina snaps out of her dictator role. "I know why it is that Asian American women are so depressed and killing themselves!" she shouts. But a female voice on the loudspeaker shuts her down: "Activity hour is over. It's time to get back to your room." Suddenly, the dictator robe looks more like a hospital gown. The outside order suggests that "Wong" has been the patient of a mental health institution all along. Or perhaps she was quietly admitted to a psychiatric facility while desperately waiting for help? Before further questions can be raised and answers given, Kristina recedes into her room. "I'm fine," are her final words. The show ends with the image of Asian subservience—or so it seems. Kristina stays in place. She's "fine." Yet the loudspeaker command relays that the protagonist's statement is not so clear, adding another layer to Kristina's ambivalent performance. Kristina never really appears to be the cheerful, accessible figure she wants herself to be. Her verbose, emotive, and agitated performances on stage refuse to provide us with catharses and introduce instead "a complication" into the field of representation[86] and a refusal to serve as a single "live" cheerleader when it comes to structural crises. By constantly returning us to the pervasive expectation that Kristina say yes to her liveness, *Cuckoo's Nest* prompts consideration precisely about what and who is at stake in U.S. institutional models of diversity and equity and their performance of inclusive pedagogy.

3

Stateless Cinema and the Undocument

Miko Revereza, *Distancing,* and *No Data Plan*

> Working with film and video, I've become increasingly
> self-aware of the irony behind recording film documents
> without my possession of living documents. Perhaps as long
> as documentation is used to exclude, deport, and incarcerate
> people by race and class lines, then our role as artists and
> thinkers is to decode, reconfigure, and subvert documents
> as conceptual play objects.
>
> —Miko Revereza, "Personal Statement," GoFundMe, 2017

Miko Revereza's life of film and video began as a young adult. Revereza notes that he was influenced by Filipino experimental cinema, the French New Wave, and Wong Kar Wai. "I didn't have access to those tools," he says about his early attempts to make films. "I just found a VHS camera at the local thrift store and just started messing around with settings on my TV, and stumbled upon experimental video art that way."[1] "You don't have to be a pro or even have access to a camera," he adds. "You can make art films with the materials . . . available to you."[2] I interviewed Miko Revereza at a café in New York City in the summer of 2019, just weeks before he received his MFA in video and film from Bard College in New York. Revereza was raised in California from the age of five. When we met for our interview, he was preparing to leave the United States permanently and move to Manila, the Filipino city where he was born. At the time he had already lived as an undocumented resident of the United States for more than twenty years. A gifted young filmmaker since his youth,

| 69

70 | STATELESS CINEMA AND THE UNDOCUMENT

Revereza was ineligible for federal student loans. Sarita See explains that when his Deferred Action for Childhood Arrivals (DACA) status expired in 2017—"the week that Donald Trump was inaugurated as United States President"—he decided to put his fee funds toward a formal degree in film. He "wrote to top university administrators . . . and asked them whether they would live up to their university's offer of sanctuary to undocumented students." After receiving multiple offers, Revereza enrolled at Bard.[3]

Revereza gained international recognition with his short film *Disintegration 93–96,* released in 2017. Compiled from his family's collection of VHS home movies, *Disintegration* is an essayistic memoir of his family's migration from Manila to Los Angeles in the 1990s. The film was filmed under the auspices of an Armed with a Camera Fellowship for Emerging Media Artists.[4] Revereza has received various film and culture grants like the Hubert Bals Fund Bright Future Award by the International Film Festival Rotterdam, Vilcek Foundation's Prize for Creative Promise in Filmmaking, and Ford Foundation's JustFilms grant.[5] At the time of this writing, he resides in the Philippines and Mexico, and is currently completing his second solo feature, titled *Nowhere Near,* about his recent return to the Philippines after years of having lived as an undocumented person in the United States. As is shown by his numerous collaborations with others, including productions with U.S. pop icon Christina Aguilera, Revereza is known for a gritty visual style that often switches back and forth between digital and analog video, and between video and celluloid film. His insistence on the right to record and create art despite one's limited resources is a reminder of what Lucas Hilderbrand has described as an "aesthetic of access," marked by a visual texture that speaks to a medium's material usage (the graininess of an old and well-viewed VHS tape, for example) that is noticeable to viewers.[6]

This chapter explores Revereza's challenge to the use of visual documentation by state border surveillance specifically with respect to U.S. immigration and border patrol laws, in his 16mm short *Distancing* and his feature-length digital video *No Data Plan.* Both completed in 2019, the films reflect on life in the United States as an illegalized immigrant. Both documentaries have been described by critics as autobiographical essays as experimental and avant-garde slow cinema that challenge the formal conventions of mainstream storytelling. Where these discussions tend to focus on the artist's aesthetic choices insofar as they serve to accurately reflect Revereza's authentic experiences of travel, migrancy, and displacement, I argue that his ambivalent and precarious self-designation as an "undocumented-documentary filmmaker"[7] echoes the specificity of visual documentation as an official form of U.S. state identification, one that has been historically wielded on behalf of U.S. immigration law and policy to control Asian border crossings into the United States since the nineteenth century.[8]

In *Distancing* and *No Data Plan,* Revereza carefully and selectively inserts photographic shots of himself that appear more as "second hand" shots—a portrait in a passport, an Instagram selfie displayed on an iPhone. We do not see his face otherwise. This tactical use of "photographic identity portraits" is his response to the common expectation and demand for authentic, realist, and biographical visibility of ethnic and minority visual artists and specifically the undocumented artist.[9] In crafting this response he obscures a recognizable view of his face to the audience, by not only recording hard-to-see photographs but withholding any direct shots of his face via the moving image camera. We thus observe his personal control over his filmic persona as one that refuses to serve as visual evidence of equal access to the American Dream. By playfully framing his filmic persona with his own visual absence and fleetingness, Revereza undermines demands for official visual documentation—passport photos are a prime example—that feed state-sanctioned truths (like legal entry into a nation's borders), in order to show how these demands undergird mainstream documentary storytelling. Indeed, his use of different visual media technologies, from 16mm film to digital video files, effectively denaturalizes the ways that visual media technologies have been exploited as instruments of state border surveillance.[10]

This chapter also draws on the filmmaker's concept of "stateless cinema," a call for the tactical evasion of visual capture and for "performances of creative fugitivism" that preempt his detection by the camera.[11] It examines how *Distancing* and *No Data Plan* visually recast official state documents and related media forms in ways that render them as unserviceable for institutional identification of minority subjects. In Revereza's films, moving images of documentation that continue to serve U.S. state technologies of capture and control are rather steered into an aesthetic practice that cares less about neoliberal ideals of American multiculturalism and togetherness than about the relationality between the filmmaker's present

72 | STATELESS CINEMA AND THE UNDOCUMENT

and ongoing histories of violent place making, survival, and minoritarian insurgency.

Distancing

> I am trading access to the U.S.—which has excluded me my whole life—for access to the rest of the world. I can finally attend film festivals with my film. I can finally revisit the Philippines. Why that line is so heartbreaking is because this decision would exile me from my family, friends, and place where I grew up. It's also heartbreaking to compare circumstances with my own family and recognize the privilege that I've managed to accumulate for myself from being a cultural producer.[12]

Born in Manila in 1988, Revereza arrived in California with his mother as a young child to reunite with his father, his grandparents, and other members of his family. His father decided that they would all overstay their tourist visas. When I met with the filmmaker in New York, he relayed his anger and fatigue about a never-changing immigration-prison system as the impetus for his departure, although he was excited about the next chapter of his life. A few weeks later, he left for the Philippines. According to U.S. immigration law, undocumented persons may be banned from returning to the States for a decade, which for Revereza means being separated from family, friends, and the place of his upbringing.

Distancing begins with the voice of Aurora, Revereza's grandmother, discussing the best airfare from California to the Philippines. Neither the filmmaker nor his *lola* is visible in the frame. While we hear her voice, we read subtitles on a black screen that features the English translation of his *lola* speaking in Tagalog. Responding in English, Revereza tells her about the good deal he found online. Aurora is surprised. In Tagalog: "So cheap! Is it a good airline? Did he ask if the price is correct?" Revereza replies in English that "there's no one to ask" on the internet, and reminds her that his ticket to Manila is one-way. It takes a moment for his *lola* to register this. "Oh! You're not coming back!" she says. "You can't even come back." Her voice does not reveal any sorrow about her grandson's impending departure, although the casual tone of their conversation changes as the black screen shifts into haunting close-ups of the filmmaker's grandfather. Revereza's *lolo* is struggling with advanced Parkinson's and dementia.[13] His mouth is wide agape, as his eyes stare at the ceiling. A series of shots show the grandfather strapped securely to his bed, and his body framed from various angles. We see where his *lolo*'s head touches the mattress, his soft strands of hair, his strained neck. Caressing his grandfather's fragile body with the lens of the camera, Revereza's recording is nervous, even fearful, as if afraid to forget the details of what his *lolo* looks like. Each shot transmits a sense of Revereza's impending loss. We hear the filmmaker's voice-over in broken Tagalog. "If I ever return here, maybe he won't be here. Maybe most things will also disappear or change completely." His voice comes to us as in hesitant and faltering fragments. I don't know if the words are only spoken by Revereza; the words seem to multiply, echo, and blur into each other, just as the images of his grandfather's face begin to bleed into another on the screen. I am reminded of Ackbar Abbas's "déjà disparu" as a cinematic trope in Hong Kong New Wave cinema of that which is already lost: a present filled with ghosts, something always already other, or something that is always already someplace else.[14] The washed-out, faded colors of *Distancing* suggest a past that is more easily forgotten than vividly remembered.

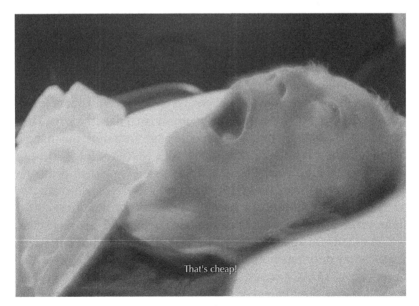

Figure 12. Revereza's *lolo*; screenshot from *Distancing*.

74 | STATELESS CINEMA AND THE UNDOCUMENT

From the home of his *lolo* and *lola,* we move to cruising shots of LAX, Los Angeles's airport, and hear Revereza's voice reminisce over his arrival to the United States as a young boy. Revereza tries to find the proper words to say something in Tagalog, but it is difficult, as if narrating the past lacks a proper language. He starts again several times, as if stuttering. The subtitles translate, "It's not . . . Without . . . There's no . . . we don't have. . . ." The words fail him. "Everything I'm saying is wrong." His voice fails to tell us what his memory knows. We only learn that he and his mother arrived many moons ago, at night. This is reflected in the film's shots of the airport, taken in the evening. They are of terminals and parking lots, baggage claim areas, escalators and exits, and people waiting.

The Undocument

"To counter this current immigration police state," writes Revereza, "stateless artists must contort themselves into meticulous performances of evasion; performances of creative fugitivism enacting a repertoire of stateless imagination."[15] *Distancing* introduces us to Revereza's newly acquired Filipino passport. We observe his brown fingers carefully turn every page. Instead of sensing any relief or fulfillment from some security of national citizenship to which the official document alludes, we only see a hazy passport on screen. The book is held open by Revereza's hand, of which we only have a partial view. His brown fingers press against the passport's pages and spine, holding it open against a flat surface as his fingers obscure the document number printed across its pages. Overexposed and out of focus, the glass desk beneath the document appears to reflect the artist's immediate surroundings, the glaring sun through a window, the shadow of a plant. There is no trace of the artist with which to clearly identify him, other than his partial hand and fingers pressing their prints on the passport pages and the glassy, scanner-like surface beneath it. Inaccessible to the viewer, the invisible prints evoke mandatory state fingerprint documentation scans, systems of biometric surveillance, and demands for speedy processing that allow or forbid a person's lawful entry into state boundaries, and that are required to apply for or renew one's DACA status. The passport is illegible; its background is the rattle of the filmmaker's 16mm camera. The rendering of the official document as an on-screen cinematic object both alters and dissolves the passport's institutional function.

The haziness of the passport and its empty pages present viewers what Laura Harris calls an *undocument*. An undocument, Harris observes, is not a certification that works to bolster any state apparatus. Revereza's cinematic images of "proper" documentation are unable to safely vet his citizenship. His filmic undocument rather lends to a "critical noncitizenship"[16] that works to "record and disturb the conditions of [its] own production."[17] The brown hand visible within the frame evokes the filmmaker's illegalized presence in the United States. No words are spoken, yet it is as if he is telling us: "Catch me if you can." The scene pokes fun at popular fears about persistent migrant encroachment and the "browning of America," problems that the proper management of official state documentation is designed to curtail.[18] The filmmaker's visual self-insertion is highly controlled in ways that "escape" the eye of the viewer—as the scope of the frame mimics the authoritative purview of the state in undocument-able ways. In 2019, Revereza also completed his film *Biometrics,* which was inspired by his experience of providing his fingerprints to immigration for DACA.[19] The 16mm short shows the stains of his inky fingerprints on the film reel. In *Distancing,* he purges the passport of its conventional service of identification and surveillance. The artist evades the accurate visual capture of his face and thus his real, accurate, and biographical identification. To cite his stateless cinema manifesto, he has created a film that "shares the same precarious motions of a fugitive."[20]

Rapid processing and quick access to data to identify and locate individuals are demands of border policing and practices of state surveillance. Revereza expresses concern about wearing his "clunky" Bolex camera as he moves around Los Angeles airport, where the risk of appearing suspicious and being accosted by police or regular bystanders are looming.[21] "Fuck it," he says in resignation, "if I get detained and if I get deported . . . [this is] what I'm doing anyway." Revereza's camera, like his legal status, goes wherever he goes. Each act of filming bespeaks his tactical maneuvering and transgression with respect to the law:

> I've learned to navigate this country in relation to what I am systematically excluded from. Growing up, it was a driver's license,

Figure 13. The passport becomes a cinematic object; screenshot from *Distancing*.

an ID, a social security number, legal employment.... growing up within these circumstances has taught me how to pull shit like that off. How to hack the system. How to circumvent the structural borders working against me.[22]

Demands to show and prove one's legal documentation, Revereza observes, are not limited to state authorities.

DREAMer Storytelling

Media productions by undocumented artists have gained increasing popularity in the wake of the DREAMer movement. Radha Hegde has observed that many feature powerful first-person stories that "emphasize the moral standing and worth of undocumented youth hoping to participate in the American Dream."[23] DREAMers entered U.S. public discourse alongside widespread fears of freeloading aliens looking to siphon resources from proper citizenry. Named after the American Dream, the 2001 Development, Relief and Education for

Alien Minors Act, or DREAM Act, sought to make citizenship more available for young undocumented immigrants. Though the bill has not passed into law, the term "DREAMer" has become widely used to describe young undocumented immigrants who arrived to the United States as children.

Visual narratives that strategically support the DREAMer movement tend to spotlight representations of undocumented youth by highlighting their youthful excellence, assimilation, and innocence.[24] Rebecca Schreiber has observed that alongside advancements in video access, post-9/11 undocumented media productions have increasingly put the camera into the hands of migrant communities. With a particular focus on video self-recordings by Mexican and Central American immigrants in the United States, Schreiber observes that "labor unions, nonprofit social service organizations, advocacy groups, filmmakers, artists, and activists developed documentary projects that . . . envisioned self-representation as a way for members of these groups to portray themselves on their own terms, and thus differently from how they were presented in the mainstream media or by documentary photographers and filmmakers."[25] These uniquely personal video documentaries often portray the abjection of migrant illegality in ways that challenge how expansive networks of visual media technologies—namely, photography, video, and other modes of facial recognition and visual identification—are managed by state authorities to accurately identify and detain individuals and working families without proper documentation to allow them to live and work within the borders of the economically developed state.

Pulitzer Prize–winning journalist and documentary filmmaker Jose Antonio Vargas is perhaps the most publicly recognized DREAMer activist in the United States. Born in Antipolo, Philippines, in 1981, Vargas came out to the United States as gay and undocumented in his 2011 *New York Times* piece "My Life as an Undocumented Immigrant." In his article the Filipino American Vargas discusses how his successes in the United States have been complicated by the trials of retaining an anonymity with respect to the state. DREAMers and advocates of citizenship for the undocumented have indeed been known for the savvy use of print, analog, and digital media outlets and social networks. The use of first-person storytelling is a pervasive aspect of DREAMer movement media. Hegde describes many of these visual narratives as "short diaristic entries" that strategically draw on traditional nuclear family values in ways that resonate with many Americans, and realist biographies of exemplary immigrants, especially children and young people, and individual sacrifice.[26] These tropes effectively "elicit compassion and action" and affectively move voters and politicians to support changes to policy and law. "Over the past 14 years," writes Vargas,

> I've graduated from high school and college and built a career as a journalist, interviewing some of the most famous people in the country. On the surface, I've created a good life. I've lived the American dream. But I am still an undocumented immigrant. And that means living a different kind of reality. It means going about my day in fear of being found out. It means rarely trusting people, even those closest to me, with who I really am. It means keeping my family photos in a shoebox rather than displaying them on shelves in my home, so friends don't ask about them. It means reluctantly, even painfully, doing things I know are wrong and unlawful.[27]

An indisputable advocate of increased public support for DREAMer advocacy and public critique of U.S. immigration law and policy, Vargas carefully frames his undocumented status and exclusion from U.S. citizenship. He must leverage his public visibility in ways that depict his public persona as an outstandingly high-achieving DREAMer. In *Undocumented* (2013), Vargas and codirector Ann Lupo explore his successes of his personal life, his fraught relationship with American citizenship, and the injustices of the U.S. immigration system. Revereza, on the other hand, contests the U.S. production and maintenance of immigrant illegality in his films, writings, and interviews. He complicates more conventional approaches to DREAMer self-representation and advocacy in the public eye. "Out of the 11 million undocumented, I am one of the 2 million in the generation that politicians patronizingly label as 'Dreamers' and out of those Dreamers I am of the small but mighty 5–10% pursuing higher education."[28] Rather than present himself as law abiding, Revereza repudiates legal documentation as the ultimate goal. His documentary film practice unravels and denaturalizes the ways in which visual documentation is coopted by state identificatory mechanisms and institutional claims to absolute objectivity:

> There's a reason they call us dreamers. They've been projecting this "dream," this hallucination, this delusion my whole life. To be documented, to be an American citizen if you're good enough. But really they call us Dreamers because they want us to keep asleep, work for cheap and rob us with our eyes closed.[29]

Documentary Expectations

Documentary film is most simply understood as a visual narrative form that shows us and represents reality, which Patricia Aufderheide describes as telling "a story about real life, with claims to truthfulness."[30] Though it boasts no singular style or aesthetic, documentaries are expected to adhere to a common set of elements—objectivity, immediacy, and reflexivity (in the form of the filmmaker's self-awareness, for example)—to establish its claims of reality and truthfulness. These are, of course, aspects contingent on historical and technological context. Pooja Rangan observes how filmic techniques that create a sense of urgency and crisis deliver "truth effects" that have come to define the documentary narrative as one of "actuality rather than creative artifact."[31] Market forces and trends also matter. The commercial success of the nonfiction film format in the twenty-first century now tends to prioritize readily consumable stories that whet our desires for relatable heroes and "neatly linked conflicts and resolutions."[32]

Alex Juhasz and Alisa Lebow note that a good documentary will often highlight "individuals over collectivities, people over their environments, human will over systemic forces." As for spectators, the documentary often works to elevate "feelings over analysis and passivity over action."[33] Revereza's documentary work strays from these templates, and offers no palpably identifiable hero or neat narrative resolution. He rather draws attention to the traditional aspects of conventional documentary storytelling, as he interrogates its reliance on identificatory paradigms of the democratic state and its individual rational citizen, not to mention that of the undocumented aspirational DREAMer who bears a very discreet and unequivocal relationship to the law.[34] For Revereza and critics like him, singular promotion of the outstanding immigrant exemplar only works to figure a limited selection of migrants and causes as worthy of attention and protection, and others as undeserving:

> I hope that more undocumented and stateless voices will step forward and tell their own stories in their own uncompromising vision. Because if we don't, our stories will be extracted, edited and commodified for us by "socially conscious" documentary filmmakers flattening our experiences into a singular social issue. We have to make better films than these grant-hogging assholes banking on our sad situations, since as stateless people we're often excluded from the eligibility of these grants.[35]

The mainstream documentary form, for Revereza, is the cultural equivalent to state-sanctioned documentation, a form that bears a historical connection to racialized state surveillance and territorial border claims.

Proper Documentation

Since the September 11 attacks of 2001, which continue to be frequently cited as the reason for strident antiterrorism laws and "the securitization of immigration enforcement and policy," rates of U.S. immigrant detention and deportation have risen.[36] Established as part of the Homeland Security Act of 2002, the Department of Homeland Security (DHS) is a massive bureaucratic apparatus that continues to control immigration and patrol U.S. borders through three main agencies, Customs and Border Protection (CBP), Immigration and Customs Enforcement (ICE), and U.S. Citizenship and Immigration Services (USCIS). Since its founding, the DHS has absorbed an estimated $333 billion to carry out its mission, tripling the number of staff to 50,000 border and interior enforcement officers and over 84,000 ICE and CBP employees as of 2021.[37] While immigrant deportations peaked under Obama's presidency (2009–2017), the Trump administration (2017–2021) continued to fuel the cycle of arrests and removal in order to strategically reduce formal numbers of legal immigration.[38] Trump's government allocated billions of dollars to erect his vision of his proverbial "big beautiful wall" along the U.S.-Mexico border, to stop unauthorized entry of illegal aliens. The rise of social media networks and online data brokerage has also enabled unprecedented forms of immigrant policing and punishment. In 2017, says Revereza, "the United States Department of Homeland Security quietly announced the monitoring and collection of social media accounts of potentially all immigrants regardless of legal or naturalization status." He adds: "In the months that followed, aggressive new tactics of immigration detainment revealed [themselves] to be linked to the triangulation of GPS data points, linking aliases to IP addresses to login times," thus making immigrant capture that much easier.[39]

Part of an ongoing history of racist and institutional violence in the United States that includes systemic mass incarceration and the growth of the private prison industry,[40] procedures of visual U.S. immigrant detention today have evolved from the early state-driven identification measures of the late nineteenth century. Photography has been a vital part of "national gatekeeping" since 1875,[41] the year the former U.S. Immigration Bureau began to integrate photographic documentation into federal regulatory identification procedures. Presumed to be unbiased, objective, and true, portrait photographs have served the institutional administration of migrants seeking to enter the United States since the Exclusion Era, whose timeframe begins with the 1882 Chinese Exclusion Act. "As the federal government introduced a series of racialized immigration restrictions, visual systems of observation and documentation became essential to their implementation and expansion," writes Anna Pegler-Gordon;[42] "these processes of observation, documentation, and representation helped reinforce popular and official understandings of different immigrant groups, as well as their differential treatment under immigration law." The first race-based law to restrict the entry of "illegal aliens" into the United States, the 1882 Exclusion Act categorized "Asian immigrants [as] the country's first 'illegal aliens,' excluded through both immigration and citizenship law for decades."[43] Its enforcement was facilitated by the photographic capture of Chinese faces and new modes of visual recordkeeping that would become part of today's extensive system of personal identification designed to control the entry of unwanted migrants (and really, anyone). Starting with Chinese women, Chinese immigrants, followed by U.S. citizens of Chinese descent,

82 | STATELESS CINEMA AND THE UNDOCUMENT

photographic immigration identification was extended to regulate the Chinese community long before it was used with other immigrant groups. The U.S. Immigration Bureau used the early photographic identification of the Chinese as a model for their expansion of photographic documentation to Mexican border crossers in the 1910s and European immigrants in the 1920s.[44] As U.S. nationals under U.S. colonization (1898–1946), Filipinos were initially allowed entry into the United States and thus exempted from Asian exclusion. A series of laws in the 1930s would later restrict Filipino immigration by revoking the national status of Filipinos and turning them into aliens ineligible for U.S. citizenship.[45]

As Revereza's fingers hold down his blurry Philippine passport, *Distancing* makes a connection between Asian exclusion and immigrant illegalization in the United States, a relationship largely obscured by pervasive perceptions of foreign illegality and unlawfulness, and yet also of certain Asian Americans as "*documented,* educated, and desirable (albeit perpetually foreign)."[46] Asian Americans' racialized proximity to the law indeed makes them a blueprint for DREAMers often expected, like Vargas, to aspire toward and aptly achieve legal documentation. While the figure of the DREAMer carefully symbolizes the dream of American togetherness, no iteration of the DREAM Act has yet been approved by Congress. It has instead given way to the expansion of immigrant surveillance laws. For Revereza, the DREAMer need not readily abide by or represent U.S. law. The filmmaker stages his and his family's brown bodies in ways that sabotage expectations for conventional DREAMer narratives. As an undocumented Filipino American, he also sabotages the classical Asian American model minority narrative with his Southeast Asian DREAMer status and by complicating DREAMer narratives like those of Vargas—and as we shall see, by leaving the United States altogether. *Distancing* puts distance between its viewer and the expectation to fully see and know its maker. It foregrounds a documentary practice based on Revereza's evasive dis/appearance that follows the "precarious motions of a fugitive."[47] Yet he continues to insert himself against this looming abjection, and into the bordered time-space of the contemporary United States. This malleable, shapeshifting quality is a cinematic translation of the daily survival practices of Revereza as a policed yet stateless person in ways that undermine the state-serving documentary image.

Moving Images and Moving Migrants: "Towards a Stateless Cinema"

In his written literary manifesto "Towards a Stateless Cinema," Revereza reflects on the intimate connection between the movement of images and that of migrants. This explorative text about filmmaking as an act of border crossing is one that frames everyday experiences and practices of migrancy as a unique positionality from which to dispute the violent policing and surveillance of state borders.[48] The artist cites home video tapes sent from the Filipino diaspora to the motherland as an example of the entangled and mutually constitutive movement of images and people. He recounts how the circulation of these tapes from North America to the Philippines fueled the dream of American prosperity and "inspired waves of migration to the States including my family's own." The shipped analog videotape as an inspiration to move overseas has recently been replaced by more user-friendly long-distance video calls that, despite their graininess, lagging audio, and "images of partners with missing frames," continue to link people across continents and compel cross-border migrations. In short, Revereza narrates moving images as artifacts that not only bear the material imprints of border transgression but also incite its performance and, indeed, perform it.

Distancing introduces us to "a lineage of statelessness in cinema" that includes references to filmmakers like Chantal Akerman, Michael Curtiz, Jonas Mekas, and Wong Kar Wai.[49] In lieu of seeing excerpts from the oeuvre of these directors, however, Revereza records his computer screen. The screen features a DVD-ripping program that duplicates his personal canon of stateless cinema classics. As he converts the filmic data to computer files in preparation for his impending move to Manila, he captures the virtual on-screen process with his 16mm camera. The shot of a computer screen features a film title, spinning disc symbol, and status progress bar, with occasional audio extracts, evoking bootlegging as an illicit creation of access. Sarita See considers Revereza's play with "the illicit and the faulty" in his films as an act of "residency bootlegging" that snatches access without proper documentation. Drawing on Hilderbrand's study of videotape bootlegging as "a set of practices and textual relationships that open up alternative conceptions of access, aesthetics, and affect,"[50] See calls

Figure 14. During the process of ripping, the moving image appears as a computer file; screenshot from *Distancing*.

particular attention to Revereza's visibility beyond what she calls the "flawless" DREAMer image.[51] "The narrative of the ideal DREAMer," she writes, "is bound up with the state's demand for compliant workers who can be easily integrated and whose labor can be smoothly extricated, and so it is important to pay attention to Revereza's creation of a DREAMer narrative that is not so easily recognized and not so easily consumed."[52]

Distancing thus enables "alternative conceptions of access, aesthetics, and affect" that underscore Revereza's everyday practices of survival and what he calls "stateless performance" under racialized border surveillance. He contrasts statelessness with enforced illegalization, as a creative reworking of state-appropriated technologies of identification to subvert American lawfulness, "a form that functions like fake IDs and forged documents [and] hacks into our bureaucratic reality. In order to survive and navigate a bordered control society, the malleability of identification is utilized in life and image production practices."[53] As Revereza converts his DVD movies in order to rip them all on his computer hard drive, the moving image appears both fleeting and multiple—as a 16mm film shot, a computer screen,

STATELESS CINEMA AND THE UNDOCUMENT | 85

and a digital file. This "shape-shifting" of the moving image format rather replicates Revereza's required adaptive and evasive flexibility, the way he navigates everyday barriers and the risk of detection. It is not meant to record and report, but rather "To be visible and invisible at the same time." The ripping scene is accompanied by short audio clips from a selection of his copied movies that, replaying English, French, and Cantonese dialog, reminds me of Revereza's voice-over performance in broken Tagalog as also a staged resistance to fit into a single story. In a similar vein, Revereza's manifesto, anchored as it is in "performances of evasion" and "free human movement," evokes a legacy of Black resistance, a fugitivism that forefronts "a desire for and a spirit of escape and transgression of the proper and the proposed,"[54] an evocation of Tina Campt's fugitives, people who "cannot or will not submit to the law; cannot or do not remain in their proper place, or the places to which they have been confined or assigned."[55] Like these critics and their objects, Revereza and his stateless documentary practice prioritizes the ephemeral, creative, and subversive. Rejecting the embrace of a settled legal status, he radically revises how we identify by hacking the violent technologies of state identification.

No Data Plan

Rather than set up an exemplary individual success story to stage a demand for equal belonging with respect to U.S. immigration law, *No Data Plan* features Revereza's *undocumentary* storytelling. His first feature-length film, *No Data Plan* breaks with relatable immigrant representations and engages the moving image formally in ways that distances viewers from the story he tells. In a virtual zoom-out, the moving image breaks away from state-sanctioned forms of visual capture and instead subtly invokes ethnic histories that have been violently erased throughout the history of U.S. imperial place making. As an undocumented person in the United States, Revereza cannot easily visit doctors, drive a car, or travel long distances without the specters of identification, surveillance, or detention. Without a passport, undocumented people cannot travel by plane. In this context, the act of successfully filming with his digital camera for three long days on the train is a stubbornly triumphant one. *No Data Plan* asserts Revereza's bodily presence in the United States and undocumentably obscures his visual detection by viewers. These distancing tactics thwart expectations for an authentic or accurately biographical narration of a single, lovable hero.

No Data Plan captures the monotony of Revereza's train ride across the United States from Los Angeles to New York. Time feels glutinous, spaces feel limited and claustrophobic, and images become quickly repetitive. During his journey, Revereza points his digital Sony A7S camera at anything that catches his attention. Without Wi-Fi access for most of the three-day ride, we follow the somewhat uninspired camera direction of the filmmaker, who has time to kill. The result is a no-budget video blending America's signature landscapes of sculptured mountains, vast open plains, and desolate industrial towns, into the dull experience of waiting, of being in limbo, in the swaying body of the train, on platforms, in waiting rooms. We also see subtle details from within the carriage like, in Revereza's words, "water residue on the window, scratches on the glass, handprints, light moving through the train's interior."[56] As in *Distancing,* the filmmaker is invisible to the viewer and never steps in front of the camera. With scenes more or less arranged in chronological order, the documentary offers no sense of development, plot, or narrative guidance. Part observational and part experimental documentary video, *No Data Plan*'s qualities of stillness and long duration hint at the influence of the genre of slow cinema with its stretched-out temporality, while the iconic landscape scenery passing by outside the window cites the grandness and exceptionalism of the American frontier so popularly depicted in the U.S. Western film—but without subscribing to it.

Other than occasional shots of scenic vistas outside the train window, nothing narratively or visually notable occurs in *No Data Plan*'s visual frame for most of its seventy-five minutes. That is, until the film's final ten minutes, when an unexpected U.S. Border Patrol security check throws the artist into an unexpected panic. Revereza's papers have expired under an increasingly harsh U.S. immigration regime. Even as he does not turn the camera toward himself, his presence feels abruptly hypervisible as both target and index of historical state violence. While the artist ultimately slips the monitoring gaze of law enforcement, the moment of imminent detection stays engraved in his bodily movement, as documented by the camera's heavy shaking after the agents have left the car. "Yet, that shakiness was the only camera movement that made sense in the moment. . . . I am witnessing my cinematography break down as I realize the inseparability

STATELESS CINEMA AND THE UNDOCUMENT | 87

Figure 15. One of the iconic landscape shots taken from inside the train; screenshot from *No Data Plan*.

between my moving image and my moving body."[57] The documentary image materializes the body's captivity, drawing attention to an otherwise unspectacularized border security apparatus that circumscribes the right to properly belong in the United States.

No Data Plan creates a connection between filmic documentation and state identification practices in ways that reckon with the forceful delimitation of national boundaries. By exploiting digital video's accessibility, Revereza's recording insists on modes of presence and movement that cross separating borders. His recording signals his self-insertion in both moving image culture and into national territory by traversing the physical space of the United States. "If movement becomes one's only sense of normalcy, it is appropriate that we have placed our existences in the moving images."[58] I read the scene of the filmmaker's near capture (to which I return again at the end) as a subversion of "documentation" as a technology of state capture and the controlling of migrant bodies. This occurs, however, without the happy promise of universal equality. Instead, *No Data Plan* highlights the seemingly opposite affects of boredom and shock, from lying low, waiting in limbo for legal approval, and the simultaneous violence of the law, as well as ambient anxiety and chronic wakefulness that may not be as familiar to those with the privilege of proper documentation. The border patrol scene in *No Data Plan* and the various

88 | STATELESS CINEMA AND THE UNDOCUMENT

claustrophobic shots from inside the train mimic the legal, spatial, and representational confinements of undocumented groups whose histories also remain outside the frame of official History. Revereza's own visual inconspicuousness in *No Data Plan*'s images reminds us that the border is constantly staged and affirmed through violent acts of "seeing and sorting" that determine who can stay and who disappears.[59]

The Mother's Story

Revereza reveals an illicit familiarity with, and a break from, conventional documentary storytelling. His thinly sketched characters, interspersed subtitles, and disjointed audio bites from the filmmaker's conversation with others invite viewers to "unsee" how we commonly know the moving image and relate to it from a distance, that is, through silence and boredom and a general sense of detachment. Vivian Huang's study of affect, moved by long-distance shots in the photographs of Tseng Kwong Chi, observes distance not as "antithetical to sociohistorical significance or memory"[60] but as an open-ended and "promiscuous"[61] engagement with history, place, identity, and community, one that those are most familiar with "who know home not by a specific coordinate but by a constellation of sought-out coordinates."[62] *No Data Plan*'s "distant" or seemingly detached storytelling also suggests how different forms of agency can emerge when leaving behind the demands of legal citizenship. The film begins with a shot of a train station's crowded platform. English subtitles appear that are neither audio transcriptions nor translated dialog, however, but rather assume the role of a (silent) narrative voice throughout the film. The subtitles inform us that "Mama has two different phone numbers." One is for her Obama Phone, which she uses to make most of her calls, and the other is the phone she uses to discuss immigration issues with family and friends. The lines we read are Revereza's, identifying the artist's position as the son, and one of economic and legal precarity. The Obama Phone, a government-funded cell phone service for low-income families, has no data plan, which lessens the risk of detection for its user. The filmmaker has also discussed having boarded trains without a data-plan device, in order to evade mobile tapping and geolocation tracking by ICE and Border Patrol. The film's title suggestively appears against the voice of the conductor asking for IDs, showing the ubiquitous demand for state documentation.

Revereza's mother uses the phone without a data plan to chat with her son—and to confess her romantic involvement with another man. "I was the only person she confided to about her affair," the subtitles read. The camera cuts to the inside of the train. It starts to move. Here, a story of the undocumented experience begins with a double betrayal: the mother's betrayal of her husband's loyalty and the filmmaker's betrayal of his mother's trust by sharing her secret confessions with an audience. Following lines elaborate how Revereza's mother meets her lover on a Craigslist rideshare. The lover is a young male driver, only twenty-three, and somehow involved with "a local Vietnamese crime organization." When the two elope (she will eventually return), the relatives cannot stop gossiping about her. We learn "she's been depressed for years . . . even before Papa's affair." Rather than opting for more conventional framings of immigrant deservingness that rely on expected DREAMer personas and tropes of familial proximity, *No Data Plan* introduces the story of a broken family, and does so through visual means that further diminish viewer relatability.

The screen's captions silently come and go. They flash over images mostly devoid of human beings—seats, the dining car, a trash can, train tracks in the dark—offering no visual match to the onscreen text. We hear the rattling sound of the train. Elsewhere, Revereza has cited technical issues as the reason for using narrative subtitles in *No Data Plan*—to avoid his voice-over having to compete with the noise of the train—but the absence of an audible speaker also instills a sense of detachment, a felt difficulty on the part of the viewer to relate to the thinly documented characters.[63] The subtitles are not devoid of emotion, however. Revereza is angry. The first time he met his mother's lover, we read, "I stared at this fucker's face . . . which looked younger than mine." Directed at the driver, his anger betrays a paternalistic impulse to reclaim his mother. Revereza does not try to stop the couple. Two months into the relationship, his mother receives a threat from one of her lover's acquaintances, a "meth addict" who threatens to kill her and report the family to immigration. She panics. The driver gives her some pills to calm down. "Later that night she calls me barely coherent. Right after she sent a text intended for the driver to Papa." By refraining from personal blame or making a moral

90 | STATELESS CINEMA AND THE UNDOCUMENT

argument about maternal duties, the subtitle draws attention to the suffocating nature of the nuclear family. Lacking a space of her own, the mother can only spend time with her lover in public, and risk being found out. Even the couple's "private" retreat in his car parked in the neighborhood raises suspicion by local residents. Through the mother's undocumentably documented story, we notice the patriarchal structures of Revereza's family and the undocumented community. The subtitles are also rich with conflicting emotions: anger, disappointment, worry—and Revereza's ongoing refusal to control the mother's life. The subtitle's detached form registers indeed a care of sorts. Care not expressed as a warm invitation but as an act of stepping back, making and giving space, avoiding narrative control. As Huang observes, too, distance equals noncaring only when proximity becomes the single gauge of meaningful relations.

No Data Plan intimates care by changing the spatial patterns of relating. One evening Revereza's mother comes home with a giant plush Totoro (the spirit character from Hayao Miyazaki's 1988 anime, *My Neighbor Totoro*). The subtitle reads: "Papa didn't notice. She's been depressed for years, even before Papa's affair." The minimal subtitles make me imagine the ecstatic mother burying herself beneath the giant stuffed Totoro, gleeful from having gone to the local fair with her lover. Once home, she disappears into the oppressive still-life of the nuclear family. Totoro in the matrimonial bedroom becomes the mother's act of defiance. The caption dismissively reads: "As a housewife you don't need a driver's license or documents to work or to worry about being captured by ICE out in the world." As women are often expected to stay home to take care of home and family, their explorations "out in the world" are perceived as a betrayal against a hard-working spouse and the entire family. Whose voice are the subtitles capturing here, the filmmaker's, the father's? Are the lines meant to represent a community? I take a step back, moved by the video into an act of caring.

No Data Plan unmakes and remakes relations of proximity and distance, and prompts care, or "a feeling *with,* rather than a feeling for" another, as in the fleeting phone conversations between Revereza and his mother in which we witness Revereza care from a distance, at arm's length.[64] Taking his mother's call, he mostly listens, passively. We sense that the filmmaker feels little tenderness, and yet his film insists on making his mother heard. Attentive subtitles turn viewers into witnesses of his mother's pleasure and grief in response to the spatial governance that enshrines patriarchal violence on both sides of the law. *No Data Plan* thus creates intimate connections despite the pull of affective proximity and empathy, dismissing the presumption that we can only relate when feeling exactly what someone else is experiencing. As a viewer, I relate by taking a step back, too, and keeping my own distance from the mother rather than having to identify with her. The video's undocumenting narrative intimates a caretaking practice that refuses to replicate the "patrilineal underpinnings" of territorial (border) claims and structures of belonging in filmic form.[65]

Lola *Aurora's Memories*

We get to know *lola* Aurora through various sound bites in Tagalog, subtitled in English. Occurring intermittently throughout the film, moments with her offer surprising insights into the dynamics of the artist's family, and how they relate to historical pasts:

> If your Dad didn't come to America, his life would've been better there [in the Philippines]. His position at the bank might've been Vice President now. When he first started, they really liked him there. . . . You would go to a good school. . . . I didn't like that. . . . I remember crying. . . . That's where it was molded, in the Philippines: his pride.

Aurora's Tagalog throws in the occasional English phrase. Her words are not accompanied by any images of her or her son, Revereza's father. We may be surprised to hear more about Revereza's heritage. Aurora reveals her son to have been an ambitious, white-collar professional in the Philippines. He gave up his job security and left behind his family to pursue a better life in the United States. If it weren't for his ego, says Aurora, the filmmaker would likely be part of a social elite, without financial or legal woes. The story tells of a failed attempt to "make it" in the United States. However, Aurora's criticism of her son also gives away the false promise of American prosperity, and her sporadic switch to English serves as a reminder that the continuous flow of Filipino migrants to the contemporary United States is underwritten by a history of U.S. colonization of the Southeast Asian

92 | STATELESS CINEMA AND THE UNDOCUMENT

archipelago.[66] The audio of Aurora's voice unfolds against a series of window shots. As in many scenes in *Distancing,* not much seems to transpire in the frame, other than water drops on the window's surface. A window cleaner, a Black man, wipes the windows of a car parked near an unnamed train station. Yet this seemingly random shot suggests a connection of sorts between the present of the train ride, the historical past of the grandmother's account, and the unrealized future that she remembers. Could this be Revereza's father now?

Aurora's father, Revereza's great-grandfather, was a propertied governor during the Spanish colonial period, with lots of servants. "He acquired so much land. If they didn't have any helpers he'd summon the tenants to serve." *Lola* Aurora uses the word "*kasama . . .* you know *kasama*? Tenants?" She is referring to the feudal land-tenure system in the Philippines established under Spanish colonialism. Through the *kasama* system, landowners frequently required personal services from tenants without compensating them. "Like when you get home you say 'My slippers!'" Aurora goes into more detail. "Pretend the helper's name is Belen. 'Belen, my slippers!'" Her performance relays a previous life and social position that is impossible now. "Back then there were such things as the bourgeoisie." Aurora's voice has a tinge of regret. "That's how things were. Now we're here in America and it's different. Everyone is equal." Her ride from Filipino past to U.S. present is bumpy, and creates a sense of confusion and grief with respect to the family's restricted mobility in the United States. Her past colonial privilege adds a bygone dimension to repeated images of restricted mobility that allude to her family's current precarity and undocumented status.

We continue to hear Aurora's voice as we see shots of Revereza's train now traveling from La Junta, Colorado, to Dodge City, Kansas. The camera turns toward the mesmerizing landscape outside the window. A majestic shoreline unfolds, as land and water blend. Post-sunset light amplifies its grandeur. A sudden cut to black changes the mood: "Everyone is equal." The subtitle visually lingers into the following shot of a train station. Blurred by the darkness of the evening and the reflection of the train window, the station's sign reads "Dodge City, KS." Known especially for the legendary Wild West legend and Western icon Wyatt Earp, the Kansan city has provided the backdrop for many film productions that celebrate the Western frontier. In *No Data Plan,* everything whizzes by in ways that do not simply celebrate U.S. expansion but render the moving image into a bearer of the haunting residue of settler occupation. Before arriving in Dodge City, we witness the train pulling in to La Junta. Colorado and parts of Kansas were seized from native people by New Spain before being annexed to the United States.[67] One might note that New Spain also held jurisdiction over the Philippines from 1565 to 1821. In a virtual zooming out that accompanies serial shots of the shoreline passing by, we might also observe that the U.S. annexation of Spanish colonies, and the transposition of "conquest and colonization from the Native communities of the West to its overseas empire"[68] echoes the Philippine *kasama* system under Spanish rule that Aurora mentions, as this system of shared tenancy restructured the local population through forced expropriation and servitude. *No Data Plan* connects these modes and uncanny moments of oppression and colonial seizure—between here and there, now and then.

Lola Aurora turns to her elderly nanny Tia Eling, who long ago became part of the household as part of Aurora's dowry. We learn that Tia Eling worked over several generations for Aurora's family, and that she did so without pay. Her parents were grateful for finding a reputable place for their daughter Eling, as she was also a single mom. "Servants of socialites were respectable positions," explains Aurora. "They'd take pride in it." In fact, "They didn't want to get paid," she adds, because they "counted as family." Aurora also wonders if laboring for free really makes Tia Eling "like family"—or could it be "technically slavery?" She compares Tia Eling's position with that of a *katulong,* a paid domestic servant, and remains unsure about which of the two is preferable. The segment closes with a ninety-second recording of the train tracks from within Revereza's halted train, and a never-ending freight train speeding rhythmically by.

Aurora's equivocal thoughts on domestic servitude and its likening to "slavery" are framed by images of Revereza's journey by train, evoking complicated and ongoing colonial and imperial subjugations. The seeming omnipresence of the train tracks summons the specter of the transcontinental railroad as a landmark of North America's modern infrastructure. Historians have detailed how Chinese indentured workers, or coolies, worked under hazardous conditions alongside Indigenous and other indentured laborers during the 1860s to erect this landmark, frequently facing death.[69] "To be a Chinese worker," Manu Karuka maintains, "was definitely not to be a slave, the property of another. It was, however, a reduction to the status of a tool for grading earth and drilling a mountain. It was to be expendable, interchangeable, replaceable."[70] Working and occupying Indigenous land, Chinese railroad workers were also rendered as a "tool" for the forced displacement measures of the settler-colonial state.

No Data Plan documents the present in ways that can be differently conceived through and alongside its "distant" histories. The imperial U.S. border police state is a settler-colonial state built on ongoing border and land claims. As such, it prods the question, what is the role of nonwhite settlement in sustaining the state's violent erasure of Indigenous lifeworlds? Iyko Day details how the trope of "claiming America," meant to challenge historical Asian exclusion, also replays settler colonialism's territorial entitlement.[71] The claim to America is in fact central to the history of immigrant rights movements, including DREAMer activism, and liberal rights discourse at large. Whereas the legal protection of minorities is not up for debate, the problem of "claiming America" lies in the logic of ownership as the only and just way to belong. What Kim Tallbear terms "American Dreaming," that is, the dream of a nation built on multicultural success, builds on colonial expropriation.[72] She emphasizes, "Dream in any form, whether White supremacist or 'progressive,' cannot be our guiding hope."[73] Entwining Aurora's bourgeois family story with recurring shots of land and the train motif, *No Data Plan* unsettles the great U.S. origin story and offers an ambiguous tension with respect to the filmmaker's undocumented positionality and the agentive power of his video recording. I approach this tension as a productive interlinking of the layered histories of U.S. state violence and their vital imbrication with minoritarian realities of survival, fugitivism, and insurgency, in ways that complicate simplified framings of unity or opposition.[74] *No Data Plan* allows us to advance a relational politics that speaks to minority histories in both their frictions with each other but also in their shared embedding in histories of colonial violence and racial capitalism. The kinds of relationality that *No Data Plan*'s storytelling introduces call for collective yet differentiated historical responsibility. Like Tallbear's vision of a shared commitment to social justice that yet requires different forms of accountability—she writes of "caretaking relations"[75]—*No Data Plan*'s relational politics pivot on care as a thing of uneven access and improper relations, without claiming equality or relatability.

Revereza recalls the frequent passing by of cargo trains on his journey—like the one that concludes Aurora's scene—drawing a parallel between the transportation of people and goods: "We travel along the same arteries as the constant flow of commodities—countless shipping containers in passing: lumber, coal, crude oil, ethanol, soap, corn, wheat, rice, French fries, canned goods, pharmaceuticals, frozen chicken, salt, sugar, phosphate, sulfur ammonia, steel, gravel, crushed stone, plastics, glass, clothing, footwear, electronics, and auto parts."[76] Undocumented immigrants, the filmmaker points out, hold less mobility than cheap consumer goods. "It shouldn't be this complicated for people to get around when we can get cat litter delivered to our doorsteps in two days." In a different interview, Revereza expands his critique of forced immobility to the immigrant detention industry that has excessively grown since the 1990s, peaking again under Trump's presidency at the time of the film's making:

> As long as there are private prison corporations turning a profit, there will be mass immigration detainment. As long as affiliated corporations are dependent on cheap goods produced by prison labor, and as long as politicians are beholden to the interests of private prison corporations, there will be no significant change on a broken immigration system.[77]

The artist's comment circles us back to the lucrative nature of produced illegality in the United States. High rates of immigrant detention mean high profits for private prison companies, which mean more tax income for the state.[78] *No Data Plan,* too, allows us to see how colonial pasts linger into the present moment, in their continuously permutating iterations.

Undocumented Selfies

The border patrol agents have left the train. Revereza is on the phone, with his right fist pressing against his leg. "Did you see my Story?" He may be speaking to his mother, that is, about Instagram Stories, Instagram's slideshow feature that saves photos and videos for followers for twenty-four hours. Speaking on the phone, his voice is increasingly agitated as he unfolds his worst nightmare come true:

I saw that there was this white SUV with the words "Border Patrol" on the side of it, and I was like what the fuck did I just see that, and then as it slowed down on the other end I saw another one that said "Border Patrol" inside of it, and someone getting out of it. It was a uniformed fucking border patrol agent.

The artist wipes his nose with his hand. We see a closeup of his right thumb. And now his knee. He sniffles, still in shock. "And I was just thinking, fuck, you know, this is it. Like, this is where they catch up to me." The filmmaker's sniffling somehow overlaps and interferes with his own speaking voice, suggesting that the phone call was recorded at a different time. Like his mother, Revereza owns two phones. He's done with the burner phone, and pulls out his iPhone. His thumb swipes through the slideshow, pausing on photos that he selects for the camera to record. Some reveal his face. Starting with the most recent, the first selfie we see features Revereza partially covered by shade and looking dead serious. Text on the screen reads: "I think they're gone. Walked right past me." Flipping forward, he rests his thumb on another selfie with a similarly grim expression. "Help: do I decline questions of citizenship???" The Instagram picture indicates

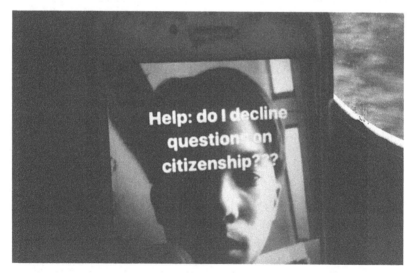

Figure 16. Revereza replays his Instagram Stories in front of the video camera; screenshot from *No Data Plan*.

a timestamp of twenty-one minutes ago. Merely twenty-one minutes separate us from the filmmaker's initial panic, as he ran through every possible scenario in his head. We again hear his voice on the phone. "I was just freaking out because I didn't know if I should lie to them, because if I lie to them, and they found out, then they could... detain me for like lying to a federal agent. But if I told them, 'No I'm not an American citizen,' then, like, they can just detain me, too." He continues, "This is what I always imagined might happen, and it just happened." And: "I just saw this car, this SUV, and just froze, and no matter how much I thought about it prior to this, I just wasn't prepared for it." The artist flips back and forth between images now. One of them says "Fuck These Fools," another one, "WTF America," and finally, "I'm OK." What the filmmaker cannot exclaim in public, he uploads to Instagram Stories, turning the platform into his (not so) secretive megaphone.

Far from naïve, Revereza understands the risks of using social media as an undocumented person, and that geolocation technologies can give him away to the DHS. His Instagram Stories video is a momentary hacking of institutional surveillance that does not record his face in properly detectable fashion. If the integrated state-market

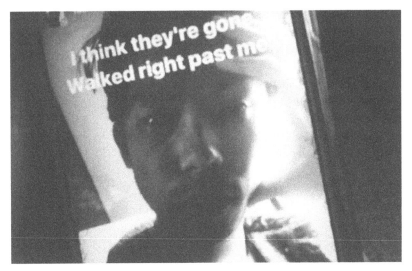

Figure 17. The filmmaker's Instagram post right after the Border Patrol agents have left the train; screenshot from *No Data Plan*.

nexus of surveillance renders immigrant online activity into a "motion data picture" that detects and traps the undocumented immigrant, Revereza turns the visual document into a conceptual object that sabotages its institutional designation and "assumes the motions of a fugitive."[79] Switching from iPhone to Instagram and to Sony A7S, his Instagram selfie is hypervisible, but still obscured and difficult to make out. Overlaid with glib emojis, Revereza's photograph pokes fun at the entangled institutional (DHS) and media (Instagram) demands for his identification and capture. Like the passport in *Distancing, No Data Plan*'s selfie is an undocument, freeing images from the demand to capture and identify, and from the expectation of relatable and authentic story.

Revereza's work deemphasizes the liberal individual by alluding to larger connections between capitalism, migrant and undocumented labor, and histories of settler colonialism. Back on the train, Revereza continues to evade the roving eyes of the state officials. As "the only non-white and black person" in the car, his complexion could give him away. But to his surprise, not much else happens. "I just put on my Bard lanyard and . . . I don't know what it was. I crossed my legs, played it cool, and they walked right past me." Anticlimactically, we feel no liberation or lingering relief. As the film ends, there is no more audible dialogue, only the rattling sound of the train. Subtitles silently and distantly appear as the filmmaker calls his mother. She is on the road somewhere with her lover.

I tell Mama my plan to leave the States a year from now.
I can tell she believes me.
She weeps through the shitty speaker.
"I just wish I could do that, too."

4

Migrant Erotics

TIWA's *Lesbian Factory* and *Rainbow Popcorn*

> At first we just wanted to record the struggles of the migrant workers, but as we were filming, many sweet lesbian couples appeared in the film. So this documentary accidentally developed into a love story.
>
> —*Lesbian Factory*

It was a humid and hot December Sunday in Taipei City. Early protestors were already bustling around the Taiwanese Presidential Office Building, where the 2015 biannual march and rally for migrant labor were scheduled to begin at 1 p.m. Early participants were almost done setting up the stage, testing technical equipment, and running through final rehearsals, as the number of people gathering increased from dozens into the hundreds. The rally's main organizer was the Taiwan International Workers' Association, also known as TIWA. Its protest march and rally would be joined today by further local NGOs, migrant workers, migrant worker advocacy groups, a handful of reporters, and many friends and allies. Meticulously planned and rehearsed for months in advance by TIWA members and staff, the protest boasted a remarkable army of volunteers recruited via word of mouth and social media. All were flawlessly executing their assigned tasks, from handing out bottled water to reviewing cues for performing groups. As the number of gatherers continued to multiply, we could all feel the electrifying power of the crowd. The march started up with a proclamation of the theme of the protest, "Justice in Caring," a call for more attention to be paid to the often invisible yet essential labor of low-wage foreign migrant workers in Taiwan.

99

The now enormous crowd began to move in the direction of Taipei's Central Station, where the public sit-in and rally were scheduled to take place. The mass of people gradually moved downtown toward the headquarters of Tsai Ing-wen, the chair of the Democratic Progressive Party and then presidential candidate of Taiwan. Noticeably absent, weeks later she would be elected as president. (At the time of this writing, Tsai continues to serve as the first female president of Taiwan.)

The events having reached an astounding day's total of one thousand participants, the finale was an on-stage reading of a letter addressed to Chair Tsai and the citizens of Taiwan. Collectively written by migrant workers and activists, the letter was read into the microphone by various migrant workers and TIWA staff in five different languages—Mandarin, Tagalog, Vietnamese, Indonesian, and Thai, languages commonly spoken by different migrant workers in Taiwan. The letter made special note of the vital role of Southeast Asians as Taiwan's largest migrant labor force. To productively contribute to the economic and social well-being of the nation as a whole, it read, the Taiwanese government had to do better at recognizing and protecting the lives and the livelihoods of its essential migrant workers.

The above is my participant observation of TIWA's 2015 iteration of its biannually organized protest, now known as the largest migrant worker advocacy event in Taiwan's history. I traveled to Taiwan on three occasions between 2015 and 2017 to research TIWA's social organization and projects, and interviewed migrant workers and TIWA employees about their struggles and concerns regarding their lives, jobs, and working conditions. These unique experiences led to this chapter's discussion of two documentaries created by TIWA members with a digital camcorder: *Lesbian Factory* (2010) and *Rainbow Popcorn* (2013). Both videos feature a group of migrant workers from the Philippines who, thanks to their shared experiences of working abroad in Taiwan, have also become romantic couples and dear friends.

As of 2022, approximately 700,000 legally employed foreign workers live in Taiwan, whose population amounts to 23.4 million. Though it is said that "Taiwan" better describes the major island of the official archipelago, and that the "Republic of China" (ROC) better reflects its dispute over sovereignty with China (also known as the People's Republic of China, or PRC), I use "Taiwan" and "ROC" interchangeably here. The majority of Taiwan's foreign workers hail from poorer nations of Southeast Asia, namely, Vietnam (212,000), the Philippines (120,000), Indonesia (84,000), and Thailand (63,000).[1] Like many migrants from the Global South who opt to work abroad in more economically developed countries, they are commonly seen by the Taiwanese state and many of its citizens as intruders who deplete local resources.[2] Migrants rarely draw attention otherwise in Taiwan, and ostensibly lack relevance in the face of more pressing issues related to cross-strait relations, governmental elections, and civic freedoms. Southeast Asian workers who enjoy and utilize public spaces in Taiwan are legally subject to state monitoring. Further fueled by public opinion about the parasitic nature of migrant workers, the government of Taipei City has repeatedly attempted to forbid foreign contract workers from congregating at Central Station on their days off from work, arguing that they disturb the peace and create a public nuisance.

Over the years, TIWA's migrant advocacy initiatives have tailored its responses to institutionalized discrimination, for example, through a strategic move which I call *sentimental activism*: the tactical use of affective theatrical performance in ways that seek to humanize migrant workers, in the case of TIWA, by pulling on the heartstrings of the general Taiwanese public. A TIWA organizer confirmed to me that the biannual march and rally had indeed become increasingly theatrical over the years in order to increase awareness about migrant workers and to depict them as a legitimate part of Taiwan's general public. Such performances were used to direct public emotion toward specific goals regarding their protection—at the 2015 march and rally, the letter-reading ceremony, for example, turned into a commemoration of overseas workers who had died in Taiwan. Some workers had died by suicide. That year, another particularly memorable performance featured a giant float of a diabetic senior in a wheelchair. Pulled along by forty migrant workers in blood-stained T-shirts, the float was loudly cheered along by fellow protestors. Like other performances that day, it was ingeniously designed to draw attention to the oppressive labor conditions under which Southeast Asian contract workers in particular have continued to steadfastly care and sustain many aspects of comfortable living for citizens of the ROC.[3]

The 2015 TIWA protest attracted a great deal of bystander attention with its one thousand protesters who marched through Taipei's

102 | MIGRANT EROTICS

city center streets with megaphones chanting protest slogans and staging the above-mentioned performances. The police were also present, closely monitoring the proceedings until the very end. In the raised hands of many in the crowd were smart phones and cameras that snapped pictures and recorded videos from all angles, with protesters, journalists, bystanders, and police officers also recording on their phones at any given moment. Thankfully no hostile conflicts arose during this event that successfully prioritized awareness and empathy over antigovernment rhetoric. After 5 p.m., after the street had been cleared of people, picket signs, banners, and garbage, TIWA staff invited its volunteers to have dinner back at the office, where a hotpot was already bubbling in the kitchen. In a virtual sequel to the day's events, at the office everyone logged into their social media accounts to upload pictures and videos, to comment on each other's posts, and to check what was on the news. We searched through the office TV's channels looking for any official coverage of the protest. "If they don't broadcast it tonight, they won't broadcast it at all," mused a fellow NGO worker. And he was correct. The TIWA-inspired protest and its thousand bodies were mentioned in neither Taipei's local print papers nor on national television—not even on the following day. The lack of news coverage, especially via major Taiwanese news outlets, shows how migrant worker issues continue to be neglected by those in power.

This chapter investigates how TIWA's activist documentaries *Lesbian Factory* and *Rainbow Popcorn* uniquely navigate a fine line between political change and state cooptation by engaging sentimental rhetorics of bliss and pain, between the goals of its activism and the demands of an increasingly neoliberal Taiwan. This is to say that the archipelago's status as a liminally sovereign nation in the eyes of the United Nations and the global eye motivates its public treatment of minority groups and migrant workers at this historical moment. When possible, I home in on the language of rights and recognition as it pertains to TIWA's videos and curious reliance on certain kinds of migrant visibility, and on how this visibility is used for its political ends. The language of rights and recognition is a powerful and necessary medium in democratic states through which individual and collective protections can garner political security, and readily identify the good (as opposed to the bad) global players in the current political landscape. The Taiwanese government's embrace of explicitly liberal political discourse since the late 1980s bespeaks its historical effort to claim de jure independence from mainland China, and to join a world league of properly democratic decision makers. Dutifully sponsored by state-based cultural establishments, TIWA's activist media must walk a difficult line between creating political videos that encourage public care of and nonhostility toward Taiwan's minorities, and participation in liberal discourses by public institutions funded by the state. Whereas media convergence scholarship elaborates on how media texts signify through evolving practices of industry and user groups, this chapter examines how the ROC demonstrates its multicultural agenda to the world and its citizens by promoting activist documentaries about minority subjects.[4] I argue that TIWA's activist videos rather exploit this rhetoric and its embrace of multicultural visibility in ways that speak to Taiwan's majoritarian desires while also insisting on an agenda of structural transformation that centers the lives of migrant workers.

The TIWA video *Lesbian Factory* and its sequel *Rainbow Popcorn* follow and narrate the lives of a group of queer Filipina and trans migrant workers who meet as foreign workers in Taiwan. In both videos, sentimental activism manifests largely in tropes of love and suffering that pull on viewers' sense of justice by framing the protagonist workers as relatable subjects worth standing up for. Rather than rely on ontological claims of being human, as much of sentimental liberal rights discourse does, however—stating that we are all the same and therefore equally deserving—the films eschew a rhetoric of sameness and equal deservingness through which minorities are plugged into existing structures and passively deserve and receive others' care. The documentaries center migrant working-class women and trans and gender-nonconforming individuals from the Global South as historical protagonists in the global struggle for equal rights and social justice. Both videos deliberately support the multicultural rhetoric of the state, yet their emphases on queer migrancy and transnational networks of care also carefully distance them from Taiwan's rhetoric of patriarchal nationalism, and from the region's ordering into competing sovereign territories. Where the Chinese title of *Lesbian Factory*, T婆工廠 (*t-po gong chang* in Mandarin), refers to the subjects of female same-sex partnerships as a mix of lesbians and "T-Po" (an English-Chinese hybridization of T for "tomboy" and po for "wife"), this chapter engages the term *queer* to name the multiple

104 | MIGRANT EROTICS

and open-ended forms of nonnormative sociality that the videos put forth. Here, the notions of "lesbian" and "Filipina," frequently used by the filmmakers and migrant workers I talked to, gestures to a women-majority social space that is yet not defined by fixed cisgender identities.[5]

Taiwan's Imperial Underbelly

After centuries of serial colonization, including Han-Chinese settlement, Japanese occupation, and nearly four decades of martial law under the Kuomintang regime exiled from mainland China (1949–1987), the ROC has emerged as an Asian model of democracy and global market integration. Throughout the 1990s, its transformation from a one-party military regime to a democratically elected government has given rise to new policies designed to protect the rights of minorities in Taiwan.[6] The state's visible promotion of its Indigenous population and sexual diversity is a case in point that has received praise from allied minority groups around the world and powerful governing institutions like the United Nations.[7] Yet such validations still have not led to the ROC's recognition as a sovereign nation-state, and it continues to exist under the shadow of the PRC. (Taiwan's original seat in the United Nations was passed on to China in 1972.) Taiwan's precarious global position incites the state to continuously assert its progressive commitment to the UN and its international audience, and it has chosen to do so primarily through its assertion of human rights and minority inclusion. Taiwan's exemplary status, in other words, hinges on its ongoing embrace of Western-style democracy and liberalism. This embrace tends to conceal the ongoing devaluation of local minorities in Taiwan, among them Indigenous, queer, and migrant worker populations that historically have been denied the rights of citizens, and that do not necessarily conform to accepted social norms. As Petrus Liu maintains, the government's "rhetoric of tolerance, liberalism, and progress is a political ruse designed to win over the sympathy of the American public, since Taiwan's continuous de facto and imagined future de jure status as a sovereign nation-state depends on American military protection and support."[8]

The dominance of the United States in the United Nations has played a critical role in Taiwan's liberalization and its national imaginary. With significant military and economic aid to Taiwan during the Cold War, the United States secured the archipelago as a strategic military access point and ally against the Red Bloc[9] and created a relationship of Taiwanese dependency that allowed President Jimmy Carter to pressure the Taiwanese government into adopting a U.S.-authored human rights policy.[10] The ROC's "democratic exemplarity" here emerges as a liberalism that is autonomous from the PRC[11] and that endorses both U.S. military-capitalist presence in the Asia Pacific and Taiwan's "subimperial" expansion into areas of the Global South.[12] Entrenched in neoliberal ideals of global governance and democracy, the universalizing language of imperial U.S. human rights discourse, to echo scholars of critical Asian studies and transnational American studies, promises independence for diverse people and groups insofar as it can reproduce its paradigms of domination and imperial control.[13] The high concentration of overseas Filipino workers (OFWs) in Taiwan is a direct result of U.S.-supported liberalization in the Asia Pacific and the emergence of regional migrant labor regimes in the latter twentieth century. Here the politico-economic reinvention of Taiwan and its aggressive southward expansion combined with the Philippines' forging of a state-led labor export system designed to alleviate national debt and high unemployment rates.[14] Regional modernization, in other words, emerges as state investment in the stability of capital accumulation and a simultaneous disinvestment from citizen care, which in Taiwan is generally outsourced to migrant workers from Southeast Asia.[15]

The exemplarity of the on-demand Asian is twofold against this backdrop. Important for my argument is to understand, first, Taiwan's complicated standing among advanced industrialized nations as a praiseworthy yet nonsovereign democracy, and second, the Taiwanese state's targeted management of the visibility of its migrant workers from the Global South in order to demonstrate to the world its clear capability in maintaining a democratic civil society. In this context, I employ the concept of sentimental activism to explore how *Lesbian Factory* and *Rainbow Popcorn* effectively mobilize an affective lexicon of rights and recognition for radical ends. These documentaries push for change on the ground by using familiar-feeling modes and narratives of representation; and they simultaneously recalibrate viewers' familiar feelings by drawing on migrant workers' life-making practices, their capacious forging of queer transnational socialities, to offer us new models of the social.

106 | MIGRANT EROTICS

If documentary radicality describes the inherent ability of documentaries to register the material conditions of social relations (including its own positionality) and "prepar[e] the political moment," as Jane Gaines maintains, the radicality of *Lesbian Factory* and *Rainbow Popcorn* lies in unfolding queer migrants' everyday lives in ways that affirm and extend alternative world-making practices.[16] That these practices at times seem more accommodating than revolutionary does not foreclose their transformative potential. Rather, they make possible ways of inhabiting existing institutional structures that do not reproduce the same old forms of sociality. As a direct response to the historical conditions that undergird the ROC's seemingly benevolent mobilization of new migrant visibilities for its own exemplary visibility as a Western-style democracy, TIWA's activist videos then also afford a vantage point to reimagine hegemonic mappings of national sovereignty, and the region, queerly—that is, beside official state discourse and the directives of capital flows.[17]

Lesbian Factory and the Queerness of Taiwan's Public Television Service

Lesbian Factory (2010, 57 min.) was produced by the Public Television Service (PTS), Taiwan's major public broadcasting network, which continues to be funded directly by state entities. PTS owns the distribution rights for *Lesbian Factory,* though its sequel *Rainbow Popcorn* (2013, 63 min.) was independently produced by TIWA without government funding, so that the NGO could retain control over its production and dissemination.[18] The filming of *Lesbian Factory* took place over five years from 2004 to 2009, and was directed by TIWA staff members Susan Chen and Jingru Wu. It features Susan, Jingru, and their foreign factory-worker colleagues as they organize and advocate for better migrant labor rights in Taiwan. *Lesbian Factory* opens with a scene of a live protest, as a group of approximately sixty Filipina workers gather behind a picket sign that reads: "Fastfame Company Abused Migrants. No Salary. No Food. No Jobs. Please Help!!!" They are protesting against computer-parts manufacturer Fastfame Technology, a company that has just closed down its Taiwanese branch and dismissed its 125 Filipina workers without payment. Like many other Taiwanese businesses, Fastfame decided to relocate its factory to mainland China to stay solvent. The workers' protest is directed at the Council of Labor Affairs (now part of the Ministry of Labor) to intervene and help get the contract laborers paid. Recounting how the migrant workers turned to TIWA for support in the face of the government's noninterventionist silence, questions arise. "Will workers be repatriated? How will they survive without food allowance? How can they get back their salary arrears? Can migrant workers get severance pay?"[19] Though their once-legal stay in Taiwan is now in jeopardy and the possibility of receiving their final wages nearly impossible, the worker protagonists appear surprisingly cheerful and excited on screen. They giggle and chat between chanting protest slogans and take pictures of one another in front of protest banners. The atmosphere at times feels more like that of a giddy high school reunion. The documentary alternates between scenes of the workers' cheer and gravity, just as it does between their public activism and intimate life, reflecting the naturally complex textures of their ordinary lives in Taiwan. "At first we just wanted to record the struggles of the migrant workers," says the voice-over, "but as we were filming, many sweet lesbian couples appeared in the film. So this documentary accidentally developed into a love story."

Figure 18. Workers unite and cheer in front of the camera; screenshot from *Lesbian Factory*.

108 | MIGRANT EROTICS

Journalist and labor activist Susan Chen founded TIWA in the mid-1980s, with the goal of compensating for the lack of institutional and state support available for Southeast Asian workers in Taiwan, a population whose numbers surged as a result of the government's neoliberal Go South policy. (Chen has also produced *Hospital Wing 8 East* [2006], a documentary about a Filipina migrant caregiver in Taiwan.[20]) As the go-to NGO for migrant labor issues in Taiwan, TIWA is run by about a dozen full-time employees, all of whom identify as feminist, and most of whom identify as women and/or queer. Having learned a great deal from the intersectional practices of earlier progressive women's groups in Taiwan, TIWA is well connected with many minority rights groups and organizations throughout Asia. An out lesbian, Jingru cites her friendships with queer migrant-worker colleagues at TIWA as the inspiration for *Lesbian Factory*. Film workshops are also available at TIWA thanks to Susan and Jingru, an example of the organization's creative learning opportunities offered to migrant workers, and are a supplement to services like legal counseling, language classes, and other recreational activities.

Filmed on digital video, *Lesbian Factory* recalls a tradition of Taiwanese activist documentary whose emergence in the late 1980s coincides with the rise of video as a popular grassroots technology, and with various antiauthoritarian civil rights movements in Taiwan. Critics Kuei-fen Chiu and Yingjin Zhang observe that activist films came to be through regular citizens learning to express themselves through video, and thus played a pioneering hand in the imagination and formation of Taiwanese civil society as it is understood today.[21] Where early Taiwanese documentaries of this period were generally shot by male street protesters as they advocated for grassroots civil and democratic reform (and often sold for little money on the spot), *Lesbian Factory* focuses on women, trans, and gender-nonconforming migrant workers who explore queer desire while working in Taiwan. How are we to reconcile this documentarian realpolitik with the emotional schmaltz of bliss, romance, and pain? Reminiscent of how the category of Asian American film and video has been actively sponsored from the 1970s onward in the United States,[22] TIWA's lively media activism is promoted and subsidized by the ROC in order to democratically showcase national diversity and multiculturalism to its citizens. Indeed, *Lesbian Factory*'s own postproduction was funded by Taiwan's Public Television Service, the network established by the ROC's post–martial law government in 1998. Much like PBS in the United States, which was created to help foster a new and civic-minded public, PTS is one of few Taiwanese networks that feature queer content. As stated by the country's 1997 Public Television Act, public television "belongs to the entire body of citizens. It shall operate independently without interference, and shall observe the . . . principles of freedom, democracy, and . . . diversity."[23] Despite its commitment to the people and "the rights and interests of disadvantaged groups,"[24] however, media critics tend to agree that Taiwan's PTS remains a top-down, "elite-driven" project.[25] Today the Public Television Service Foundation receives nearly half of its annual budget from government appropriations, and approximately 40 percent from other state-funded grants. This precedent was established in the 2010s, when the conversion of analog to digital television infrastructures was cost prohibitive and depended on state subsidies.[26] Access to TV frequencies today is still regulated by the ROC's Ministry of Defense, which closely monitors public use of the broadcast spectrum. The selection of the foundation's supervising members must be confirmed by the national parliament (Legislative Yuan) and tend to be aligned with the ruling party. PTS's formal claim that "personnel operations, editorial rights, [and] program content" are completely autonomous from the government is therefore questionable.[27]

The network was initially hesitant to use the term *lesbian* in the title of *Lesbian Factory*. Scholars and activists note that despite Taiwan's official proclamations of LGBTQ tolerance—as the first state in Asia to legalize gay marriage, for example—actions that explicitly curtail the rights of sexual and gender-nonconforming minorities continue to persist throughout Taiwan.[28] Public television's "will to institutionality," its absorption of difference into institutional agendas,[29] has certainly boosted the circulation of *Lesbian Factory* across different media platforms. After being shown on one of PTS's prestigious documentary programs in 2010, the documentary was viewed at government-sponsored screening events and as part of a national documentary showcase, and had limited local theatrical release. Screened over two hundred times to Taiwanese audiences before, it then entered the international film festival market, where it circulated not only as a work of queer and migrant labor activism but also as a product uniquely made in the ROC.[30] Minority activism in *Lesbian Factory* converges with state-curated dissemination and policies,

110 | MIGRANT EROTICS

and turns the visual documentation of a government's neglect toward protecting its foreign workers into a national democracy-loving showcase. Critics like Inderpal Grewal, Petrus Liu, and Josephine Ho situate a global rights discourse within the history and afterlife of Cold War hierarchies, and I contend that *Lesbian Factory*'s institutional and international circulations also create a strong and legitimating currency by way of its media depictions of liberal politics. *Lesbian Factory*'s international visibility is ostensible proof of the ROC's care for its minorities and foreign workers, an antithetical contrast with respect to mainland China's notorious record of human rights violations and media censorship. Its ability to show and elicit emotion is advantageous when it comes to accruing global support and symbolic capital for the liminally independent nation of Taiwan. As the documentary travels from the activist camera into the lenses of national media outlets and international festivals, it becomes an example of how progressive movements can be coopted by neoliberal visions of democracy and capital. The film's distinctly affective and activist circuitries, however, continue to create potentialities for other progressive relationships to emerge.

Sentimental Stories of Activism

Scenes of intimacy and coming out about queer life elicit viewers' empathy with the protagonists of *Lesbian Factory*. They incite our wishes to know more about the ups and downs of their experiences, and especially to laugh with them. *Lesbian Factory* solicits our sentimental hankerings for both bliss and difficult struggle, and our desires to stand up for the relatable characters of the documentary. We learn more about *Lesbian Factory*'s migrant protagonists as they answer questions about their lives as couples. How did their relationships begin? How did each know that the other liked them back? "If somebody likes you, you will recognize it easily. It's different from friends," says Bing, a T-presenting Filipina who describes the beginning of her relationship with fellow worker Yam. Asked how she knew for sure that Yam was more than just a friend, she responds: "Because she made me like that," and encircles Yam with her arms, mimicking a big hug. Laughter percolates through the whole room. We meet Lan, who is a star organizer like Bing and Yam. She explains how she wanted her mother to retire from working in Kuwait and move to Taiwan, so that she could rest and Lan could take over as the family breadwinner. Her girlfriend Pilar ("the very fat one," smiles Lan), was going to return home to the Philippines, but when Lan needed to stay longer, she extended her stay as well. "You know, I love her very much," Lan says about Pilar. Her statement is followed by clapping and cheering in the background. Further far-from-home migrant confessions follow, now from Ellen and Elsa. Ellen, who is addressed as a queer woman in *Lesbian Factory* and identifies as male in the film's sequel, tells the interviewer how he also came to Taiwan to support his family, and met Elsa during that time. Ellen says he is "so lucky" to have met Elsa, and remembers his own overwhelming shyness. "I see her, and I didn't say anything, I didn't say Hi, hello. I can't say a word because I am too shy to see her." Elsa recalls what it was like to realize that she wanted to be with another woman, and not a man. "No I don't like you"— she insisted—"because we are the same sex." But it was meant to be. "Every time if I see her, I'm happy." Elsa's account is accompanied by loud happiness from everyone in the room—with the exception of Ellen, who starts to cry. "So touching," Ellen says, wiping his tears.

Figure 19. Elsa *(left)* and Ellen *(right)* tending to each other during the protest; screenshot from *Lesbian Factory*.

112 | MIGRANT EROTICS

In both Taiwan and the Philippines, sentimental storytelling bears a strong cultural association with state censorship.[31] *Lesbian Factory* pulls on viewers' heartstrings with its narratives of love and suffering, through engaging conventional narratives of filial piety and female vulnerability. It stands out in its pragmatic use of sentimental affect that both moves and mobilizes viewers while challenging heteronormativity and nationalism in ways that underwrite most liberal conceptions of social justice. As it does so it underscores, in pragmatic fashion, sentimentality's usefulness in social struggles for inclusion that strive to bring about scenes that such liberal-humanistic logic seems to foreclose. Though its propriety and effectiveness are contentiously debated, the use of sentimentality for political ends is nothing new. Maneuvering sentimentality has a long tradition in progressive aesthetic production. While documentary is conventionally defined as a "serious" film form that refrains from an excessive use of emotions,[32] certain genres of socially "committed" and especially human rights-based documentary are known for their sentimental affect.[33] Often labeled as "mawkish, nostalgic, and simpleminded" due to its deliberate manipulation of viewer emotions, sentimentality is a tactic that is used by state and public media in order to leverage public opinion and to keep viewers, however (un)comfortably, watching from their seats.[34] When Jingru asks Lan and Pilar about how they became a couple, they respond "We talk talk talk talk talk, and then one day, we're together." Jingru asks for more detail. "That's too simple," she counters. "Nobody will be satisfied with your answer like that," she says. What an audience wants (or what is needed to get at them), her statement implies, is a juicy love story ending in the women's unification. Conveying a shared experience, love becomes a narrative device that emotionally organizes viewers around the precaritized workers. Feelings of romantic love offer a sense of common belonging for the viewers as well. Especially through sentimentality, love makes subjects legible and relatable.[35]

Lesbian Factory's queer stories as channeled through patriarchal ideals of dutiful daughters and caring members of the OFW community uncannily overlap with Philippine state propagations of women as reproductive citizens. Especially since Corazon Aquino's presidency in the mid-1980s, female OFWs have been hailed as "the new heroes of the nation" heeding demands for Christian piety and good womanhood.[36] Vicente Rafael maintains that featuring sentimental

Figure 20. Pilar *(left)* and Lan *(right)* coyly share their love story with the filmmakers; screenshot from *Lesbian Factory*.

narratives of the Filipina diaspora, also a tactic of official state rhetoric, makes it easier to gloss over "the inability of the state to provide for its people."[37] It also tends to presume that the proper role of Filipina women is to engage in various norms of self-sacrifice. Love for one's family and for the nation, for example, may be expressed through cycles of difficult absence that allow for the ongoing deliverance of remittances. Gluing together fractured and transnationally dispersed families, love, to cite Elizabeth Freeman, "binds a socius."[38] Freeman advances a critique of how the temporal rhythms of human bodies and their lives streamline "toward maximum productivity."[39] Her concept of "binding" helps us grasp how feelings of "coherently collective" love can powerfully synchronize relationships between people and create "socially meaningful embodiment," thereby enabling the biopolitical projects of nation building and capital accumulation (as also inherently spatializing projects).

Feminist labor studies have also been critical of how economies of labor have learned to monetize affect. Arlie Russell Hochschild argues that in the particular field of care work often staffed by OFWs,

114 | MIGRANT EROTICS

love is the "new gold" lately mined along with other resources and commodities from the Global South.[40] The intimate and the private become targeted for capital accumulation in the hegemonic North; what Hochschild's intervention risks normalizing, however, is an ideal of love as "pure" human property originally divorced from market economies and nationalist ideologies that belongs with the patriarchal family. *Lesbian Factory* makes use of love's binding for its activist ends.

The Taiwanese Council of Labor Affairs rejects the workers' appeal for support—perhaps unsurprising given the role of the high-tech industry that includes Fastfame in Taiwan's economic success history. In the 1960s before political liberalization, Taiwan's electronic industry boomed as a result of strategic government sponsorship whose goal was to develop an open, export-oriented market that could meet increasing offshoring demand from the West. "Taiwanese entrepreneurs spearheaded the rapid development of high-tech assembly lines first in Taiwan and later along coastal China," notes Yu-Fang Cho, "making Taiwan one of the world's biggest suppliers of electronic products."[41] Nowadays, Taiwanese companies frequently outsource large chunks of their production process to Southeast Asia (and, as we have seen, to Southern working bodies on the archipelago). Penalizing Fastfame for moving overseas and abandoning its blue-collar foreign contract workers would thus mean setting a precedent for limiting free market rein and putting the ROC's economic future at risk. In this future, the labor of migrant Filipinas is indispensable, but not their lives. Their image might circulate through public broadcasting, local theaters, and international film festivals, proving the ROC's "inclusive" public space. Yet, through existing legal mechanisms, their corporeal bodies are rendered transient, removable, and biologically unthreatening (how convenient that the "lesbian" in TIWA's documentary won't reproduce with local men). Once they are gone, so is the abject (sexuality) that they signify. Ironically, the repetition of uneven inclusions, by which the ROC itself remains outside a league of independent nation-states, is what makes the archipelago's liberal sovereignty legible or at the least imaginable.

Responding to the council's noninterventionist politics, TIWA and its migrant workers attempt to make their grievance public and organize a protest in front of the government building. Between shots of demonstrating workers, the camera lingers on the protagonists taking breaks as they rest and lean against each other and tease each other. By crosscutting images of raised fists and speeches with intimate moments, and interspersing these among the couples' narrative anecdotes, *Lesbian Factory* offers a deeply humanizing portrayal of its migrant protagonists not only as loving and lovable but also as human beings who deserve rights and a proper private life. Love becomes a primary reason for better labor rights. If workers have no say with regard to their job assignments, they are likely to be separated and randomly posted to new positions across the main island. No human rights, no right to future love—to love is to be human.

Only For Taiwan: Migrant Erotics

As *Lesbian Factory*'s migrant couples continue to answer questions about the initial sparks and confusions that occurred when they first started to fall in love, Jingru asks everyone a pointed question: How it is possible to make love in a room shared by other workers? The interviewees giggle loudly and display intrigue, shock, and embarrassment about the question. Pilar hides behind a bunch of pillows, and Lan tries to suppress her giddiness by covering her mouth with a tissue. With a big grin, Lan implies that the act is difficult—because Pilar "is very noisy." Yam and Bing chuckle along, further delaying the secret to having sex in a shared common space. Bursts of laughter and affect run through love's governing circuitry and bind the roommates in a "socially meaningful embodiment" that runs counter to hegemonic demands for "maximum productivity" (24/7 factory work) as well as reproductive togetherness (the hetero family).[42] Somewhere between high-pitched giggling and thick laughter, Jennet reveals the answer to Jingru's question. When other roommates are also messing around and making out—especially the noisy ones—having sex isn't that difficult. Plus, there is always spooning. "So what we do is just do it the silent way. Side view or. . . ." Loud laughter dominates the audio before Jennet can finish her explanation. But the takeaway is clear: sometimes quiet shifts in positioning is all it takes to navigate one's spatio-social settings, and to give a partner pleasure.

Life in the workers' crowded dormitories show that spatial intimacy among the cast of *Lesbian Factory* can be erotic and sexual, a kind of intimacy in which "people are bound to one another, engrouped, made to feel coherently collective," yet not only in the ways

116 | MIGRANT EROTICS

demanded by state and capital.[43] In her critique of the streamlining of bodies and their intimate acts into productive and reproductive "schemes of events" that include marriage and the "accumulation of health and wealth for the future" as well as brief moments of recuperation to continue fulfilling the demands of work,[44] Freeman describes the uniqueness of queer intimate attachments as able to challenge such "seemingly ordinary bodily tempos and routines."[45] During time off work in the dorms, away from the factory, dorm sex bespeaks a *migrant erotics,* intimacies that highlight the curious temporal and spatial dimensions of queer migrant lifeworlds whose physical and affective movements do not depend on straightness nor state and market validation.

Migrant erotics also manifests in queer liaisons that appear to only take place while working abroad. As we revisit *Lesbian Factory* through *Rainbow Popcorn,* for some protagonists, returning to the Philippines is also a return to identifying as straight cisgender women at home. There is a specific acronym for liaisons between what might be conceived as temporary migrant lesbianism—OFT, "only for Taiwan"—as Amie Parry has also noted.[46] Though one might presume these intimate relationships to be a temporary experiment of labor migration that end once our subjects return to the Philippines, *Lesbian Factory* and *Rainbow Popcorn* offer a more complex picture that shows how the protagonists inhabit multiple and conflicting identities and social relationships, doing away with the notion that homecoming equals returning to normal.

Rainbow Popcorn

Rainbow Popcorn features the majority of *Lesbian Factory*'s original migrant cast members, and continues to track their unpredictable itineraries and experiences after they have left Taiwan. While finishing the film in just two years (*Lesbian Factory* took five), filmmakers Susan and Jingru followed their colleagues to the Philippines, and on to new international workplaces like the United Arab Emirates. The documentary showcases the drama of living and being in inside spaces. Its title derives from the English translation of *caihong bale* (彩虹芭樂), or "rainbow guava"—a term bound to stoke viewer interest. In the Philippines, "guava" popularly connotes the satisfaction of guilty pleasures and of sensational, thrilling narratives. *Rainbow*

Popcorn's focus on domestic spaces is pragmatic: Wu explained to me that opportunities to film the protagonists while they worked were scarce, and foiled shooting permissions, visa rejections, and financial restrictions also made it difficult for the filmmakers to gather their intended labor-related material for the screen. *Rainbow Popcorn* thus evolved toward more intimate dialogue, frequently featuring conversations between friends and colleagues inside homes and hotel rooms. The film cites its predecessor *Lesbian Factory* in its scenes in ways that comment on the reflexivity of its own documentary form. *Lesbian Factory* footage in *Rainbow Popcorn* often appears in black and white, with serial shots of *Rainbow Popcorn*'s protagonists watching themselves on a small screen viewing *Lesbian Factory*. Intended to create continuity between the two documentaries, these directorial choices also serve to heighten viewer awareness with respect to the cast's labor struggles and emotional worlds.

Bing objects to the concept of OFT and the idea that migrant women's same-sex relationships are just about being away from home. She maintains that environmental factors might play a role for some, yet "for me, it's in my reality already," "it's in your body already." For Bing, queer desire is not about choice, but committing to it is. She rejects a narrative of lark lesbianism that would tend to reduce Filipinas' migrant intimacies to circumstantial need and suggests the "issue" will be resolved once back home. Ellen challenges conventional norms of gender in a different way, by way of his male identification. Jingru inquires about Ellen's experience as a transgender man in the care industry in the Middle East. Wu asks, "When you applied to Bahrain as a nurse or caregiver, did the agency or the broker, or anyone else, ask why you look like this?" A shot of the bountiful dinner table that has been prepared by Ellen for his special guests reminds us of the deep friendship between filmmakers and their subjects, inviting viewers into the conversation and its intimate setting. Ellen responds that no one has ever bothered him, not even his employer, who knew Ellen only from agency files that manipulated his profile picture to look more feminine. Ellen's speech is humorous and playful as he describes how he hardly recognized himself with long black hair that had been photoshopped without his consent. He calls it "ugly," making him look neckless and fat. "I lost my neck there," he laughs and grips his neck. Ellen then recalls being once questioned by a Filipina agent about his gender identity. "She asked me. . . . Yeah, I am," is how

118 | MIGRANT EROTICS

he quickly rehearses the moment. Wu follows up, "What did she ask you?" to which Ellen replies, "Are you a she or a he?" Without using the terms "man" or "male," he then reenacts the full conversation, from his initial evasive "Whatever," to committing "I'm a *he*," to explaining that he knows he is a he "because I love *she*."

Viewers of *Rainbow Popcorn* follow the protagonists to a funeral in a somber church. "This is Alice's funeral. She was thirty-two years old," narrates *Rainbow Popcorn*. Survived by her partner, her family, and her friends, Alice (whom viewers may remember from *Lesbian Factory*), has passed away from chronic health issues. The documentary follows Susan and Jingru as they visit the Philippines for Alice's memorial. We further learn that two other protagonists from *Lesbian Factory*, Bonjong and Jenet, for undisclosed reasons have also passed. Given the absence of institutional care and protection in the OFW economy, it is not surprising that OFWs chronically suffer from deteriorating health. (Suicide rates are also alarmingly high, the film conveys. Prompted by their visit to the United Arab Emirates in 2010, the filmmakers reference the example of Dubai in *Rainbow Popcorn*: here 80 percent of the population are foreign workers, with an annual suicide rate of over 100.) Watching Susan and Jingru reunite with their migrant colleagues, we learn more about the toll labor migration takes on the protagonists' lives after returning home. Ellen, who viewers may recognize as the delightfully pudgy character from *Lesbian Factory* and who now identifies as male, appears emaciated and aged. He is missing several teeth, and we learn that he has suffered a stroke. Ellen is still deeply melancholic about having broken up with Elsa—who is now married to a cisgender man and is also a mother. In *Rainbow Popcorn*, none of the initially filmed couples of *Lesbian Factory* is still together, though all ex-lovers explicitly affirm their ongoing care and even longing for one another. Elsa tears up in front of the camera whenever Ellen comes up. She shares that while she had to consider the future and opt for security, she remains deeply heartbroken over their separation. No one will ever know her as deeply as her ex, she confesses with tears, not even her husband. And as Ellen watches *Lesbian Factory* and its scene that features Elsa's confession of love for him, he cannot hide his pain. Asked by Wu to share how he feels, Ellen grieves over the loss of past joy, but concedes, "It's okay. You can no longer turn what is done." Where documentary reflexivity is often used as a distancing device that brings to attention filmic

Figure 21. Old lovers and comrades gather in the filmmakers' hotel room; screenshot from *Rainbow Popcorn*.

form, that is, the way it narrates and represents, *Rainbow Popcorn*'s reflexive qualities are more about revisiting the joys of past queerness, highlighting the protagonists' unwavering attachment even after incisive changes.[47]

Lan and Pilar—the latter described in *Lesbian Factory* as the "fat one" who is also the "most flirtatious" of the group—have broken up. After working in Kuwait together, Pilar decided to return to the Philippines to raise her child. She chuckles that she's not sure who the father is. Lan is based in Kuwait, where she is in a relationship with another Filipina woman who used to work in Taiwan. Nonetheless, Lan and Pilar continue to regularly chat online, to check in with each other, and, both as flirtatious as ever, to assert their mutual love—emphatically, and with heart emojis. Pilar tells Jingru on screen that Lan is the person whom she really wants to be with. Finally, Yam and Bing have also decided to go their separate ways. After the power couple of Taiwan's migrant labor movement realized their traditional families would never accept their relationship, Yam married an old friend and had a baby. Yam's appearance has noticeably changed. Her tomboy look from *Lesbian Factory* has now softened with her maternal appearance and long, feminine haircut. Like most of the now-separated couples, Yam and Bing are still friends, and their attachment brings us back to migrant erotics as queer intimate forms of life making that transpire outside institutional legibility and validity, "tempos and routines."[48] The lingering bonds of queer love and desire in *Rainbow Popcorn* have lasted years beyond the filming of *Lesbian Factory*, revealing lateral kinships and queer desires that stubbornly persist alongside hegemonic orders and social imaginaries. Migrant erotics are detached neither from nationalist and patriarchal identity scripts and the social forms that uphold them, nor from heterosexual marriage and the traditional family (additionally protected by the absence of divorce laws in Catholic-dominated Philippines).[49] But *Rainbow Popcorn* suggests, however, a blurring between friendship, romantic love, and erotic desire that challenges the norms of Filipina womanhood, the nuclear family, and the patriarchal ideal of national Filipino futurity. Here supposedly natural caretakers frustrate the expectation that they serve "privileged forms of sociality" like "human media."[50] *Rainbow Popcorn* extends *Lesbian Factory*'s sentimental activist endeavor of affording visibility, pleasure, and visible pleasure to depreciated migrant bodies. The protagonists appear as sentimental subjects that hold on to and insist on forms of sociality that may not be meant to last, and in so doing also rework the collective order that romantic love and its prevailing narrative of reproductive nationalism uphold.

Separations and Reunions

"The morning of separation," a caption reads. We are back in *Lesbian Factory* and witness the protagonists moving out of the dormitory and gathering in a different building to learn about their new jobs. "If you can't be in the same factory . . . ," the filmmaker anticipates, voicing what occupies everyone's mind in the room. Yam immediately responds, "Miserable. I don't want to answer that question. . . . Look at our eyes, we cannot sleep tonight." With puffy eyes she and her partner Bing try to smile and act playful before the camera. However, when Bing stops to say, "I feel bad. I don't like that we separate," Yam breaks out in tears. Chen refuses to turn off the camera and continues to capture the gravity of feelings as the group assembles in a large hall where the lottery's job placements will be announced. "Each migrant worker has an assigned number," explains a voice-over. "Agents choose workers by picking numbers from the booklet. Migrant workers have no rights to express their wishes and do not know where they will go." Only two out of the film's seven couples end up at the same company, and their expression of gratitude—as Ellen says, "God is so good to us. This is our destiny"—is in stark contrast to the grief of other tearful faces. "Good friends and gay partners were heartlessly separated," the voice-over summarizes. "Those who were chosen by the same factory were like hitting the jackpot." Chen pans the camera across the lottery "losers," despite their apparent discomfort about being filmed at this very moment. Only as Yam hides behind a seat and waves Chen's camera away, does she stop filming. By exposing migrant workers' intimate life for political mobilization—sometimes with positive feelings as in their sharing of love-making secrets, sometimes with felt brutality as in the exhibition of their pain—*Lesbian Factory* prompts a reconsideration of video activism through the lens of documentary ethics. Upon whose affective labor and visual availability does the potential of social justice rely? When do attachment and visibility—as acts of public inclusion—become a violent force?

For Paula Rabinowitz, "shedding tears is central to the labor documentary"[51] because it mobilizes public sentiment against "political authority."[52] Pooja Rangan takes a close look at the pervasive trope of suffering in humanitarian documentaries. She argues that the rationale of rescue and emergency can quickly "turn into an alibi" for subsuming "the particular, embodied facts of difference" into a norm of universal humanness.[53] Recent writings in feminist and queer cultural studies from Taiwan echo Rangan's claim. Authors such as Josephine Ho, Jen-peng Liu, Naifei Ding, Hans Tao-Ming Huang, and Petrus Liu offer a powerful critique of sentimental discourse in seemingly progressive movements. These authors show how Taiwan's state feminism has traditionally relied on a rhetoric of female victimhood to further marginalize populations like local sex workers and low-income foreign workers.[54] Sentimentality here equals social exclusion, moral discipline, and state surveillance. *Lesbian Factory* approaches sentimentality not as the deadening of social life but as a means to attend to and extend minoritarian world-making practices. For one, since the workers' payment depends on institutional support, their visualized suffering can sway more conservative audiences and pressure a neoliberal government into a consideration of human

122 | MIGRANT EROTICS

rights. By keeping its protagonists relatable, *Lesbian Factory* asserts OFWs' equal standing with local citizens while also insisting on a more just and livable present for those outside the paradigms of normal citizenship. TIWA's documentary work consistently mobilizes around forms of what we may describe as not necessarily reproductive transnational belonging. Repeated scenes of socializing among migrant workers and TIWA staff further amplify this claim. Back at the workers' dormitories, we witness a close-knit, queer diasporic community eating, drinking, and singing together.

One night, the protagonists approach Chen to hand over a secretly prepared gift. The director lets go of the camera to accept a collective donation to the NGO. Chen is visibly moved in the frame. With everyone squeezed together on bunk beds, the intimate gathering undeniably blurs the roles of filmmakers and filmed, again suggesting ways of being with each other beyond patriarchal and liberal citizen-state renderings. A similar scene takes place in *Rainbow Popcorn,* showing a dozen cast members snuggled on the filmmakers' hotel beds. It is the filmmakers' last night in the Philippines and, as the voice-over summarizes, "the old comrades who'd fought together" have gathered to bid farewell. The cozy atmosphere of the reunion quickly gives way to "romantic gossip." Old friends and lovers take rounds asking each other questions and sharing personal stories of heartbreak and love. What happens if your partner wants to have a baby? What's the difference between being ditched for a man or a woman? Except for Elsa's husband Oscar, who remains for the most part quiet (and looks clearly intimidated), the group is entirely queer. Alice figures prominently in the scene, her future death (with which the documentary opens) still unthinkable. This is her coming out night, where she introduces everyone to her girlfriend, Mildred. The questions do not end. Where did they meet? Why did Alice hide her sexuality all these years? Isn't she proud of her girlfriend? Alice calmly responds to query after query, making clear that she did not feel the need "to explain to everybody." For some, Alice's lesbianism has always been obvious. "You know, if you're the same, you will smell it," one of her friends shares. Her remark prompts someone in the back to call out, "We don't take a shower?" to which everyone laughs. Further comments ensue, and the camera goes back and forth between Alice (Mildred sitting in her lap) and the different inquisitors. In between these shots, we glimpse earlier pictures of Alice in Taiwan, which turns the sequence into a tender commemoration of a beloved member of the queer Filipina-Taiwanese community. TIWA's affective documentary work emerges here as an archive and product of queer collective caretaking that bridges the two archipelagoes of the Philippines and Taiwan; the activist instrument of the camera exposes vulnerable subjects to the public's gaze.

After the protagonists' assignments to different companies across the main island of Taiwan, several of the new working places turn out to be scams. In other cases, our protagonists are sent to the heavy industry sector where they are given the most demanding and dangerous jobs. They are miserable. Alternating shots of a metal factory and the workers' account of the heavy physical labor they were asked to perform relay clear exploitation. Just when there seems to be no hope for betterment, however, the collaborative effort of TIWA, Yam, Bing, Lan, and others finally pays off. The Council of Labor Affairs adjusts its foreign labor regulations. From now on, blue-collar migrant workers have a say in their assignment process and can change workplaces without leaving the country (each time spending large amounts of money on brokers and placement agencies, travel, and readmittance). In addition, hiring companies are preexamined for fraud. Migrant workers have rewritten labor history. *Lesbian Factory* concludes with a teaser of *Rainbow Popcorn*'s future queer drama, reminding us of the unfinished work of social justice. Ultimately, by conjuring queer migrant spaces of pleasure, erotics, and care, TIWA's videos affectively alter and deterritorialize hard geopolitical boundaries and majoritarian perceptions of place.

5

Me llamo Peng

Self-Care with a Camcorder

> There were only Chinese people in the kitchen, and I was having quite a good time with them. . . . As we talked about our interest in their culture, one of them—Peng—told me he had made "a film of his life." The next week he brought me eight DVDs. I entered into Peng's life, and he entered into mine.
>
> —Jahel Guerra Roa, codirector of *Me llamo Peng,* "Journal du Réel #2" (my translation)

Me llamo Peng (My name is Peng, 2010, 29 min.) is a self-recorded documentary by the Chinese migrant worker protagonist Peng Ruan. In 2002, Peng traveled from Weihai, Shandong province, to Western Europe, where he embarked on a journey to the various sites of his temporary contract employment between France and Spain. Like Miko Revereza's camera in chapter 3, Peng's camcorder goes wherever Peng goes. This chapter discusses the virtual dialogue between *Me llamo Peng* and its directors Jahel Guerra Roa and Victoria Molina de Carranza, who are respectively from Venezuela and Spain.[1] They feature Peng's creative impulses as guided by his contagiously aspirational attitude and hopes to succeed, which take us along with him from job to job and affectively help us to bear with his hard times. And yet, one cannot help but wonder how this Asian Century narrative of self-making continues to feed Peng's precarious and low-paid labor into a regime that only amplifies his need for solvency and his need to continue moving between temporary jobs. How are we to reckon with this dialog?

The camcorder is Peng's closest companion. It accompanies him

| 125

126 | ME LLAMO PENG

to and after work, and during his time off, thus enabling him to share his hard-earned and happy moments—his excitement about having purchased a new pair of leather shoes, for example, or about his nature hike on one of his days off. We enjoy watching him eat a steaming bowl of fresh noodles, listening to him muse over the meaning of life, and swearing in frustration about the endless demands of his job (for instance, when he has to cook just one more unexpected banquet dish, after midnight on a New Year's Eve). The camcorder inspires him to explore scenes beyond work and to have fun within his cramped quarters, as we can see when Peng masquerades around in his boss's traditional Chinese garb, but only after everyone has left the restaurant. With the camcorder Peng creatively captures his joys and discomforts, his "different ways of being able to move," and his desire "to solve problems, have ideas, be joyful about the present, [and] make things."[2]

Me llamo Peng is the result of Guerra and Molina de Carranza's careful distillation of sixty hours of footage that Peng shot over the course of six years, on a secondhand analog camcorder that he purchased in France. As he recorded his working travels, he mailed most of his tapes back home to China as his way of staying in touch with family back home. His filmic letters[3] are a reminder of Sasha Costanza-Chock's observation that migrant workers are often "early adopters" of various media technologies.[4] Roughly divided into four parts respectively dedicated to the different worksites along his itinerary, the film jumps back and forth between nonconsecutive years and offers an impression of the long duration of Peng's travels, rather than a chronologically linear journey. "The place or the order didn't matter," explain the directors, who were especially interested in "our main character's life and his close relationship with the camera."[5] Viewers will find Peng talking to his camcorder late at night, after he is able to wrap up a long shift and finally turn it on again. Exhausted, he often eats alone in his cramped quarters to tell us how he is feeling, sometimes even documenting the visual novelty of some work-related injury.

The Directors

Guerra and Molina de Carranza met as film students at the Creative Documentary Program at the Autonomous University of Barcelona.[6]

Their final thesis collaboration sought to document the everyday lives of Chinese immigrants in Spain. "The idea," Molina de Carranza told me, with respect to the lives of regular Spanish citizens and the Chinese immigrant community in Spain, "was to break this imaginary wall that keeps us apart, and . . . to give voice to different members of our Chinese community who decided to start a new life thousands of miles away from their homes."[7] When Guerra mentioned their project to a Chinese coworker (at the Japanese restaurant where she worked in Barcelona), it was Peng who promptly brought her his comprehensive recordings of his recent working life. Gifted with Peng's footage, the women had to come up with a storyline that could feature significant aspects of his awesome recordings. Without an adequate knowledge of Mandarin, the directors were additionally faced with narrating hours of Peng's video journals that had been shot "without any aim."[8] Guerra and Molina de Carranza decided to structure the short with regard to Peng's "life philosophy," which they encapsulated with the phrase (as noted in the press packet): "Where there's money, I'll go."[9] We thus follow Peng's journey from job to job—to Paris, where he works in the kitchen of a Chinese restaurant, and to three locales in Catalonia: Biscarri, where he works at a rural pig farm; Tarragona, where he works at a dry cleaning business; and Amposta, where he works as a construction worker. Despite the money-guided philosophy ascribed to Peng by Guerra and Molina de Carranza, they believe the work of their protagonist is incredibly motivated by his strong optimism and desire to explore. As a child, Peng was always watching films:

> He never missed a new release because his mom worked at the movie theater selling tickets. As the years passed, Peng began to see his monotonous surroundings "in black and white." That's why . . . he decided to search for the colors he needed. He packed his suitcase and headed for Europe to begin his own adventure. After his arrival, Peng invested in a second-hand camera that would go with him from town to town as he worked on whatever job available. He always says: "Where there's money, I'll go," but it's his desire to change his life and see what lies beyond his limits that keeps him moving forward. In most circumstances, Peng answers with, "Everything, always very good." With this positive attitude and constant collaboration, we were able to move on with *Me llamo Peng.*[10]

128 | *ME LLAMO PENG*

Peng hungers for life beyond the confines of his living quarters, as his self-recordings as featured in the documentary show his ceaseless commitment to keep moving and working as he tries his hand at new jobs. As we witness his artistic inclinations despite his difficulties at work, his perpetual lack of job security, and his tremendous isolation, we engage with Peng as a self-directed individual who overcomes the harsh realities of his arduous life of work. It is as if Peng manages to retain or even earn an individuated subjectivity against the penetration of capital into the "very souls"[11] of migrant workers. The camcorder captures his playfulness, dedication, and creativity, and is an antidote to the self-estranging labor that Peng capably performs daily, in ways that challenge stereotypes of the facelessness of Asian labor in developed economies of the Global North, and of the passivity of Chinese working bodies as the "radical opposite" to liberal Western ideas of individuality, civilization, and creative production.[12] And yet, as far as we can see in this short video that effects our praise for Peng and his flexible risk-taking and enterprising qualities, is it possible to affirm that he is living a good life? Can we affirm this without tuning out the realities of his disciplining labor and precarious valuation by a vaster neoliberal agenda of self-reliant, nonstop, on-demand productivity? Peng's precarity is also marked by his status without the close presence of friends, family, or notable community attachments, as we come to know him regarding his positionality within a regime that sustains itself at the lowest possible cost. Guerra and Molina de Carranza show how Peng's hopefulness and exploitation cruelly merge into an entanglement of precarity and drive in a paradoxical self-validation. "A relation of *cruel optimism* exists when something you desire is actually an obstacle to your flourishing," Lauren Berlant has observed. "Why is it so hard to leave those forms of life that don't work?" she asks. "Why is it that, when precariousness is spread throughout the world, people fear giving up on the institutions that have worn out their confidence in living?"[13]

Peng at Work

One of the video's first shots shows Peng working in the back of a Chinese restaurant in Paris. The video's time display shows that it is near midnight, and we see Peng wrapping up his duties in the kitchen. Now he can think about prepping his own dinner. In the following shots we learn that Peng not only works inside the restaurant, but lives there as well. He sets up his bed with a couple chairs from the dining hall, and switches on the television to catch up on news. He is so tired he can hardly sit up straight, let alone process new information. "Iraq lost the war," he mumbles to the camera. It is 2003, and Saddam Hussein has just been overthrown. Exhausted, he relays nothing more, and just shakes his head, with dark circles beneath his puffy eyes. "Before I began filming, I had so many things to say, but now. . . ." Peng shifts uncomfortably on his chair, his finger checking an alarm clock that shows the advanced hour. Frustrated and worn out, he repeats himself. "Before I began filming, I had so many things to say, but now. . . ."

We find Peng recording at an equally late hour on a different evening, smushing his fingers into the puffy edema of his legs. "There's a hole when I press down," he says, watching the impressions that his finger makes on his fluid-filled flesh. The indentations remain. Peng continues to press into his swollen legs several times, as if unable to feel his body. Long working hours have resulted in impairments of his body and mind. We observe his constant fatigue, the swelling of his legs and feet, his chronic back pain, and perhaps unsurprisingly, his nonchalance about his own self-care. Estranged from his body, Peng is more intrigued by his camcorder and the quality of his filming—did he capture all of it well enough?

At a steam-cleaning factory in Tarragona, his living quarters have been upgraded to that of a cramped dormitory. Sitting on his dorm mattress one evening, Peng reports that he has been fired—again. "It's the third time" he's been dismissed from his job in Spain, "so I'm used to it," he tells the camera. "Fuck! . . . I spent 20€ on my shoes and today some hot oil spilled all over my hand and my shoes. I don't think I can go out with them anymore. My soul hurts. I don't care about my hand. My skin will recover, but not the leather." The specter of bodily injury and of dismissal are part of Peng's ordinary life, along with the persistence of open wounds. He is not bothered at all by a blotchy red patch that has emerged on his hand. Peng appears more upset about the lost euro value of his shoes. Is it the money, or is it because he has lost a souvenir of his nonworking life? As an ethnic Chinese migrant worker, Peng belongs to the fourth largest migrant group of non-Europeans in Spain. He also belongs to the large pool of foreign workers willing to assume the most precarious of jobs that do not interest European citizens.[14] Immigrant labor is "highly segmented" in Spain, explains migration scholar Wayne A. Cornelius.[15] In each of its sectors "foreigners occupy the least skilled, most physically demanding, most dangerous, and most temporary jobs, with no promotion ladder, even though many of the new immigrants employed in such jobs are reasonably well educated and skilled workers." While the flexibility of low-paid migrant workers like Peng systematically makes them great candidates for short-term jobs, Spanish immigration law complicates their access to legal long-term residency, work permits, and healthcare. Migrant workers are often left to work informally under the table, or with "formal-sector firms" with no benefits or social security.[16] The 2008 Eurozone crisis, the European Union's "most serious economic and political crisis," further restricted Spanish immigration by limiting the entry of non-EU "low- and middle-skilled immigrants."[17]

Lisa Marie Cacho observes that the structural exploitation of immigrant and other minorities by nation-states and private corporations is undergirded by legal systems that render specific populations "legally illegible" with respect to recognition and thus protection by the law.[18] "To be ineligible for personhood is a form of social death," she writes. Disability scholar Helen Meekosha also calls attention to the ways in which capital's colonial geographies normalize the impairment of workers from the Global South and render them as surplus. "The processes of colonisation, colonialism, and neo-colonial power," she notes, "have resulted in vast numbers of impaired people in the global South. Much of this relates to the global economy; it concerns control to resources."[19] While *Me llamo Peng* is about an exemplary individual, the documentary shows how Peng is one of many surplus workers whose disposability and injurability enable the freer circulation of capital. An individual sense of self-continuity and sovereignty here appears oddly commensurate with a system's need for constant crisis and perhaps even chronic illness to keep its workers replaceable, pliable, and with little demand.[20] The less a worker legally belongs to national ground, the more exploitable that worker's labor. The video shows Peng's uneven investments—in his body, his leather shoes, his (unheeded) feelings of pain—within a form of governance that hierarchizes values of life. These investments are cruel, not only because they hurt or affectively feel painful, but because they numb a feeling of the present and spur a subject further into a relentless rhythm of work and migration. Deeply personal, Peng's self-recording is also reminiscent of Revereza's distancing aesthetic. It "zooms out" to open up our purview beyond the confines of biographical or ethnographic realist depiction of Peng and instead highlights the structures that demand his appearance and disappearance in anticipable ways, that is, in ways that are commensurate with hegemonic value economies.

Mr. Wu

After working at a pig farm in Tarragona, Peng moves on to Amposta to join a construction crew. On Christmas Eve of 2004, he returns to his sleeping quarters from another long shift. It is past midnight when he switches on the camcorder. He sounds upbeat:

> Today it's Christmas. "Merry Christmas." It's been a day. . . . I've been so busy. I'm almost done. This finger will recover soon. Look! Let's do a zoom! Does it look good? Mr. Wu used to live here. Some people called him Chenjian. Other people called him Sir Wu. It's been a week or so since he died. He had something wrong with his liver. I don't know what exactly. No one wants to live in this room. People think there's something wrong with it. But there's nothing wrong. I don't think it's contagious. I'll live here a couple of days and then I might go to Tortosa. I'll work anywhere people need me.

Peng wants to share another injury. "Look! Let's do a zoom. Does it look good?" he asks excitedly, holding out his finger to focus on its broken nail, and the dark remainder of a bruise. "I'm almost done," he smiles broadly. Using his bruised finger as a fun prop, Peng appears to be in a good mood, but abruptly begins to "remember" Mr. Wu, a migrant worker he has never met. The former tenant of Peng's current residence, Wu had been suffering from "something wrong with his liver. I don't know what exactly" (the Mandarin word Peng uses denotes hepatitis). "No one wants to live in this room. People think there's something wrong with it."

For the first time we notice that Peng is alone, in his own bedroom. It is vacant due to Wu's untimely death (and others' fear of inhabiting a space of unresolved illness). Peng's excitement fades as he nervously frowns. The occasional strange and brief smile enhances

Figure 22. Peng ponders Mr. Wu's death; screenshot from *Me llamo Peng*.

our sense of restlessness. Peng assures himself that everything will be OK, and that the show must go on.[21] Determined to "work anywhere people need me," moving on requires that Peng ignore the specter of death, even if doing so proves uncomfortable and difficult. We get no more detail about Wu or his passing.

Things That Matter: Recording Subjectivity

For Guerra and Molina de Carranza, selecting what to include in the film

> was a technological challenge that meant spending endless hours in a campsite we made without tents or a bonfire, but with magnetos, wires, and computers. We had to transfer Peng's VHS-C videotapes into another digital format that we could work with. After long days transferring footage in real time (taking notes on everything), we had a complete overview of what our main character had shot. At the same time, we analyzed and classified the footage, trying to overcome the language barrier.... After the translation

works came chaos: What did we want to show? . . . Choosing scenes, editing, and finding a suitable rhythm were our main challenges.[22]

The directors' endeavor to give Peng the visibility he deserves required a "suitable" narrative worth public attention, and a character who "made sense."[23] The protagonist's "positive" and creative subjectivity—brought into form by the directors' reassembling of Peng's footage—offers a recognizable narrative of the self-owning, rights-bearing individual. In this view, the protagonist's filmic investment in the idea and expression of his persona—manifest in a total of sixty hours of recording—is hardly surprising. As the directors shared with me, they asked Peng for feedback on the film before making it available to the public. The film is collaborative not only because it involves shared video production work but also because it reveals the visual and affective labor of all three filmmakers in creating a valued subjecthood. "He was very proud and moved to see the film, he also came to the release day and party and really appreciated it."[24] For the directors, *Me llamo Peng* "shows first-hand what an integration process in Europe looks like for Chinese people," a story that takes on special value during the 2008 Eurozone crisis, a time of increased anti-immigrant sentiment and looming anxieties with regard to Europe's borders.[25] The documentary short was picked up and produced by public television and broadcast on Televisió de Catalunya, Catalonia's Barcelona-based public television network. However, like TIWA's activist documentary discussed in chapter 4, Peng's video-recorded everyday performance exceeds institutional demands for readily accessible images of migrant precarity.

The Camcorder That Cares

In a following scene, Peng holds his hand close to the camera. On it protrudes a huge, ugly blister. "Not bad, isn't it," Peng comments, in a tone with both pride and irony. The filmmaker then begins to growl dramatically, enhancing our curiosity. The next shot is of him at a table with a pair of sharp scissors in his nonblistered hand. Adjusting the position of the blister, he checks on the camcorder once again before proceeding. We are unable to see Peng pop the blister. Instead, we watch the protagonist dry his abruptly deflated wound

Figure 23. Peng meticulously positions his hand in front of the camera to stage the blister scene; screenshot from *Me llamo Peng*.

with a tissue, before he turns toward the camera to wipe the lens clean of all fluid splatter. As usual, Peng reveals no sign of physical discomfort; he is a satisfied amateur filmmaker who has successfully staged a great act. Using his body as main character and his immediate surroundings as set, Peng creates a filmic scene, and ends it with a literal screen wipe.

Always at his side, it is the camcorder that cares for Peng and helps maintain him in ways that counter demands for his disposability. Self-care, as Sara Ahmed writes, is about creative survival. "When you are not supposed to live, as you are, where you are, with whom you are with, then survival is a radical action; a refusal not to exist until the very end; a refusal not to exist until you do not exist.... We can be inventive, we have to be inventive, Audre Lorde suggests, to survive."[26] Peng's filmic persona resists "romantic anticapitalist" notions of authenticity and agency as devoid of the powers of capital and labor.[27] The video simultaneously documents *and* participates in the messy interweaving of oppositional forces and seemingly irreconcilable desires that undergird the governance of minoritized life today. This governance engages forms of power that are enabling and that encourage collaboration but cannot be detached from the cruel optimism that perpetually transcribes a chronically injured body into the "healthy" matter of recognized subjecthood. In this sense, *Me llamo Peng* reflects a site of busy transaction between dominant value regimes and a subject's self-investment in ways that speak to the book's larger argument about Asians on Demand. On the one hand, the protagonist's visibility is deeply tied to racial, national, and economic hierarchies as well as to the norm of personhood, a socially recognizable and state-sanctioned form of being that defines the human value of a life. At the same time, Peng's own affective attachments to liberal personhood speak of his creative impulse that also sabotages his ready availability as a romanticized figure of human sovereignty.

Acknowledgments

I feel very lucky to have encountered many inspiring, kind, support-ive, and grounding people during my time researching and writing this book. *Asians on Demand* is not only a product of long hours of working alone at the desk. It is also a testimony of the time, care, and labor that my friends, colleagues, and family have generously offered me. The following record is necessarily incomplete.

My special thanks go to Arnika Fuhrmann, Grace Kyungwon Hong, Angela Xiao Wu, Heijin Lee, Pacharee Sudhinaraset, Michelle Cho, Vivian Huang, Melissa Phruksachart, Debbie Cho, Fiona Ng, Jeannie Simms, Michelle Har Kim, Erin Huang, Phi Hong Su, Chris-tiane Heidi Fränzel, Trung Hoang Le, and my Duisburg-Düsseldorf kin for their support and cheer (not only) during the last stretch of writing. I heart you all.

A big thank you to the artists and activists who inspired the mak-ing of this book, especially to Jingru Wu, Kristina Wong, Ming Wong, and Miko Revereza, who were willing to meet me in person, often repeatedly. Jahel Guerra and Victoria Molina de Carranza patiently answered my questions via email.

This book started as a dissertation at the University of Southern California, and was completed under the guidance of Akira Lippit, Anikó Imre, Kara Keeling, and Grace Kyungwon Hong. I secretly be-lieve that Akira knows how to wield magic to make the world stay calm. Anikó, Kara, and Grace gave me an intellectual home as a gradu-ate student. I am grateful for Anikó's heartfelt support and for Grace's unfailing and deeply caring mentorship even long after graduation from USC. My research has greatly benefitted from the wisdoms of Tara McPherson and Natania Meeker, from a fellowship with Viet Nguyen and Janet Hoskins's Center for Transpacific Studies, and from Rhacel Parreñas's terrific Intimate Economies seminar at USC's Center for Feminist Research. Thank you Rhacel for your continuous

138 | ACKNOWLEDGMENTS

support. Laura Isabel Serna expertly led our cross-disciplinary visual studies dissertation writing group. Thanks to the group members for valuable feedback.

My move to Los Angeles from Berlin came with unexpected culture shock, and suddenly everyone around me was wearing flip flops. Friends and co-conspirators created a nurturing environment that nearly convinced me to believe in the American Dream. I am grateful for the friendships of Crystal Mun-Hye Baik and Jih-Fei Cheng, who helped me understand the value of sharing work with each other. I fondly remember my conversations with Anne McKnight, Genevieve Yue, Alexander Chase, Ana Paulina Lee, Lindsay Rebecca Nelson-Santos, Shaoling Ma, Fiorella Cotrina, Mayumo Inoue, Patty Ahn, Viola Lasmana, Umayyah Cable, Nadine Chan, Mila Zuo, Ameeth Vijay, Karen Tongson, Jasmine Nadua Trice, Kristy Kang, Diego Semerene, Nic John Ramos, Lara Bradshaw, Alison Kozberg, Brett Service, Evan Vincent Nicoll Johnson, Brian Jacobson, Eric Hoyt, Sebnem Baran, Tim Holland, JeCheol Park, Mike Dillon, and Debjani Dutta, among many others. Jia Tan holds a special place in my heart.

Los Angeles connected me to the fabulous Eric Cho, Brian Hu, Ada Tseng, and the Los Angeles Asian Pacific Film Festival, where I had the pleasure to work as a programmer alongside Joel Quizon, Anderson Le, Abraham Ferrer, and Shinae Yoon. Fred Harig, Kelly Kawar, and Inkoo Kang—what a joy to have you in my life. A shout-out to everyone who offered me a ride when my car broke down before deciding to get stolen. All of you made L.A. more of a home.

The seeds of this book were planted during my undergraduate and graduate years at the Freie Universität Berlin, where I had the privilege to study with Alexandra Schneider, Robin Curtis, Marc Siegel, and alongside Stephan Schoenholtz and Zhan'ao Yang; but also in Beijing, where I learned so much about activist, art, and documentary filmmaking from Chen Tao and Tan Tan, and from the generous spirits of Cui Zi'en, Zhang Xianmin, and Zhu Rikun. Sun-ju Choi and Kimiko Suda invited me to join the programming team of what would become the Asian Film Festival Berlin, and they continue to inspire. It has been a pleasure to work with Jee-Un Kim and Anna Xian. Arnika Fuhrmann's friendship is the gift that keeps on giving.

I have met great colleagues and friends at the Massachusetts Institute of Technology. I am grateful for the MIT Mellon Postdoctoral Fellowship in the Humanities, and the resources provided to me during my stay there. Thank you Catherine Clark, Paloma Duong, Amah Edoh, Bruno Perreau, Ian Condry, Vivek Bald, Sasha Costanza-Chock, Paul Roquet, Heather Lee, Elizabeth Marcus, and Emma Tseng. I am fortunate to have met and spent time with Jing Wang. My heartfelt appreciation to Yu-Fang Cho, Bliss Lim, and Lisa Parks for offering me invaluable feedback at our MIT manuscript workshop. Thanks to Wendy Hui Kyong Chun, Kara Keeling, Michelle Cho, and Lilly Nguyen with whom I shared joy and discussions at the Racial Regimes and Digital Economies symposium. Thanks also to Jenn Fang for deconstructing the model minority myth for us in the classroom. Thank you, Lisa Lowe, for your kindness. Meeting Mary Kuhn was indeed a stroke of luck. I thank Alex Zahlten, Rina Zahlten, Tomiko Yoda, Kim Icreverzi, Momoko Shimizu, and Kimberly Sanders for intellectual and social community. Alex patiently read several portions of the manuscript in the making.

A research grant by the Taiwan Ministry of Education allowed me to spend the summer of 2016 in Taipei. Jingru Wu, Teri Silvio, Shu-ching Chuang, Eno Chen, Amie Parry, Chien-ting Lin, Shi-yan Chao, Andy Wang, Ping Wang, Naifei Ding, Chun-yen Wang, Chiwei Cheng, Chia-chi Wu, and Chun-chi Wang all played a role in making my trip a great success.

At New York University, I have been blessed to work alongside many supportive souls whose advice, company, and encouragement have been invaluable: Zhen Zhang, Anna McCarthy, Bob Stam, Marina Hassapopoulou, Laura Harris, Toby Lee, Juana Suárez, Josslyn Luckett, Ed Guerrero, Dana Polan, Dan Streible, Howard Besser, Claudia Calhoun, Chris Straayer, Antonia Lant, William Simon, Allen Weiss, Manthia Diawara, Mara Mills, Paula Chakravartty, Lily Chumley, Angela Zito, Aisha Khan, Jini Kim Watson, Crystal Parikh, Thuy Linh Tu, Amita Manghnani, Radha Hegde, Tzu-hui Celina Hung, Susan Murray, Juan Piñon, Gayatri Gopinath, Amy Zhang, Yoon Jeong Oh, Thomas Looser, Naomi Clark, Robert Yang, and Nicole Starosielski. Karen Shimakawa is a one-of-a-kind mentor, colleague, and dear friend. I am also grateful for the fruitful exchanges with colleagues at the NYU Center for the Humanities under the thoughtful guidance of Ulrich Baer and Molly Rogers. A Tisch Initiative for Creative Research Conference Fund and an Innovation and Anti-Racism Micro Grant by the Office of Global Inclusion have further provided funding for research and writing. The A/P/A Studies Working Group

140 | ACKNOWLEDGMENTS

sponsored by the Asian/Pacific/American Institute at NYU offered a space for fertile discussion. Thank you to the Global Asias Summer Workshop members, Heijin Lee, Pacharee Sudhinaraset, and Hentyle Yapp, for their incisive writing feedback. The workshop was made possible with funding from the Asian Film and Media Initiative in Cinema Studies at NYU. Heijin and Pach have offered a wonderful mix of friendship and intellectual companionship over the years. I would not have made it here without Angela Xiao Wu's friendship and comradeship. Kenneth Sweeney, Liza Greenfield, Melanie Daly-Castilla, and Cristina Cajulis have expertly helped me navigate the administrative labyrinth. Working with the students at NYU has been one of the most rewarding parts of my job. E. K. Tan, Alexandra Juhasz, Meenasarani Linde Murugan, Ying Qian, Neferti Tadiar, Nurhaizatul Jamil, Wendy Muñiz, Brandy Monk-Payton, and Tina Wu have offered intellectual community beyond NYU.

I am so grateful for the generosity of the people who read portions of the manuscript and inspired me in other ways: Bhaskar Sarkar, Joshua Neves, Mila Zuo, Tess Takahashi, Tomiko Yoda, Weixian Pan, Franz Prichard, Sabine Haenni, Homay King, Marc Steinberg, Ma Ran, Jenny Chio, Christopher Patterson, Lily Wong, Danielle Wong, Isabela Seong Leong Quintana, Cheryl Naruse, Dredge Byung'chu Kang, Brian Bernards, Calvin Hui, Thy Phu, Kien Nghi Ha, Anja Sunhyun Michaelsen, Noa Ha, Rosalia Engchuan, Eng-Beng Lim, Thomas Lamarre, Christine Bacareza Balance, Clara Iwasaki, Nishant Shah, Yuri Furuhata, Kandice Chuh, Betsy Huang, Hwa-Jen Tsai, Hye Jean Chung, Jasper Verlinden, Alvin Wong, Franco Lai, Lucetta Kam, Tina Chen, Chang Tan, Lana Lin, Alexandra Chang, Bakirathi Mani, Brian Larkin, Jane Gaines, Heather Love, Claudia Breger, Nanna Heidenreich, Brigitte Kuster, Leslie A. Adelson, Juan Llamas-Rodriguez, Ipek Celik, Victor Fan, Fan Popo, Mirae Rhee, Ishita Tiwary, Genevieve Clutario, Hae Yeon Choo, Carlos Jimenez, Shannon Mattern, Chaitanya Lakkimsetti, Hongwei Bao, Jin Haritaworn, Jan Padios, Ronak Kapadia, Angelica Fenner, Eli Haschemi, Sylvia Schedelbauer, Aykan Safoğlu, Kris Mizutani, Sarah Mai Dang, and Mita Banerjee. My unbounded thanks to Steven Chung and Hoang Tan Nguyen for their insightful, kind, and highly constructive manuscript comments.

I feel lucky to have found a brilliant interlocutor in Michelle Har Kim.

It has been a pleasure to work with Leah Pennywark at the University of Minnesota Press and the rest of the team that includes Anne Carter, Rachel Moeller, Wendy Holdman, and Shelby Connelly. Thank you for taking great care with this project.

Asians on Demand is written in loving memory of Franziska Ottilie Heberer, Wang Wenxuan, Liu Feng, and Wang Xiaobing. I am glad for the time I get to spend with Wang Xiaoling. This book is dedicated to Thomas Heberer, Jing Wang, and Linlin Heberer with all my love.

Notes

Introduction

My special thanks to Steven Chung, Grace Kyungwon Hong, and Hoang Tan Nguyen for instrumental feedback on the introduction.

1. Hito Steyerl. *Strike II*. HDV, 2012. https://www.youtube.com/watch?v=m1tA6eOgRt4.

2. Catherine A. Steinmann, "Visceral Exposure: Melanie Gilligan, Hito Steyerl, and the Biopolitics of Visibility," (PhD diss., University of British Columbia, 2015), 23.

3. "Refusal to represent" is the written description for the uploaded video *Strike II.*

4. Eve Oishi, "Bad Asians: New Film and Video by Queer Asian American Artists," *Countervisions: Asian American Film Criticism,* ed. Darrell Y. Hamamoto and Sandra Lui (Philadelphia: Temple University Press, 2000), 221.

5. Grace Kyungwon Hong, "Speculative Surplus: Asian American Racialization and the Neoliberal Shift," *Social Text* 36, no. 2 (2018): 107–22.

6. Colleen Lye, *America's Asia: Racial Form and American Literature, 1893–1945* (Princeton, N.J.: Princeton University Press, 2005), 7. See also Aihwa Ong, *Neoliberalism as Exception: Mutations in Citizenship and. Sovereignty* (Durham, N.C.: Duke University Press, 2006); and Helen Heran Jun, *Race for Citizenship: Black Orientalism and Asian Uplift from Pre-Emancipation to Neoliberal America* (New York: New York University Press, 2011).

7. *Online Etymology Dictionary, s.v.* "exemplar," accessed June 22, 2021, https://www.etymonline.com/word/exemplar; and *Online Etymology Dictionary, s.v.* "example," accessed June 22, 2021, https://www.etymonline.com/word/example.

8. Homay King, *Lost in Translation: Orientalism, Cinema, and the Enigmatic Signifier* (Durham, N.C.: Duke University Press, 2010), 2. See also Lisa Nakamura, *Digitizing Race: Visual Cultures of the Internet* (Minneapolis: University of Minnesota Press, 2008); Danielle Wong, "Dismembered Asian/American Body Parts in *Ex Machina* as 'Inorganic' Critique," *Transformations* 29 (2017): 34–51; Anne Anlin Cheng, *Ornamentalism* (New York: Oxford University Press, 2021); Vivian L. Huang, *Surface Relations: Queer Forms of Asian American Inscrutability*

144 | NOTES TO INTRODUCTION

(Durham, N.C.: Duke University Press, 2022). Other scholars who have taught me to think critically through Asian media images include Oishi, "Bad Asians"; Richard Fung, "Looking for My Penis: The Eroticized Asian in Gay Video Porn," in *How Do I Look? Queer Film & Video,* ed. Bad Object-choices (San Francisco: Bay Press, 1991), 145–68; Gina Marchetti, *Romance and the Yellow Peril: Race, Sex, and Discursive Strategies in Hollywood Fiction* (Berkeley: University of California Press, 1993); Celine Parreñas Shimizu, *The Hypersexuality of Race: Performing Asian/American Women on Screen and Scene* (Durham, N.C.: Duke University Press, 2007) and *Straitjacket Sexualities: Unbinding Asian American Manhoods in the Movies* (Stanford, Calif.: Stanford University Press, 2012); Glen Mimura, *Ghostlife of Third Cinema: Asian American Film and Video* (Minneapolis: University of Minnesota Press, 2009); Hoang Tan Nguyen, *A View from the Bottom: Asian American Masculinity and Sexual Representation* (Durham, N.C.: Duke University Press, 2015); Lily Wong, *Transpacific Attachments: Sex Work, Media Networks, and Affective Histories of Chineseness* (New York: Columbia University Press, 2018); Crystal Mun-hye Baik, *Reencounters: On the Korean War and Diasporic Memory Critique* (Philadelphia: Temple University Press, 2020); Mila Zuo, *Vulgar Beauty: Acting Chinese in the Global Sensorium* (Durham, N.C.: Duke University Press, 2022).

9. Wendy Hui Kyong Chun, "Introduction: Race and/as Technology; or, How to Do Things to Race," *Camera Obscura* 24, no. 1 (2009): 9.

10. Grace Kyungwon Hong, *Death beyond Disavowal: The Impossible Politics of Difference* (Minneapolis: Minnesota University Press, 2015), 17, emphasis added.

11. Kara Keeling, *The Witch's Flight: The Cinematic, the Black Femme, and the Image of Common Sense* (Durham, N.C.: Duke University Press, 2007), 11. Cf. Lynne Joyrich and Wendy Chun, eds., "Race and/as Technology," special issue, *Camera Obscura: Feminism, Culture, and Media Studies* 24, no. 1 (2009); Nakamura, *Digitizing Race*; Lisa Nakamura and Peter Chow-White, eds., *Race After the Internet* (New York: Routledge, 2013); Shaka McGlotten, "Black Data," in *No Tea, No Shade: New Writings in Black Queer Studies,* ed. E. P. Johnson (Durham, N.C.: Duke University Press, 2016), 262–86; Safiya Umoja Noble, *Algorithms of Oppression: How Search Engines Reinforce Racism* (New York: New York University Press, 2018); Ruha Benjamin, *Race After Technology: Abolitionist Tools for the New Jim Code* (Cambridge: Polity, 2019).

12. Keeling, *The Witch's Flight,* 19.

13. See also Kara Keeling, *Queer Times, Black Futures* (New York: New York University Press, 2019), 122.

14. Hollywood declared digital video its main production technology in 2013. See Stephen Follows, "When and How the Film Business Went Digital," January 9, 2017, https://stephenfollows.com/film-business-became-digital/.

15. Film and analog video both store information by way of a direct relation to the world, such as the celluloid film strip's exposure to light or the camcorder's storing of signals in their original form. Digital media code information

NOTES TO INTRODUCTION | 145

into computable sequences of 0s and 1s that are often seen as a rupture in the analogical relation between image and world and thus the representation of reality. Some helpful readings, including critical revisions of such common perceptions, include Laura U. Marks, *Touch: Sensuous Theory and Multisensory Media* (Minneapolis: University of Minnesota Press, 2002); D. N. Rodowick, *The Virtual Life of Film* (Cambridge, Mass.: Harvard University Press, 2007); and Homay King, *Virtual Memory: Time-Based Art and the Dream of Digitality* (Durham, N.C.: Duke University Press, 2015). Digital compression is also commonly known for making information storage much easier than analog media in terms of storage space, although scholars like Jancovich and Keilbach complicate this observation. See Marek Jancovic and Judith Keilbach, "Streaming against the Environment: Digital Infrastructures, Video Compression, and the Environmental Footprint of Video Streaming," in *Situating Data: Inquiries in Algorithmic Culture,* ed. Karin van Es and Nanna Verhoeff (Amsterdam: Amsterdam University Press, 2023), 85–102. On the relation between the digital image and racial representation in particular, see Kara Keeling, "Passing for Human: Bamboozled and Digital Humanism," *Women & Performance: A Journal of Feminist Theory* 15, no. 1 (2005): 237–50, and "I = Another: Digital Identity Politics," in Grace Kyungwon Hong and Roderick A. Ferguson, eds., *Strange Affinities: The Gender and Sexual Politics of Comparative Racialization* (Durham, N.C.: Duke University Press, 2011), 59; and Nakamura, *Digitizing Race.*

16. Joshua Neves and Bhaskar Sarkar, "Introduction," in *Asian Video Cultures. In the Penumbra of the Global,* eds. Joshua Neves and Bhaskar Sarkar (Durham, N.C.: Duke University Press, 2017), 6. Lucas Hilderbrand offers another capacious definition of video, "as an umbrella term for *technologies* (broadcast signals, electro-magnetic videotape, cathode-ray tubes, streaming digital data, camcorders, editing software, playback decks), *content* (programming and 'art'), and *institutions* (networks, cable providers, tape rental outlets, galleries, festivals, file-sharing communities, event videographers). Video as a medium is constituted by all these factors." Lucas Hilderbrand, *Inherent Vice: Bootleg Histories of Videotape and Copyright* (Durham, N.C.: Duke University Press, 2009), 6f. For Marita Sturken, video likewise uniquely encompasses and bridges various institutions, politics, and practices, including "art and technology, television and art, art and issues of social change, collectives and individual artists, the art establishment and anti-establishment strategies, profit and non-profit worlds, and formalism and content." Marita Sturken, "Paradox in the Evolution of an Art Form. Great Expectations and the Making of a History," in Doug Hall and Sally Jo Fifer, eds., *Illuminating Video. An Essential Guide to Video Art* (New York: Aperture, 2005), 108. See also Michael Z. Newman, *Video Revolutions. On the History of a Medium* (New York: Columbia University Press, 2014).

17. Ming-Yuen S. Ma and Erika Suderburg, "Introduction. Another Resolution: On Global Video," in *Resolutions 3: Global Networks of Video,* ed.

146 | NOTES TO INTRODUCTION

Ming-Yuen S. Ma and Erika Suderburg (Minneapolis: University of Minnesota Press, 2012), xv. On video's intermediality see also Thomas Lamarre, *The Anime Ecology: A Genealogy of Television, Animation, and Game Media* (Minneapolis: University of Minnesota Press, 2018).

18. Hilderbrand, *Inherent Vice,* 7.

19. Zhang Zhen, "Introduction: Bearing Witness: Chinese Urban Cinema in the Era of 'Transformation,'" in *The Urban Generation: Chinese Cinema and Society at the Turn of the Twenty-First Century,* ed. Zhang Zhen (Durham, N.C.: Duke University Press, 2007), 20. See also Ishita Tiwary's discussion of the introduction of analog video technology in India in the 1980s, and the ways that video formats and infrastructures both shaped and responded to the preexisting sociocultural context of the time. Ishita Tiwary, *Analog Memories: A Cultural History of Video* (New Delhi: Oxford University Press India, forthcoming).

20. Hilderbrand, *Inherent Vice,* 7f. See also Zhang Zhen and Angela Zito, eds., *DV-Made China: Digital Subjects and Social Transformations after Independent Film* (Honolulu: University of Hawai'i Press, 2015); and Lori Kido Lopez, *Asian American Media Activism: Fighting for Cultural Citizenship* (New York: New York University Press, 2016).

21. Kate Horsfield, "Busting the Tube: A Brief History of Video Art," in *Feedback: The Video Data. Bank Catalog of Video Art and Artist Interviews,* ed. Kate Horsfield and Lucas Hilderbrand (Philadelphia: Temple University Press, 2006), 8. See also Alexandra Juhasz, *AIDS TV: Identity, Community, and Alternative Video* (Durham, N.C.: Duke University Press, 1995). Sasha Costanza-Chock makes a compelling case for understanding how the everyday media uses of migrant communities have served as a precursor to contemporary practices of media activism, with respect to immigrant rights movements. Sasha Costanza-Chock, *Out of the Shadows, Into the Streets! Transmedia Organizing and the Immigrant Rights Movement* (Cambridge, Mass.: MIT Press, 2014), 101.

22. For writings on video art see Alexandra Juhasz, "Video Art on YouTube," in *Resolutions 3: Global Networks of Video,* ed. Ming-Yuen Ma and Erika Suderburg (Minneapolis: University of Minnesota Press, 2012), 310. Johannes Birringer further elaborates on video art's emergence with critical arts movements in his article, "Video Art/Performance: A Border Theory," *Performing Arts Journal* 13, no. 3 (1991): 54–84. See also Lucas Hilderbrand, "Moving Images: On Video Art Markets and Distribution," in *Resolutions 3: Global Networks of Video,* ed. Ming-Yuen Ma and Erika Suderburg (Minneapolis: University of Minnesota Press, 2012), 1–17.

23. Kathleen Collins, *From Rabbit Ears to the Rabbit Hole: A Life with Television* (Jackson: University of Mississippi Press, 2021), 185. See also Amanda D. Lotz, *The Television Will Be Revolutionized* (New York: New York University Press, 2007), and *Netflix and Streaming Video: The Business of Subscriber-Funded Video on Demand* (Cambridge: Polity, 2022); Chuck Tyron, *On-Demand Culture: Digital Delivery and the Future of Movies* (New Bruns-

wick, N.J.: Rutgers University Press, 2013); and Kevin McDonald and Daniel Smith-Rowsey, eds., *The Netflix Effect: Technology and Entertainment in the 21st Century* (New York: Bloomsbury Academic, 2016).

24. Laura Marks, Stephen Makonin, Radek Przedpełski, and Alejandro Rodriguez-Silva, "Tackling the Carbon Footprint of Streaming Media," technical report, Simon Fraser University, 2021, https://www.sfu.ca/sca/projects---activities/streaming-carbon-footprint.html. See also Cisco Annual Internet Report (2018–2023), white paper, updated March 2020, https://www.cisco.com/c/en/us/solutions/collateral/executive-perspectives/annual-internet-report/white-paper-c11-741490.html.

25. Hilderbrand, *Inherent Vice*, 10.

26. Hilderbrand, *Inherent Vice*, 10.

27. Rutvica Andrijasevic, Julie Yujie Chen, Melissa Gregg, and Marc Steinberg, "Introduction: Platform Capitalism Has a Hardware History," in *Media and Management* (Lüneburg and Minneapolis: meson press and University of Minnesota Press, 2021), xiii.

28. Rutvica Andrijasevic, Julie Yujie Chen, Melissa Gregg, and Marc Steinberg, "Coda: Closures and Openings," in *Media and Management,* 98f.

29. Andrijasevic et al., "Introduction," xiv. Given Japan's prominent role in advancing video technology and inventing VHS, it would be interesting to further pursue how the invention of JIT production might have shaped video's on-demand uses beyond platform streaming. See also Marc Steinberg, "Management's Mediations: The Case of Toyotism," in *Media and Management,* 1–30, and his article, "From Automobile Capitalism to Platform Capitalism: Toyotism as a Prehistory of Digital Platforms," *Organization Studies* 43, no. 7 (July 2021): 1069–90.

30. Niels van Doorn, "Platform Labor: On the Gendered and Racialized Exploitation of Low-Income Service Work in the 'On-Demand' Economy," *Information, Communication & Society* 20, no. 6 (2017): 899.

31. Lisa Gitelman, *Always Already New: Media, History, and the Data of Culture* (Cambridge, Mass.: MIT Press, 2008), 7.

32. Mark Williams, "Real-Time Fairy Tales: Cinema Pre-Figuring Digital Anxiety," in *New Media: Theories and Practices of Digitextuality,* ed. Anna Everett and John T. Caldwell (New York: Routledge, 2003), 162.

33. Gitelman, *Always Already New,* 138.

34. Sybille Krämer, *Medium, Messenger, Transmission: An Approach to Media Philosophy* (Amsterdam: Amsterdam University Press, 2015), 36.

35. Sarah Kember and Joanna Zylinska, *Life after New Media: Mediation as a Vital Process* (Cambridge, Mass.: MIT Press, 2012), 19. John Durham Peters describes media as "civilizational ordering devices" that establish the parameters for human relating and include the ocean, fire, the sky, making mediation an elementary dimension of human life and, indeed, of understanding humanness itself. John Durham Peters, *The Marvelous Clouds: Toward a Philosophy of Elemental Media* (Chicago: University of Chicago Press, 2015), 5. Richard

148 | NOTES TO INTRODUCTION

Grusin in "Radical Mediation," *Critical Inquiry* 42, no. 1 (2015): 124–48, maintains that "all bodies (whether human or nonhuman) are fundamentally media and life itself is a form of mediation" (132). For him, mediation encompasses "flowers, trees, rivers, lakes, and deserts; microbes, insects, fish, mammals, and birds; digestion, respiration, sensation, reproduction, circulation, and cognition; planes, trains, and automobiles; factories, schools, and malls; nation-states, NGOs, indigenous communities, or religious organizations; rising sea levels, increased atmospheric concentrations of CO_2, melting icecaps, intensified droughts, violent storms" (145). In short, "there is nothing that is not *mediation*" (135). This book engages mediation in its mutual imbrications with realities of race and Asian racialization specifically.

36. Krämer, *Medium,* 31.

37. Krämer, *Medium,* 36. Weihong Bao offers a related, albeit slightly differing, overview of concepts of mediation, namely, as transmission, intermediary, and environment. See Weihong Bao, *Fiery Cinema: The Emergence of an Affective Medium in China, 1915–1945* (Minneapolis: University of Minnesota Press, 2015), 8ff.

38. Wendy Cheng, "Strategic Orientalism: Racial Capitalism and the Problem of 'Asianness,'" *African Identities* 1, no. 2 (2013): 149, emphasis added. See also Lisa Lowe's discussion of the racialized labor category of the coolie as "an intermediary form of Asian labor, used both to define and to obscure the boundary between enslavement and freedom, and to normalize both." Lisa Lowe, *The Intimacies of Four Continents* (Durham, N.C.: Duke University Press, 2015), 25.

39. See Kuan-hsing Chen, *Asia as Method: Toward Deimperialization* (Durham, N.C.: Duke University Press, 2010); Jin-kyung Lee, *Service Economies: Militarism, Sex Work, and Migrant Labor in South Korea* (Minneapolis: University of Minnesota Press, 2010); Viet Nguyen and Janet Hoskins, "Introduction: Transpacific Studies: Critical Perspectives on an Emerging Field," in *Transpacific Studies: Framing an Emerging Field,* ed. Janet Alison Hoskins and Viet Thanh Nguyen (Honolulu: University of Hawai'i Press, 2014), 1–38; Brian Bernards, *Writing the South Seas: Imagining the Nanyang in Chinese and Southeast Asian Postcolonial Literature* (Seattle: University of Washington Press, 2015); Brook Larmer, "Is China the World's New Colonial Power?," *New York Times,* May 2, 2017, https://www.nytimes.com/2017/05/02/magazine/is-china-the-worlds-new-colonial-power.html; Kwaku Opoku Dankwah and Padmore Adusei Amoah, "Gauging the Dispositions between Indigenes, Chinese and Other Immigrant Traders in Ghana: Towards a More Inclusive Society," *Asian Ethnicity* 20, no. 1 (2019): 67–84; Wasana Wongsurawat, *The Crown and the Capitalists: The Ethnic Chinese and the Founding of the Thai Nation* (Seattle: University of Washington Press, 2019); Yoon Jung Park, "Playing the China Card or Yellow Perils? China, 'the Chinese', and Race in South African Politics and Society," *Asian Ethnicity* 21, no. 4 (2020): 464–83; Melissa Lefkowitz, "(Re)Mediating China in Kenya: Chinese Youth, Kenyan Hosts, and the Quest for Global Connection" (PhD diss., New York University, 2022).

NOTES TO INTRODUCTION | 149

40. I find Bao's description of the intermediary as what "separates two distinct entities but brings them into a relationship" on point, but add to that, that the medium renders its own process invisible. Bao, *Fiery Cinema,* 11.

41. Cheng, "Strategic Orientalism," 135. See also Claire Jean Kim, "The Racial Triangulation of Asian Americans," *Politics & Society* 27 (1999): 105–38; Vijay Prashad, *The Karma of Brown Folk* (Minneapolis: University of Minnesota Press, 2000); Nadia Kim, "Critical Thoughts on Asian American Assimilation in the Whitening Literature," in *Racism in Post-Racism America: New Theories, New Directions,* ed. Charles A. Gallagher (Chapel Hill, N.C.: Social Forces, 2008), 53–66; and Jun, *Race for Citizenship.*

42. Iyko Day, *Alien Capital: Asian Racialization and the Logic of Settler Colonial Capitalism* (Durham, N.C.: Duke University Press, 2016), 34.

43. Neferti Tadiar, "Decolonization, 'Race,' and Remaindered Life under Empire," *Qui Parle* 23, no. 2 (2015): 152.

44. See also A. Aneesh, *Virtual Migration: The Programming of Globalization* (Durham, N.C.: Duke University Press, 2006); Nitin Govil, *Orienting Hollywood: A Century of Film Culture Between Los Angeles and Bombay* (New York: New York University Press, 2015); Dal Yong Jin, *Digital Platforms, Imperialism and Political Culture* (New York: Routledge, 2015); Nicole Starosielski, *The Undersea Network* (Durham, N.C.: Duke University Press, 2015); Jack Linchuan Qiu, *Goodbye iSlave: A Manifesto for Digital Abolition* (Champaign: Illinois University Press, 2016); Jan Padios, *Nation on the Line: Call Centers as Postcolonial Predicaments in the Philippines* (Durham, N.C.: Duke University Press, 2018); Mary L. Gray and Siddharth Suri, *Ghost Work: How to Stop Silicon Valley from Building a New Global Underclass* (Boston: Houghton Mifflin Harcourt, 2019); Sarah T. Roberts, *Behind the Screen: Content Moderation in the Shadows of Social Media* (New Haven, Conn.: Yale University Press, 2019); Joshua Neves, *Underglobalization: Beijing's Media Urbanism and the Chimera of Legitimacy* (Durham, N.C.: Duke University Press, 2020); Christopher B. Patterson, *Open World Empire: Race, Erotics, and the Global Rise of Video* (New York: New York University Press, 2020).

45. Grace Kyungwon Hong, *Death beyond Disavowal,* 17.

46. Krämer, *Medium,* 215.

47. Krämer, *Medium,* 84, emphasis added.

48. Krämer, *Medium,* 36.

49. Tadiar, "Decolonization," 152.

50. Melissa Phruksachart, "The Bourgeois Cinema of Boba Liberalism," *Film Quarterly* 73, no. 3 (2020): 61.

51. This term has gained increasing popularity after 2010. See for instance, Rajat M. Nag, "The Asian Century," keynote address at the Indian Council for Research on International Economic Relations in New Delhi, India, November 15, 2010, https://www.adb.org/news/speeches/asian-century; Peter Petri and Thomas Vinod, "Development Imperatives for the Asian Century," Asian Development Bank (2013), http://hdl.handle.net/11540/2309; Aimee Bahng,

150 | NOTES TO INTRODUCTION

Migrant Futures: Decolonizing Speculation in Financial Times (Durham, N.C.: Duke University Press, 2018); Parag Khanna, *The Future Is Asian: Commerce, Conflict, and Culture in the 21st Century* (New York: Simon & Schuster, 2019); Valentina Romei and John Reed, "The Asian Century Is Set to Begin," *Financial Times*, March 25, 2019, https://www.ft.com/content/520cb6f6-2958-11e9 -a5ab-ff8ef2b976c7. On neoliberal market developments in Asia, see Vedi Hadiz, "Empire, Neo-liberalism, and Asia: An Introduction," in *Empire and Neoliberalism in Asia*, ed. Vedi Hadiz (London: Routledge, 2006), 1–20.

52. Hong, "Speculative Surplus," 111.

53. Jodi Melamed, *Represent and Destroy: Rationalizing Violence in the New Racial Capitalism* (Minneapolis: University of Minnesota Press, 2011), 1. Melamed categorizes the different phases of this modernity loosely into "racial liberalism (1940s to 1960s), liberal multiculturalism (1980s to 1990s), and neoliberal multiculturalism (2000s)." While she focuses on the specific context of the United States, she also makes a case for the global impact of the distinct ways in which racial difference is managed through U.S. capitalist forms.

54. Roderick A. Ferguson, *The Reorder of Things: The University and Its Pedagogies of Minority Difference* (Minneapolis: University of Minnesota Press, 2012), 13.

55. Melamed, *Represent and Destroy*, 12.

56. Nishant Shah, "Weaponization of Care," *Heinrich Böll Stiftung: Heimatkunde. Migrationspolitisches Portal*, May 11, 2021, https://heimatkunde.boell .de/de/2021/05/11/weaponization-care?fbclid=IwAR1WfF8uGCX6O1Isc7 DDM_35mgGmDLBi5icGNvpuR3E5_rCV-pZ7GJLR0Z4; Sara Ahmed, *On Being Included: Racism and Diversity in Institutional Life* (Durham, N.C.: Duke University Press, 2012). Note the productive slippage that the term "image" registers between an institutional reputation and brand, and visual representations of diversity.

57. Keeling, "I = Another," 59. See also King's critique of common assumptions that digital video images are less biased or more objective than analog media representations, and thus implicitly pro-minority, because they are founded on "computational, quantitative ways of thinking—ways of thinking that can be expressed by a mathematical notation system" that appear as "the best or the only truly accurate ways of thinking." King, *Virtual Memory*, 9.

58. Phruksachart, "The Bourgeois Cinema of Boba Liberalism," 61. See also Corinne Mitsuye Sugino, "Multicultural Redemption: 'Crazy Rich Asians' and the Politics of Representation," *Lateral* 8, no. 2 (2019), https://csalateral.org/ issue/8-2/multicultural-redemption-crazy-rich-asians-politics-representation -sugino. In a similar vein, the now standard supply of Asian and specifically South Korean dramas on global U.S. video streaming platforms conveys a new global literacy on the part of their users. Here, too, however, the value of Asians, while not measured through traditional identifiers of labor and production, remains contingent on their racialized proximity to capital. Moreover, scholars have linked the recent surge in South Korean dramas on U.S.

NOTES TO CHAPTER 1 | 151

platforms to the expansive and imperial industry practices of U.S. media and tech corporations. See H. J. Stephany Noh, "South Korea," Global Internet TV Consortium, October 2020, https://www.global-internet-tv.com/south-korea; Dal Yong Jin, "Netflix's Corporate Sphere in the Digital Platform Era in Asia," in *The Routledge Handbook of Digital Media and Globalization,* ed. Dal Yong Jin (London: Routledge, 2021), 167–75. Ji Hoon Park, Kristin April Kim, and Yongsuk Lee, "Netflix and Platform Imperialism: How Netflix Alters the Ecology of the Korean TV Drama Industry," *International Journal of Communication* 17 (2023): 72–91.

59. Sasha Torres, "Television and Race," in *A Companion to Television,* ed. Janet Wasko (Malden, Mass.: Wiley-Blackwell, 2010), 407. See also Herman Gray, *Watching Race: Television and the Struggle for "Blackness"* (Minneapolis: University of Minnesota Press, 1995); and Sarah Banet-Weiser, *Kids Rule! Nickelodeon and Consumer Citizenship* (Durham, N.C.: Duke University Press, 2007). While the references in this section go beyond the age of online streaming, the authors collectively demonstrate the steadily broadening methods of monetizing diversity, onscreen and off, under a neoliberal economy.

60. On the conflation of moving images with political representation see also Keeling, *The Witch's Flight,* 42ff.; and Kristen J. Warner, "Plastic Representation," *Film Quarterly* 71, no. 2 (2017), https://filmquarterly.org/2017/12/04/in-the-time-of-plastic-representation. Hentyle Yapp offers another compelling critique of representational politics in an international frame that developed from Western liberalism and continus in neoliberal demands for diversity. Hentyle Yapp, *Minor China: Method, Materialisms, and the Aesthetic* (Durham, N.C.: Duke University Press, 2021).

61. Hong, "Speculative Surplus," 112.

62. Rey Chow, "When Reflexivity Becomes Porn: Mutations of a Modernist Theoretical Practice," in *Entanglements, or Transmedial Thinking about Capture* (Durham, N.C.: Duke University Press, 2012), 14.

63. Keeling, *Queer Times,* 19.

64. José Esteban Muñoz, *Cruising Utopia: The Then and There of Queer Futurity* (New York: New York University, 2009), 91. See also Keeling, *Queer Times.* Further inspirations hail from Curtis Marez's critique of futurism in his book, *Farm Worker Futurism: Speculative Technologies of Resistance* (Minneapolis: University of Minnesota Press, 2016). I am also thinking alongside Gayatri Gopinath's notion of the "impossible" in her critique of queer diasporic culture. Gayatri Gopinath, *Impossible Desires: Queer Diasporas and South Asian Public Cultures* (Durham, N.C.: Duke University Press, 2005), 15f.

1. Improper *Asiatische Deutsche*

1. The title of Wong's video is in both English and German: *Lerne Deutsch mit Petra von Kant / Learn German with Petra von Kant.*

2. Fatima El-Tayeb, *European Others: Queering Ethnicity in Postnational*

152 | NOTES TO CHAPTER 1

Europe (Minneapolis: University of Minnesota Press, 2011), xviii. See also Axeli Knapp, "Resonanzräume—Räsonierräume: Zur transatlantischen Reise von Race, Class und Gender," in *Gender Mobil? Geschlecht und Migration in transnationalen Räumen*, ed. Helma Lutz (Münster: Westfälisches Dampfboot, 2009), 215–33. Writings by German activists and critics of color that have influenced my thinking further include Kien Nghi Ha, Nicola Lauré al-Samarai, and Sheila Mysorekar, eds., *re/visionen. Postkoloniale Perspektiven von People of Color auf Rassismus, Kulturpolitik und Widerstand in Deutschland* (Berlin: Unrast, 2007); Maureen Maisha Eggers, Grada Kilomba, Peggy Piesche, and Susan Arndt, eds., *Mythen, Masken und Subjekte. Kritische Weißseinsforschung in Deutschland* (Münster: Unrast, 2009). Kandice Chuh is also helpful in thinking through the limited paradigms by which we understand race as an object of critique, in "It's Not about Anything," *Social Text* 32, no. 4 (2014): 125–34.

3. Fatima El-Tayeb, " 'Gays Who Cannot Properly Be Gay': Queer Muslims in the Neoliberal European City," *European Journal of Women's Studies* 19, no. 1 (2012): 89. My discussion draws from El-Tayeb's notion of "queering ethnicity" as a "constant mixing of genres and styles [that] reflects a resistance to notions of purity and uncomplicated belonging." El-Tayeb, *European Others,* xxx.

4. Peter Rainer in Alexandra Juhasz, "Video Art on YouTube," in *Resolutions 3: Global Networks of Video,* ed. Ming-Yuen Ma and Erika Suderburg (Minneapolis: University of Minnesota Press, 2012), 310. See also book introduction.

5. Eve Oishi, "Bad Asians: New Film and Video by Queer Asian American Artists," in *Countervisions: Asian American Film Criticism,* ed. Darrell Hamamoto and Sandra Liu (Philadelphia: Temple University Press, 2000), 221–41.

6. Rey Chow, "When Reflexivity Becomes Porn," in *Entanglements, or Transmedial Thinking about Capture* (Durham, N.C.: Duke University Press, 2012), 13–30.

7. Ming Wong, *"Lerne Deutsch mit Petra von Kant / Learn German with Petra von Kant,"* accessed June 28, 2022, http://www.mingwong.org/lerne-deutsch-mit-petra-von-kant-learn-german-with-petra-von-kant.

8. For a historical overview of the demographic shifts in postwar Kreuzberg—from its migrant worker ghetto to becoming a locale of urban innovation and transnational capital, and its brand as a hip and queer district today—see Jin Haritaworn, *Queer Lovers and Hateful Others: Regenerating Violent Times and Places* (London: Pluto Press, 2015), 57ff.

9. El-Tayeb, *European Others,* xxix.

10. Homay King, *Virtual Memory: Time-Based Art and the Dream of Digitality* (Durham, N.C.: Duke University Press, 2015), 136. Wong's alignment with a damaged white lesbian figure also reminds me of Hoang Tan Nguyen's notion of "bottomhood" or queer-feminist positionality, insofar as Wong's performance tactically joins the image of sexless Asian masculinity and frivolous lesbianism into a reparative form of coming together beyond the limiting forms of race and nation. See Hoang Tan Nguyen, *A View from the Bottom: Asian*

NOTES TO CHAPTER 1 | 153

American Masculinity and Sexual Representation (Durham, N.C.: Duke University Press, 2014).

11. Birgit Rieger, "Porträt Ming Wong: In fremden Kleidern," *Der Tagesspiegel Online,* July 29, 2018, sec. Kultur. https://www.tagesspiegel.de/kultur/portraet-ming-wong-in-fremden-kleidern/22857982.html. My translation. Wong also exploits the common assumption of Asians' proximity to whiteness to offer performances of unexemplary Asianness and improper whiteness.

12. David Theo Goldberg, "Racial Europeanization," *Ethnic and Racial Studies* 29, no. 2 (2006): 331.

13. "Germany's PISA Shock," OECD, https://www.oecd.org/about/impact/germany-pisa-shock.htm; see also Kimiko Suda and Sun-ju Choi, "Asian Film Festival Berlin: 'Imagine(d) Kinships and Communities,'" in *Asiatische Deutsche: Vietnamesische Diaspora and Beyond*, ed. Kien Nghi Ha (Berlin: Assoziation A, 2012), 246–57.

14. See, for example, Martin Spiewak, "Das Vietnamesische Wunder," *Zeit Online,* August 3, 2009, http://www.zeit.de/2009/05/B-Vietnamesen.

15. See Heinz Gollwitzer, *Die Gelbe Gefahr: Geschichte Eines Schlagworts: Studien Zum Imperialistischen Denken* (Göttingen: Vandenhoeck & Ruprecht, 1962); John Kuo Wei Tchen and Dylan Yeats, eds., *Yellow Peril! An Archive of Anti-Asian Fear* (New York: Verso, 2014). Contrary to popular opinion, Germany colonized large parts of Africa and acquired protectorates in the Asia Pacific including areas of China. See Charles Stephenson, *Germany's Asia-Pacific Empire: Colonialism and Naval Policy 1885–1914* (Rochester, N.Y.: Boydell, 2009); Sebastian Conrad, "Rethinking German Colonialism in a Global Age," *Journal of Imperial and Commonwealth History* 41, no. 4 (2013): 543–66; Bradley Naranch and Geoff Eley, eds., *German Colonialism in a Global Age* (Durham, N.C.: Duke University Press, 2014); Hartmut Berghoff, Frank Biess, and Ulrike Strasse, eds., *Explorations and Entanglements: Germans in Pacific Worlds from the Early Modern Period to World War I* (New York: Berghahn Books, 2018).

16. Jana Hensel, "Vietnamesen in Sachsen. Werben um Khanh," *Zeit Online,* March 27, 2011, http://www.zeit.de/2011/13/S-Vietnamesen/seite-1.

17. "Angela Merkel und die Muslime und Türken Multi Kulti is Tot," YouTube video, 1:50, from kabeleins news, posted by "pommescurry1," October 16, 2010, https://www.youtube.com/watch?v=Xuq0Bnw1DzQ. Translation. Similar rhetorics have been used by leading German politicians since the 1970s, perhaps most infamously by chancellor Helmut Kohl's public statement that "We are not an immigrant country. And we cannot become one." See also Deniz Göktürk, David Gramling, Anton Kaes, Andreas Langenohl, eds., *Transit Deutschland: Debatten zu Nation und Migration* (Konstanz: University of Konstanz Press, 2011); Tiffany Nicole Florvil, *Mobilizing Black Germany: Afro-German Women and the Making of a Transnational Movement* (Urbana: University of Illinois Press, 2020).

18. Goldberg, "Racial Europeanization," 344.

154 | NOTES TO CHAPTER 1

19. Jin Haritaworn, Tamsila Tauqir, and Esra Erdem, "Gay Imperialism: Gender and Sexuality Discourse in the 'War on Terror,'" in Adi Kuntsman and Esperanza Miyake, eds., *Out of Place: Interrogating Silences in Queerness/Raciality* (York, UK: Raw Nerve Books, 2008), 78. The authors elaborate how majoritarian constructs of Muslim homophobia racialize Muslim populations as antidemocratic and antagonistic to European identity. See also El-Tayeb, "'Gays Who Cannot Properly Be Gay.'"

20. The position of South Asian Germans overlaps yet is distinct from the kinds of Asian rendering I focus on here and deserves a separate discussion. Regarding the racialization of South Asians in Germany see Urmila Goel, Jose Punnamparambil, und Nisa Punnamparambil-Wolf, eds., *InderKinder. Über das Aufwachsen und Leben in Deutschland* (Heidelberg: Draupadi Verlag, 2012); Urmila Goel, *Das Indernet. Eine rassismuskritische Internet-Ethnografie* (Bielefeld: transcript, 2020).

21. Robert E. Rhoades, "Foreign Labor and German Industrial Capitalism 1871–1978: The Evolution of a Migratory System," *American Ethnologist* 5, no. 3 (1978): 553–73; Robert Miles, "Labour Migration, Racism and Capital Accumulation in Western Europe since 1945: An Overview," *Capital & Class* 10, no. 1 (1986): 49–86; Rita Chin, *The Guest Worker Question in Postwar Germany* (Cambridge: Cambridge University Press, 2007).

22. Kien Nghi Ha, *Ethnizität und Migration reloaded. Kulturelle Identität, Differenz und Hybridität im postkolonialen Diskurs* (Berlin: Wissenschaftlicher Verlag, 2004). See also Hito Steyerl, "Postkolonialismus und Biopolitik. Probleme der Übertragung postkolonialer Ansätze in den deutschen Kontext," in *Spricht die Subalterne deutsch?*, ed. Encarnación Gutiérrez Rodríguez and Hito Steyerl (Münster: Unrast, 2003), 38–55.

23. Rita Chin and Heike Fehrenbach, "Introduction: What's Race Got to Do with It? Postwar German History in Context," in *After the Nazi Racial State: Difference and Democracy in Germany and Europe*, ed. Rita Chin, Heide Fehrenbach, Geoff Eley, and Atina Grossmann (Ann Arbor: University of Michigan Press, 2009), 22.

24. "No person shall be favoured or disfavoured because of sex, parentage, race, language, homeland and origin, faith, or religious or political opinions. No person shall be disfavoured because of disability." Basic Law of the Federal Republic of Germany, Article 3, "Equality before the Law," Deutscher Bundestag, accessed June 28, 2022, https://www.btg-bestellservice.de/pdf/80201000.pdf. While the principle of right of blood was extended to a conditional birthright in 2000, common sense understandings of citizens and foreigners continue to be based in the idea of a white German-blooded body. See also Nanna Heidenreich, *V/erkennungsdienste, das Kino und die Perspektive der Migration* (Bielefeld: transcript, 2015).

25. For an overview see Statistisches Bundesamt, "Migration und Integration," accessed September 19, 2020, https://www.destatis.de/EN/Themes/

Society-Environment/Population/Migration-Integration/_node.html# sprg265538.

26. On the precarious legal status of Vietnamese contract workers after German unification see Karin Weiss, "Nach der Wende: Vietnamesische Vertragsarbeiter und Vertragsarbeiterinnen in Ostdeutschland heute," *Erfolg in der Nische? Die Vietnamesen in der DDR und in Ostdeutschland,* ed. Karin Weiss and Mike Dennis (London: Lit Verlag, 2005), 77–96; Kien Nghi Ha, "The Vietnamese in Germany (Part 1 of 2)," *diaCRITICS,* March 25, 2013, https://dvan .org/2013/03/the-vietnamese-in-germany-part-i; Gertrud Hüwelmeier, "Transnational Vietnamese. Germany and Beyond," in *Asian Migrants in Europe. Transnational Connections,* ed. Sylvia Hahn and Stan Nadel (Göttingen: Vandenhoeck and Ruprecht, 2014), 81–94; Phi Hong Su, *The Border Within: Vietnamese Migrants Transforming Ethnic Nationalism in Berlin* (Stanford, Calif.: Stanford University Press, 2022). On racial politics in East German contract worker economies see Mike Dennis, "Asian and African Workers in the Niches of Society," in Mike Dennis and Norman LaPorte, *State and Minorities in Communist East Germany* (New York: Berghahn Books, 2011), 87–123; Quinn Slobodian, ed., *Comrades of Color: East Germany in the Cold War World* (New York: Berghahn Books, 2015).

27. See Maja Figge and Anja Michaelsen, "Das 'rassifizierte Feld des Sichtbaren.' Deutungen des NSU-Terrors 2004–2011," in *Zeitschrift für Medienwissenschaft* 13, no. 2 (2015): 106–17.

28. On Korean labor migration to Germany see Jung-Sook Yoo, *Koreanische Immigranten in Deutschland: Interessenvertretung und Selbstorganisation* (Hamburg: Verlag Dr. Kovač, 1996); Heike Berner and Sun-ju Choi, eds., *Zuhause: Erzählungen von deutschen Koreanerinnen* (Berlin: Assoziation A, 2006); You Jae Lee, "Glückauf der Kyopos—50 Jahre koreanische Arbeitsmigration in Deutschland," Heinrich-Böll-Stiftung, *Heimatkunde,* January 29, 2014, https:// heimatkunde.boell.de/2014/01/29/glueckauf-der-kyopos-50-jahre-koreanische -arbeitsmigration-deutschland and his edited volume, *Glück auf! Lebensgeschichten koreanischer Bergarbeiter in Deutschland* (Munich: Iudicium, 2021); Young-Sun Hong, *Cold War Germany, the Third World, and the Global Humanitarian Regime* (Cambridge: Cambridge University Press, 2015); Koreanische Frauenruppe, "30 Jahre Koreanische Frauengruppe in Deutschland," May 18, 2017, https://t1.daumcdn.net/cfile/tistory/215FC43D591DAAF510?original.

29. Mita Banerjee, "Travelling Theory, Reshaping Disciplines? Envisioning Asian Germany through Asian Australian Studies," in *Locating Asian Australian Cultures,* ed. Tseen Khoo (London: Routledge, 2008), 170.

30. Notable exceptions include Ipek A. Celik, *In Permanent Crisis: Ethnicity in Contemporary European Media and Cinema* (Ann Arbor: University of Michigan Press, 2015); Heidenreich, *V/erkennungsdienste*; Ömer Alkin, *Die visuelle Kultur der Migration. Geschichte, Ästhetik und Polyzentrierung des Migrationskinos* (Bielefeld: transcript Verlag, 2019); and Anja Sunhyun Michaelsen,

156 | NOTES TO CHAPTER 1

"Aus der Nähe? Feministische Filmtheorie und postmigrantisches Kino," *Nach Dem Film* 10 (2019), https://www.nachdemfilm.de/index.php/issues/text/aus-der-naehe-feministische-filmtheorie-und-postmigrantisches-kino. Michaelsen helpfully deploys the term *postmigrantisch* (postmigrant) that has gained traction in recent years by German cultural producers and critics to challenge the institutional and public neglect of Germany's immigrant history and pluralistic culture. See also Ömer Alkin, Jiré Emine Gözen, and Nelly Y. Pinkrah, eds., "X | Kein Lagebericht," special issue, *Zeitschrift für Medienwissenschaft* 14, no. 26 (2022), https://doi.org/10.14361/zfmw-2022-140103.

31. Ming Wong, interview, "Ming Wong: Part I," *ART iT,* August 1, 2010, https://www.art-it.asia/en/u/admin_ed_feature_e/9kgWtzQE4V1jMyluUnv3.

32. Ludwig Seyfarth, "Ming Wong: Portrait," *vonhundert,* November 2009, http://www.vonhundert.de/index.php?id=226.

33. For Kira Kosnick, German cosmopolitanism is "to be part of a worldwide network of art institutions that link Berlin to cities like Singapore, Seoul, Sao Paulo, Beijing, Mumbai, New York and Los Angeles." Kira Kosnick, "Cosmopolitan Capital or Multicultural Community? Reflections on the Production and Management of Differential Mobilities in Germany's Capital City," in *Cosmopolitanism in Practice,* ed. Magdalena Nowicka and Maria Rovisco (Farnham, UK: Ashgate, 2009), 170. World openness is thus a form of concealment: to overlay the unwanted parts of diversity with the profitable yields of global cultural flows.

34. Ming Wong, *"Angst Essen / Eat Fear,"* May 16, 2008, http://www.mingwong.org/angst-essen-eat-fear.

35. Künstlerhaus Bethanien, cofunded by the city of Berlin, subsidized *Eat Fear.* The costs for *Lerne Deutsch* were borne by the artist himself.

36. See Cherise Smith, *Enacting Others: Politics of Identity in Eleanor Antin, Nikki S. Lee, Adrian Piper, and Anna Deavere Smith* (Durham, N.C.: Duke University Press, 2011); Britta Schilling, *Postcolonial Germany: Memories of Empire in a Decolonized Nation* (Oxford: Oxford University Press, 2014); Susann Therese Samples, "Black Is Not Beautiful: The German Myth of Race," in *Relating Worlds of Racism: Dehumanisation, Belonging, and the Normativity of European Whiteness,* ed. Philomena Essed, Karen Farquharson, Kathryn Pillay, Elisa Joy White (Cham, Switzerland: Palgrave Macmillan, 2019), 223–44.

37. Anca Parvulescu, "Old Europe, New Europe, Eastern Europe: Reflections on a Minor Character in Fassbinder's *Ali, Fear Eats the Soul," New Literary History* 43 (2012): 735.

38. King, *Virtual Memory,* 136.

39. See also Claire Jean Kim, "The Racial Triangulation of Asian Americans," *Politics & Society* 27 (1999): 105–38; Nadia Kim, "Critical Thoughts on Asian American Assimilation in the Whitening Literature," in *Racism in Post-Racism America: New Theories, New Directions,* ed. Charles A. Gallagher (Chapel Hill, N.C.: Social Forces, 2008), 53–66; Viet Nguyen and Janet Hoskins, "Introduction: Transpacific Studies: Critical Perspectives on an

Emerging Field," in *Transpacific Studies: Framing an Emerging Field,* ed. Janet Hoskins and Viet Nguyen (Honolulu: University of Hawai'i Press, 2014), 1–38.

40. Kobena Mercer, "Reading Racial Fetishism: The Photographs of Robert Mapplethorpe," in *Welcome to the Jungle: New Positions in Black Cultural Studies* (New York: Routledge, 1994), 171–220.

41. On Chinese privilege in Singapore see Adeline Koh and Sangeetha Thanapal, "Chinese Privilege, Gender and Intersectionality in Singapore: A Conversation between Adeline Koh and Sangeetha Thanapal," *b2o,* March 4, 2015, https://www.boundary2.org/2015/03/chinese-privilege-gender-and-intersectionality-in-singapore-a-conversation-between-adeline-koh-and-sangeetha-thanapal/. On Singapore's diversity politics, see also Eng-Beng Lim, *Brown Boys and Rice Queens: Spellbinding Performance in the Asias* (New York: New York University Press, 2013); Chua Beng Huat, "The Cultural Logic of a Capitalist Single-Party State, Singapore," *Postcolonial Studies* 13, no. 4 (2010).

42. "Power 100," *Art Review,* 2017, accessed June 29, 2022, https://artreview.com/power_100.

43. Ministry of Culture and Education, *Hito Steyerl. Duty Free Art,* exhibition catalog (Madrid: Museo Nacional Centro de Arte Reina Sofía, 2015), 141.

44. Gutiérrez Rodríguez and Steyerl, *Spricht die Subalterne deutsch?*

45. Hito Steyerl, "In Defense of the Poor Image," *e-flux* 10 (2009), https://www.e-flux.com/journal/10/61362/in-defense-of-the-poor-image.

46. See T. J. Demos, "Hito Steyerl's Traveling Images," in *The Migrant Image: The Art and Politics of Documentary during Global Crisis* (Durham, N.C.: Duke University Press, 2013), 74–89; Nick Aikens, ed., *Too Much World: The Films of Hito Steyerl* (Berlin: Sternberg, 2014); Catherine A. Steinmann, "Visceral Exposure: Melanie Gilligan, Hito Steyerl, and the Biopolitics of Visibility," PhD diss., University of British Columbia, 2015; Jihoon Kim, *Between Film, Video, and the Digital: Hybrid Moving Images in the Post-Media Age* (New York: Bloomsbury Academic, 2016); Kimberly Bradley, "Hito Steyerl Is an Artist with Power. She Uses It for Change," *New York Times,* December 15, 2017, https://www.nytimes.com/2017/12/15/arts/design/hito-steyerl.html; Thomas Elsaesser, "The Essay Film: From Film Festival Favorite to Flexible Commodity Form?," in *Essays on the Essay Film,* ed. Nora M. Alter and Timothy Corrigan (New York: Columbia University Press, 2017), 240–58.

47. Demos, "Hito Steyerl's Traveling Images," 75.

48. Steyerl also cites Japanese art house cinema and Third Cinema as important influences. "Life in Film: Hito Steyerl," *Frieze,* April 1, 2008, https://www.frieze.com/article/life-film-hito-steyerl; and Steyerl, "In Defense of the Poor Image."

49. In her discussion of Black female media representations in U.S. popular culture, Racquel Gates offers a compelling approach to the poor image by tying divisions of low and high culture to racial politics, and specifically, what she calls via George Lipsitz the film and media industry's " 'possessive investment' in aesthetics that is tied to racial politics and racial representation." Racquel

Gates, "The Last Shall Be First: Aesthetics and Politics in Black Film and Media," *Film Quarterly* 71, no. 2 (2017): 40.

50. Celine Parreñas Shimizu, *The Hypersexuality of Race: Performing Asian/American Women on Screen and Scene* (Durham, N.C.: Duke University Press, 2007); Nguyen, *A View from the Bottom*; Lily Wong, *Transpacific Attachments: Sex Work, Media Networks, and Affective Histories of Chineseness* (New York: Columbia University Press, 2018); Genevieve Yue, *Girl Head: Feminism and Film Materiality* (New York: Fordham University Press, 2020); Mila Zuo, *Vulgar Beauty: Acting Chinese in the Global Sensorium* (Durham, N.C.: Duke University Press, 2022); Vivian L. Huang, *Surface Relations: Queer Forms of Asian American Inscrutability* (Durham, N.C.: Duke University Press, 2022).

51. Jin Haritaworn, *The Biopolitics of Mixing: Thai Multiracialities and Haunted Ascendancies* (Farnham, UK: Ashgate, 2012), 108. Haritaworn explores the rise of a fashionable "mixed race" identity category in Europe that functions similarly to Asianness.

52. Angelica Fenner and Robin Curtis, "If People Want to Oppress You, They Make You Say 'I': Hito Steyerl in Conversation with Angelica Fenner and Robin Curtis," in *The Autobiographical Turn in Germanophone Documentary and Autobiographical Film,* ed. Robin Curtis and Angelica Fenner (Rochester, N.Y.: Camden House, 2014), 38.

53. The video is freely available on the archival online platform Ubuweb. Its original screening context, under *documenta*'s official slogan "The Migration of Forms," further elucidates what I see as a rather depoliticized engagement of migration and race politics. By defining *migration,* in the curators' words, as viewers' "own movement through [the documenta] space" and their ability to forge meaning across various artworks, the term ends up repeating the ideal of the cosmopolitan intellectual—and that is, ultimately also raceless—mind. Ruth Noack and Roger M. Buergel, "Some Afterthoughts on the Migration of Form," *Afterall: A Journal of Art, Context and Enquiry* 18 (2008): 9.

54. Steyerl in Fenner and Curtis, "If People Want to Oppress You," 42.

55. Hito Steyerl, "The Essay as Conformism? Some Notes on Global Image Economies (2011)," in *Essays on the Essay Film*, ed. Nora M. Alter and Timothy Corrigan (New York: Columbia University Press, 2017), 276–85.

56. Parreñas Shimizu, *The Hypersexuality of Race,* 15.

57. Parreñas Shimizu, *The Hypersexuality of Race,* 3.

58. Nora M. Alter, *The Essay Film after Fact and Fiction* (New York: Columbia University Press), 4.

59. Elsaesser, "The Essay Film," 242.

60. Steyerl, "The Essay as Conformism?" 276.

61. Fenner and Curtis, "If People Want to Oppress You," 38.

62. Fenner and Curtis, "If People Want to Oppress You," 38.

63. Hito Steyerl, "Reise und Rasse," in *Im Handgepäck Rassismus: Beiträge zu Tourismus und Kultur,* ed. Martina Backes, Tina Goethe, Stephan Günther, and Rosaly Magg (Freiburg: Informationszentrum Dritte Welt, 2002), 32.

NOTES TO CHAPTER 2 | 159

64. Hito Steyerl, "Missing People: Entanglement, Superposition, and Exhumation as Sites of Indeterminacy," *e-flux* 38 (2012), https://www.eflux.com/journal/38/61209/missing-people-entanglement-superposition-and-exhumation-as-sites-of-indeterminacy. See also Steyerl, "The Spam of the Earth: Withdrawal from Representation," *e-flux* 32 (2012), https://www.e-flux.com/journal/32/68260/the-spam-of-the-earth-withdrawal-from-representation.

65. Hito Steyerl, "A Thing Like You and Me," *e-flux* 15, April 2010, https://www.e-flux.com/journal/15/61298/a-thing-like-you-and-me/.

2. Mental Health and Live Fictions

1. Celine Parreñas Shimizu, *The Hypersexuality of Race: Performing Asian/American Women on Screen and Scene* (Durham, N.C.: Duke University Press, 2007), 24.

2. "Interview with Kristina Wong," *Center for Cultural Innovation* (peer-to-peer blog), May 7, 2013. https://www.cciarts.org/cgi/page.cgi/_article.html/Peer_to_Peer_Blog/Interview_with_Kristina_Wong.

3. See Rachel Lee, *Exquisite Corpse of Asian America: Biopolitics, Biosociality, and Posthuman Ecologies* (New York: New York University Press, 2014), and "'Where's My Parade?' Margaret Cho and the Asian American Body," *TDR / The Drama Review* 48, no. 2 (2004): 108–32; Euni Kim, "'An Impression of Asian People': Asian-American Comedy, Rhetoric, and Identity in Ali Wong's Standup Comedy," *Rhetoric & Public Affairs* 24, no. 1 (2021): 307–32; D'Lo, "Sewing Patches through Performance," in *Q&A. Voices from Queer Asian North America,* ed. Martin F. Manalansan IV, Alice Y. Hom, and Kale Bantigue Fajardo (Philadelphia: Temple University Press, 2021), 57–63; Mila Zuo, "Sour Laughter: Charlyne Yi and Ali Wong," in *Vulgar Beauty: Acting Chinese in the Global Sensorium* (Durham, N.C.: Duke University Press, 2022), 193–233.

4. Kristina Wong, "Artist Statement," accessed January 26, 2023, https://www.kristinawong.com/about.

5. Kristina Wong, "Wong Flew Over the Cuckoo's Nest," accessed January 26, 2023, https://www.kristinawong.com/projects-blog/wong-flew-over-the-cuckoos-nest.

6. "About the Film," Flying Wong Productions, accessed July 4, 2022, http://flyingwong.com/about.html.

7. "Kristina Wong: Performer, Writer, Cultural Commentator and 'Eco-Comedian,'" Rutgers Student Affairs, accessed July 4, 2022, http://markconference.rutgers.edu/dt_team/kristina-wong/.

8. Kristina Wong, "Kristina Wong for Public Office," accessed January 26, 2023, https://www.kristinawong.com/projects-blog/kristina-wong-for-public-office.

9. "Kristina Wong: *The Wong Street Journal*," REDCAT, August 5, 2015, https://www.redcat.org/event/kristina-wong-wong-street-journal; Abe Ahn,

160 | NOTES TO CHAPTER 2

"In Uganda, a Performance Artist Confronts Her Privilege." *Hyperallergic,* November 25, 2015, http://hyperallergic.com/253800/in-uganda-a-performance-artist-confronts-her-privilege/.

10. Preeti Sharma, "Sewing as Care Work," in *The Auntie Sewing Squad Guide to Mask Making, Radical Care, and Racial Justice,* ed. Mai-Linh K. Hong, Chrissy Yee Lau, and Preeti Sharma (Oakland: University of California Press, 2021), 38.

11. Kristina Wong, email to the author, March 2, 2022.

12. *Wong Flew Over the Cuckoo's Nest,* directed by Mike Closson (Flying Wong Productions, 2011), https://www.imdb.com/title/tt1587387/?ref_=nv_sr_srsg_0.

13. Kristina Wong, "Wong Flew Over the Cuckoo's Nest." *Cuckoo's Nest* "is a National Performance Network Creation Fund Project commissioned by Asian Arts Initiative and La Peña Cultural Center. Funding for *Wong Flew Over the Cuckoo's Nest* has also been provided by the National Endowment for the Arts, The Ford Foundation, and La Peña's New Works Fund supported by The James Irvine Foundation. [It] is also a Project of Creative Capital."

14. Emphasis added.

15. Joanne Seiff, "Knit for Life: An Asian-American Artist Uses Knitting to Draw Attention to Some Disturbing Statistics," *Vogue Knitting International,* 2007. See also *Confessions of a Yarn Hoarder* (FlyingWongProd, 2011), https://www.youtube.com/watch?v=ePJoaUFn9Ro.

16. Kobena Mercer, "Black Art and the Burden of Representation," *Third Text* 4, no. 10 (1990): 62.

17. Kristina Wong, email to the author, May 11, 2013.

18. As Stephanie Nohelani Teves and Maile Arvin remind us, "the ongoing exoticization of the Pacific as a space of fantasy and freedom . . . is different than the ways Asian women are figured as representative of sexual excess rooted in Orientalism." Stephanie Nohelani Teves and Maile Arvin, "Decolonizing API: Centering Indigenous Pacific Islander Feminism," in *Asian American Feminisms and Women of Color Politics,* ed. Lynn Fujiwara and Shireen Roshanravan (Seattle: University of Washington Press, 2018), 111. Other scholars have highlighted the common problem of subsuming Pacific Islanders into Asian America. See, for instance, Vicente M. Diaz, "To 'P' or Not to 'P'? Marking the Territory Between Pacific Islanders and Asian American Studies," *Journal of Asian American Studies* 7, no. 3 (2004): 183–208; and Lisa Kahaleʻole Hall, "Which of These Things Is Not Like the Other: Hawaiians and Other Pacific Islanders Are Not Asian Americans, and All Pacific Islanders Are Not Hawaiian," *American Quarterly* 67, no. 3 (2015): 727–47.

19. Kristina Wong, "Reflections on Shitty Performance Art, Crisis, and Isolating Ourselves Intentionally After Isolating Unintentionally," MacDowell News, June 14, 2021, https://www.macdowell.org/news/reflections-on-shitty-performance-art-crisis-and-isolating-ourselves-intentionally-after-isolating-unintentionally. Author's emphasis.

NOTES TO CHAPTER 2 | 161

20. Jeffrey Santa Ana, *Racial Feelings: Asian America in a Capitalist Culture of Emotion* (Philadelphia: Temple University Press, 2015), 15.

21. Helen Heran Jun, *Race for Citizenship: Black Orientalism and Asian Uplift from Pre-emancipation to Neoliberal America* (New York: NYU Press, 2011), 9; See also Grace Kyungwon Hong, "Speculative Surplus: Asian American Racialization and the Neoliberal Shift," *Social Text* 36, no. 2 (2018): 107–22.

22. K. Hyoejin Yoon, "Learning Asian American Affect," in *Representations: Doing Asian American Rhetoric,* ed. LuMing Mao and Morris Young (Logan: Utah State University Press, 2008), 294.

23. Sharma, "Sewing as Care Work," 40.

24. Vivian L. Huang, *Surface Relations: Queer Forms of Asian American Inscrutability* (Durham, N.C.: Duke University Press, 2022), 136f.

25. Vivian L. Huang, "Inscrutably, Actually: Hospitality, Parasitism, and the Silent work of Yoko Ono and Laurel Nakadate," *Women & Performance: A Journal of Feminist Theory* 28, no. 3 (2018), 191.

26. Eve Oishi, "Bad Asians: New Media by Queer Asian American Artists," in *Countervisions: Asian American Film Criticism,* ed. Darrell Y. Hamamoto and Sandra Liu (Philadelphia: Temple University Press, 2000), 223. See also Jun Okada, *Making Asian American Film and Video: History, Institutions, Movements* (New Brunswick, N.J.: Rutgers University Press, 2015).

27. Anjali Enjeti, "Kristina Wong: Pushing the Envelope on Race, Rights and America." *The Guardian,* March 26, 2015, https://www.theguardian.com/stage/2015/mar/26/kristina-wong-pushing-envelope-art-race-america.

28. Katherine Nigh, "Interview with Performance Artist Kristina Wong," *My Year Without A Man,* podcast, 2019, https://soundcloud.com/myyearwithoutaman/kristinawong.

29. Kristina Wong, "Reflections on Shitty Performance Art."

30. Tina Chen, *Double Agency: Acts of Impersonation in Asian American Literature and Culture* (Stanford, Calif.: Stanford University Press, 2005), xviii.

31. Listen also to Kristina Wong, "Social Justice Cram School for Kids: Kristina Wong," interview by Cindy Wang Brandt, *Parenting Forward*, podcast, March 25, 2019, https://cindywangbrandt.com/podcast/episode-38-social-justice-cram-school-for-kids-kristina-wong-teddy-chao.

32. Chen, *Double Agency,* 18, her emphasis.

33. Parreñas Shimizu, *The Hypersexuality of Race,* 214.

34. Nigh, "Interview."

35. Personal conversation with the author, May 29, 2022.

36. Kristina Wong, email to the author, 2013.

37. Sianne Ngai, *Ugly Feelings* (Cambridge, Mass.: Harvard University Press, 2005), 93.

38. Mel Y. Chen, "Agitation," *South Atlantic Quarterly* 117, no. 3 (2018): 559. See also Chen's *Animacies: Biopolitics, Racial Mattering, and Queer Affect* (Durham, N.C.: Duke University Press, 2012). In her study of depression in Japan, Junko Kitanaka further reminds us that Asians have historically been

162 | NOTES TO CHAPTER 2

conceived as lacking in emotional and mental sophistication compared to the delicate Western mind. She writes that "the symptoms of depression—particularly sadness, a sense of guilt, and self-blame—were regarded as signs of maturity, even of adult selfhood. . . . By contrast, non-Westerners, it was claimed, did not possess reflexive selves and were unable to suffer from depression because their immature and nonautonomous selves did not have a capacity for introspection." Junko Kitanaka, *Depression in Japan: Psychiatric Cures for a Society in Distress* (Princeton, N.J.: Princeton University Press, 2012), 15. Ann Cvetkovich further points out how depression, through its "precursor," melancholy, became attached to Western values of enlightened subjecthood. See Ann Cvetkovich, *Depression: A Public Feeling* (Durham, N.C.: Duke University Press, 2012), 89. The assignment of mental health and illness bespeaks indeed an ongoing battle over who counts as fully human. This includes the ongoing pathologization of entire continents by the U.S. state to justify imperial expansion. See for instance Warwick Anderson, *Colonial Pathologies: American Tropical Medicine, Race, and Hygiene in the Philippines* (Durham, N.C.: Duke University Press, 2006); Christopher Bell, "Introducing White Disability Studies: A Modest Proposal," in *The Disability Studies Reader*, 3rd ed., ed. Lennard J. Davis (New York: Routledge, 2010), 275–82; Jih-Fei Cheng, *Materialist Virology*, manuscript in preparation; Nirmala Erevelles, *Disability and Difference in Global Contexts: Enabling a Transformative Body Politic* (New York: Palgrave Macmillan, 2011); Anna Mollow, "'When Black Women Start Going on Prozac': Race, Gender, and Mental Illness in Meri Nana-Ama Danquah's 'Willow Weep for Me.'" *MELUS* 31, no. 3 (2006): 67–99; Kim E. Nielson, *A Disability History of the United States* (Boston: Beacon, 2012); David Palumbo-Liu, *Asian/American: Historical Crossings of a Racial Frontier* (Stanford, Calif.: Stanford University Press, 1999); Leah Lakshmi Piepzna-Samarasinha, *Care Work: Dreaming Disability Justice* (Vancouver: Arsenal Pulp, 2018); Ellen Samuels, *Fantasies of Identification: Disability, Gender, Race* (New York: New York University Press, 2014), and Nayan Shah, *Contagious Divides: Epidemics and Race in San Francisco's Chinatown* (Berkeley: University of California Press, 2001).

39. Jonathan Metzl, "Introduction: Why 'Against Health?'" in *Against Health: How Health Became the New Morality,* ed. Jonathan M. Metzl and Anna Kirkland (New York: New York University Press, 2010), 1f. Marco Ramos highlights via Jonathan Metzl how these divisions in the United States are intimately linked with racial politics. Black and Brown patients, for instance, get disproportionately diagnosed with mental illness and emotional disturbances, a reality that goes back to prevalent psychiatric practices in the 1970s that "pathologized Black activism as 'psychosis.'" Marco Ramos, "Mental Illness Is Not in Your Head," *Boston Review,* May 17, 2022, https://bostonreview .net/articles/mental-illness-is-not-in-your-head/?fbclid=IwAR0NIpFyDq P1auPzZ-ogmbZ3rjJOBD7Y0QCxzJkeSPMNIh1aS3FsS8YpIag. Ramos here references Jonathan Metzl's *The Protest Psychosis: How Schizophrenia Became a Black Disease* (Boston: Beacon, 2009). See also Chen, "Agitation," 559.

NOTES TO CHAPTER 2 | 163

40. A survey conducted by the National Center for Education Statistics found that only 0.1 percent among "Asian" students aged three to twenty-one suffer from "emotional disturbances," under which depression is commonly filed. By contrast, the categories "Black" and "American Indian" show the highest numbers of "emotional disturbance." For the original data see National Center for Education Statistics, "Children 3 to 21 Years Old Served under Individuals with Disabilities Education Act (IDEA), Part B, by Race/Ethnicity and Type of Disability: 2010–11 and 2011–12," *Digest of Education Statistics,* June 2013, http://nces.ed.gov/programs/digest/d13/tables/dt13_204.50.asp. For a critical breakdown of these data that looks further into "who gets labeled with a disability," see Rajiv Narayan, "The Jaw-Dropping Prison Pipeline No One Talks About," *Upworthy,* June 8, 2014, http://www.upworthy.com/the-jaw-dropping-prison-pipeline-no-one-talks-about?c=ufb1.

41. Minsun Lee, Wenyue Lu, Tyrell Mann-Barnes, Jin-Hyeok Nam, Julie Nelson, and Grace X. Ma1, "Mental Health Screening Needs and Preference in Treatment Types and Providers in African American and Asian American Older Adults," *Brain Sciences* 11, no. 5 (2021): 597; Shihoko Hijioka, "Suicide among Asian Americans," Asian American Psychological Association, May 2012, https://www.apa.org/pi/oema/resources/ethnicity-health/asian-american/suicide-fact-sheet.pdf.

42. Asian American Psychological Association, "Fact Sheets," accessed July 4, 2022, https://aapaonline.org/publications/fact-sheets/.

43. National Asian Pacific American Women's Forum, "Mental Health among AAPI Women. Fact Sheet," May 2021, https://www.napawf.org/our-work/content/2021/5/26/mental-health-among-aapi-women. See also National Alliance on Mental Illness, "Asian American Teenage Girls Have Highest Rates of Depression," January 1, 2011, https://www.nami.org/Press-Media/Press-Releases/2011/Asian-American-Teenage-Girls-Have-Highest-Rates-of; Astraea Augsberger, Albert Yeung, Meaghan Dougher, and Hyeouk Chris Hahm, "Factors Influencing the Underutilization of Mental Health Services among Asian American Women with a History of Depression and Suicide," *BMC Health Services Research* 15 (2015): 1–11, 542; and Wei-chin Hwang, *Culturally Adapting Psychotherapy for Asian Heritage Populations: An Evidence-Based Approach* (Cambridge, Mass.: Academic, 2016).

44. "The Rise of Asian Americans," Pew Research Center, 2012, https://www.pewsocialtrends.org/rise-of-asian-americans-2012-analysis/overview.

45. Neil G. Ruiz and Abby Budiman, "Key Facts about Asian Americans, a Diverse and Growing Population," Pew Research Center, April 29, 2021, https://www.pewresearch.org/fact-tank/2021/04/29/key-facts-about-asian-americans.

46. James Kyung-Jin Lee, *Pedagogies of Woundedness: Illness, Memoir, and the Ends of the Model Minority* (Philadelphia: Temple University Press, 2021), 3. See also Mimi Khúc, "Open in Emergency: Queering Asian American Mental Health," *Q&A: Voices from Queer Asian North America,* edited by Martin F.

164 | NOTES TO CHAPTER 2

Manalansan, Alice Y. Hom and Kale B. Fajardo (Philadelphia: Temple University Press, 2021), and Khúc's edited special issue, "Open in Emergency: A Special Issue on Asian American Mental Health," *Asian American Literary Review* 7, no. 2 (2016).

47. Asian American Psychological Association, "Fact Sheets."

48. See also Shane Shucheng Wong, Jeanelle J. Sugimoto-Matsuda, Janice Y. Chang, and Earl S. Hishinuma, "Ethnic Differences in Risk Factors for Suicide among American High School Students, 2009: The Vulnerability of Multiracial and Pacific Islander Adolescents," *Archives of Suicide Research* 16, no. 2 (2012): 159–173; Andrew Subica and Li-Tzy Wu, "Substance Use and Suicide in Pacific Islander, American Indian, and Multiracial Youth," *American Journal of Preventive Medicine* 54, no. 16 (2018): 795–805; Andrew M. Subica, Nia Aitaoto, Bruce G. Link, Ann Marie Yamada, Benjamin F. Henwood, and Greer Sullivan, "Mental Health Status, Need, and Unmet Need for Mental Health Services among U.S. Pacific Islanders," *Psychiatric Services* 70, no. 7 (2019): 578–85; American Medical Student Association, "Mental Health in the Asian Americans/Pacific Islander Community," September 4, 2020, https://www.amsa.org/mental-health-in-the-asian-americans-pacific-islander-community/#:~:text=According%20to%20a%202019%20study,for%20the%20general%20US%20population; Brittany N. Morey, Richard Calvin Chang, Karla Blessing Thomas, 'Alisi Tulua, Corina Penaia, Vananh D. Tran, Nicholas Pierson, John C. Greer, Malani Bydalek, and Ninez Ponce, "No Equity without Data Equity: Data Reporting Gaps for Native Hawaiians and Pacific Islanders as Structural Racism," *Journal of Health Politics, Policy and Law* 47, no. 2 (2022): 159–200.

49. Lee, *Pedagogies of Woundedness*, 10; see also Jennifer Huizen, "Asian American Mental Health Stigma: Why Does It Exist?" *Medical News Today,* January 28, 2021, https://www.medicalnewstoday.com/articles/asian-american-mental-health.

50. Kristina Wong, *Wong Flew over the Cuckoo's Nest Film Press Kit,* 2013, https://www.yumpu.com/en/document/read/12129432/kristina-wong-wong-flew-over-the-cuckoos-nest-the-film.

51. Kristina Chew, "The Disabled Speech of Asian Americans: Silence and Autism in Lois-Ann Yamanaka's *Father of the Four Passages,*" *Disability Studies Quarterly* 30, no. 1 (2010), http://dsq-sds.org/article/view/1068/1233. On the role of intelligence tests to measure racial value see also Palumbo-Liu, *Asian/American.*

52. Kimberly May Jew, Canyon Sam, Denise Uyehara, and Brenda Wong Aoki, "Perspectives on Asian American Performance Art: Contexts, Memories, and the Making of Meaning on Stage. An Interview with Canyon Sam, Denise Uyehara, and Brenda Wong Aoki," *MELUS* 36, no. 4 (2011): 144.

53. Kristina Wong, *Wong Flew over the Cuckoo's Nest Film Press Kit.*

54. Suk-Young Kim, *K-pop Live: Fans, Idols, and Multimedia Performance* (Stanford, Calif.: Stanford University Press, 2018), 205.

55. Philip Auslander, "Digital Liveness: A Historico-Philosophical Perspec-

tive," *PAJ: A Journal of Performance and Art* 34, no. 3 (2012): 3–11; Suk-Young Kim, "Liveness: Performance of Ideology and Technology in the Changing Media Environment," Oxford Research Encyclopedia of Literature, March 29, 2017, https://oxfordre.com/literature/view/10.1093/acrefore/9780190201098.001.0001/acrefore-9780190201098-e-76, and *K-pop Live*; Michelle Cho, "3 Ways that BTS and Its Fans Are Redefining Liveness," May 29, 2018, *Flow Journal,* https://www.flowjournal.org/2018/05/bts-and-its-fans.

56. Kristina Wong, Facebook message to the author, July 9, 2019.

57. Kristina Wong, *Wong Flew over the Cuckoo's Nest Film Press Kit.*

58. Cinema Libre Studio, a Los Angeles–based company focusing on educational and grassroots film distribution, is *Cuckoo's Nest*'s official distributor. As of June 2018, its website shows all *Cuckoo's Nest* DVDs out of stock.

59. "Educational Info for Wong Flew Over the Cuckoos Nest," http://flyingwong.com/education.html.

60. Huang, "Inscrutably, Actually," 190.

61. José Esteban Muñoz, *Disidentifications: Queers of Color and the Performance of Politics* (Minneapolis: University of Minnesota Press), 182.

62. Sasha Torres, *Black, White, and in Color: Television and Black Civil Rights* (Princeton, N.J.: Princeton University Press, 2003), 48.

63. Chris Lam and Leo Xia, "How to Pick Up Asian Chicks," *Now, Pour the Tea,* podcast, January 8, 2018, https://www.podchaser.com/podcasts/now-pour-the-tea-589106/episodes/9-how-to-pick-up-asian-chicks-24537921. *Cuckoo's Nest* was produced through a mix of private and public funds.

64. Roderick A. Ferguson, *The Reorder of Things: The University and Its Pedagogies of Minority Difference* (Minneapolis: University of Minnesota Press, 2012), 214.

65. Okada, *Making Asian American Film and Video, 2.*

66. Okada, *Making Asian American Film and Video, 5.*

67. Okada, *Making Asian American Film and Video, 4.*

68. Kristina Wong, email to the author, 2013.

69. Jenn Fang, "Acting Up & Acting Out: The Wondrous Work of Kristina Wong," *reappropriate,* June 15, 2015, http://reappropriate.co/2015/06/acting-up-acting-out-the-wondrous-work-of-kristina-wong/.

70. Kitty Lindsay, "Kristina Wong," *Feminist Crush,* podcast, February 3, 2017, https://feministcrush.libsyn.com/s2-ep-3-kristina-wong.

71. Lee, *The Exquisite Corpse,* 121.

72. Lee, "Where's My Parade?" 115.

73. John Limon, *Stand-Up Comedy in Theory, or, Abjection in America* (Durham, N.C.: Duke University Press, 2000), 21. See also Lee, " 'Where's My Parade?' "

74. On abject humor see Maggie Hennefeld and Nicholas Sammond, "Introduction: Not It, or, The Abject Objection," in *Abjection Incorporated: Mediating the Politics of Pleasure and Violence,* ed. Maggie Hennefeld and Nicholas Sammond (Durham, N.C.: Duke University Press, 2020), 1–31.

166 | NOTES TO CHAPTER 2

75. See Anne Anlin Cheng, *The Melancholy of Race: Psychoanalysis, Assimilation, and Hidden Grief* (Oxford: Oxford University Press, 2000), and David L. Eng and Shinhee Han, *Racial Melancholia, Racial Dissociation: On the Social and Psychic Lives of Asian Americans* (Durham, N.C.: Duke University Press, 2019).

76. Karen Shimakawa, *National Abjection: The Asian American Body Onstage* (Durham, N.C.: Duke University Press, 2002), 7.

77. Shimakawa, *National Abjection*, 3.

78. Fred Moten, *Black and Blur* (Durham, N.C.: Duke University Press, 2017), 268.

79. Besides the work of Shimakawa, Ju Yon Kim's notion of the "racial mundane" as everyday bodily practices that give form to legible identities helps me articulate this claim. See Ju Yon Kim, *The Racial Mundane: Asian American Performance and the Embodied Everyday* (New York: New York University Press, 2015).

80. Kristina Wong, email to author, 2013.

81. Kristina Wong, *Wong Flew over the Cuckoo's Nest Film Press Kit.*

82. Muñoz, *Disidentifications*, 182.

83. Okada, *Making Asian American Film and Video*, 7.

84. feministkilljoy [@SaraNAhmed]. "So much power & violence works through exhaustion: the exhaustion of people's capacities to resist; the exhaustion of people's capacities to live their lives on their own Terms; the exhaustion of having to navigate systems that are designed to make it harder to get what you need," Twitter, June 6, 2022, https://twitter.com/SaraNAhmed/status/1533807998417657857.

85. Kristina Wong, *Wong Flew over the Cuckoo's Nest Film Press Kit.*

86. Nehal El-Hadi, "Ensemble: An Interview with Dr. Fred Moten," *MICE Magazine* 4 (2018), http://micemagazine.ca/issue-four/ensemble-interview-dr-fred-moten.

3. Stateless Cinema and the Undocument

1. Alexis Convento and Miko Revereza, "Filipinx Identity, Diaspora, and Art Practice with Alexis Convento and Miko Revereza," *Medium,* January 1, 2017, https://medium.com/trytobegood/alexis-convento-x-miko-revereza-f80c5c5d37b0.

2. Miko Revereza, "Pinoy Talent Helped in Making Christina Aguilera's Latest Video," interview by *CNN Philippines*, May 16, 2018, https://www.cnnphilippines.com/life/entertainment/2018/05/09/Christina-Aguilera-Accelerate-filmmaker.html.

3. Sarita Echavez See, "Dis-integration: Miko Revereza's Video Letters and the Aesthetics of Counter-Assimilation," *Amerasia Journal* 46, no. 1 (2020): 19.

4. "AWC Alumni & Projects," Visual Communications, accessed July 4, 2022, https://vcmedia.org/awc-alumni.

NOTES TO CHAPTER 3 | 167

5. "IFFR Announces Hubert Bals Fund Spring Selection 2019," *International Film Festival Rotterdam,* May 20, 2019, https://press.iffr.com/173158-iffr-announces-hubert-bals-fund-spring-selection-2019; "Miko Revereza," Vilcek Foundation, accessed July 4, 2022, https://vilcek.org/prizes/prize-recipients/miko-revereza/; "Ford Foundation Invests over $4M to Support Social Justice Documentary Film Projects in 2022," Ford Foundation, December 19, 2022, https://www.fordfoundation.org/news-and-stories/news-and-press/news/ford-foundation-invests-over-4m-to-support-social-justice-documentary-film-projects-in-2022.

6. Lucas Hilderbrand, *Inherent Vice: Bootleg Histories of Videotape and Copyright* (Durham, N.C.: Duke University Press, 2009), 15.

7. Miko Revereza, "Personal Statement," available on "Miko's BARD MFA Fund," GoFundMe, March 14, 2017, https://www.gofundme.com/f/mikos-bard-mfa-fund.

8. Anna Pegler-Gordon, *In Sight of America: Photography and the Development of U.S. Immigration Policy* (Berkeley: University of California Press, 2009).

9. Pegler-Gordon, *In Sight of America,* 13.

10. See also Elizabeth Cowie's discussion of video and surveillance in her chapter, "The World Viewed: Documentary Observing and the Culture of Surveillance," in *A Companion to Contemporary Documentary Film,* edited by Alexandra Juhasz and Alisa Lebow (Malden, Mass.: John Wiley & Sons, 2015), 580–610.

11. Miko Revereza, "Towards a Stateless Cinema," *Cine Droga,* accessed February 9, 2021, https://cinedroga.com/statement/statement.html.

12. Jordan Cronk, "Interview: Miko Revereza," *Film Comment,* April 18, 2019, https://www.filmcomment.com/blog/interview-miko-revereza/.

13. David S. Chun, "Virtual Reality Can't Take You Home. A Profile of an Undocumented Filipino-American Filmmaker," *The Towner,* June 7, 2016, http://www.thetowner.com/film-making-los-angeles-manila/.

14. Ackbar Abbas, *Hong Kong: Culture and the Politics of Disappearance* (Minneapolis: University of Minnesota Press, 1997).

15. Revereza, "Stateless Cinema."

16. Laura Harris, *Experiments in Exile: C. L. R. James, Hélio Oiticica, and the Aesthetic Sociality of Blackness* (New York: Fordham University Press, 2018), 10.

17. Harris, *Experiments in Exile,* 160.

18. Jesse Días Jr., "Prison and Immigration Industrial Complexes: The Ethnodistillation of People of Color and Immigrants as Economic, Political, and Demographic Threats to U.S. Hegemony," *International Journal of Criminology and Sociology* 1 (2012): 267.

19. See Aaron E. Hunt, "A Moment When I Forgot My Home: A Conversation with Miko Revereza," *The Criterion Collection,* August 3, 2021, https://www.criterion.com/current/posts/7483-a-moment-when-i-forgot-my-home-a-conversation-with-miko-revereza.

168 | NOTES TO CHAPTER 3

20. Revereza, "Stateless Cinema."

21. Howie Chen and Alex Ito, "Chen's [Remote] 3. Miko Revereza: Stateless Cinema," *Vimeo,* June 18, 2020, https://vimeo.com/430534406. Following quotes from this source.

22. Cronk, "Interview: Miko Revereza."

23. Radha Hegde, *Mediating Migration* (Cambridge: Polity, 2016), 34. For a detailed discussion of undocumented media activism see also Sasha Costanza-Chock, *Out of the Shadows, Into the Streets! Transmedia Organizing and the Immigrant Rights Movement* (Cambridge, Mass.: MIT Press, 2014).

24. See also Claudia A. Anguiano and Karma R. Chávez, "DREAMers' Discourse: Young Latino/a Immigrants and the Naturalization of the American Dream," in *Latina/o Discourse in Vernacular Spaces: Somos de una Voz?* ed. Michelle A. Holling and Bernadette M. Calafell (Lanham, Md.: Lexington Books, 2011), 81–99; Tracy Lachica Buenavista and Jordan Beltran Gonzales, "DREAMs Deferred: Filipino Experiences and an Anti-Militarization Critique of the Development, Relief, and Education for Alien Minors Act," *Harvard Journal of Asian American Policy Review* 21 (2010–2011): 29–37; and Kevin Escudero, *Organizing While Undocumented: Immigrant Youth's Political Activism under the Law* (New York: New York University Press, 2020).

25. Rebecca M. Schreiber, *The Undocumented Everyday: Migrant Lives and the Politics of Visibility* (Minneapolis: University of Minnesota Press, 2018), 3.

26. Hegde, *Mediating Migration,* 34.

27. Jose Antonio Vargas, "My Life as an Undocumented Immigrant," *New York Times Magazine,* June 22, 2011, https://www.nytimes.com/2011/06/26/magazine/my-life-as-an-undocumented-immigrant.html.

28. Revereza, "Personal Statement."

29. His description bears a striking resonance with Mel Chen's description of the rendering of Asian Americans as a "sleeping race." See Mel Y. Chen, "Agitation," *South Atlantic Quarterly* 117, no. 3 (2018): 559.

30. Patricia Aufderheide, *Documentary Film: A Very Short Introduction* (New York: Oxford University Press, 2007), 2. See also Elizabeth Cowie, *Recording Reality, Desiring the Real* (Minneapolis: University of Minnesota Press, 2011).

31. Pooja Rangan, *Immediations: The Humanitarian Impulse in Documentary* (Durham, N.C.: Duke University Press, 2017), 4.

32. Alexandra Juhasz and Alisa Lebow, "Beyond Story: An Online, Community-Based Manifesto," *World Records,* Ways of Organizing, 2, article 3 (March 2022), https://worldrecordsjournal.org/category/volume-2/.

33. Juhasz and Lebow, "Beyond Story."

34. Jane Greenway Carr observes that "Historically, documents become the component parts of archives, the collections of material preserved by governments and institutions to tell the stories those in power wish to record. To 'document' is to teach, but it is also to participate in the exchange

of power and subversion inherent in identifying as an individual, a member of a group, a citizen." Jane Greenway Carr, "Documentary and Documentation," *Brooklyn Quarterly,* issue 5, June 11, 2015, http://brooklynquarterly.org/documentary-and-documentation.

35. Ursula Grisham, "Miko Revereza," *Filmatique,* February 5, 2019, https://blog.filmatique.com/all/miko-revereza.

36. Livia Luan, "Profiting from Enforcement: The Role of Private Prisons in U.S. Immigration Detention," *Migration Policy Institute,* May 2, 2018, https://www.migrationpolicy.org/article/profiting-enforcement-role-private-prisons-us-immigration-detention.

37. American Immigration Council, "The Cost of Immigration Enforcement and Border Security," January 20, 2021, https://bit.ly/3f9XIfo.

38. For deportation numbers see Department of Homeland Security, "Table 39. Aliens Removed or Returned: Fiscal Years 1892 to 2019," Yearbook 2019, October 28, 2020, https://www.dhs.gov/immigration-statistics/yearbook/2019/table39; "Table 33. Aliens Apprehended: Fiscal Years 1925 to 2019," October 28, 2020, https://www.dhs.gov/immigration-statistics/yearbook/2019/table33; and Muzaffar Chishti, Sarah Pierce, and Jessica Bolter, "The Obama Record on Deportations: Deporter in Chief or Not?" Migration Policy Institute, January 26, 2017, https://www.migrationpolicy.org/article/obama-record-deportations-deporter-chief-or-not.

39. Revereza, "Stateless Cinema."

40. Días, "Prison and Immigration Industrial Complexes," 266. See also Ronak K. Kapadia, *Insurgent Aesthetics: Security and the Queer Life of the Forever War* (Durham, N.C.: Duke University Press, 2019).

41. Erika Lee, *At America's Gates: Chinese Immigration During the Exclusion Era, 1882–1943* (Chapel Hill: University of North Carolina Press, 2003).

42. Pegler-Gordon, *In Sight of America,* 7.

43. Esther Yoona Cho, "A Double Bind—'Model Minority' and 'Illegal Alien,'" *Asian American Law Journal* 24 (2017): 124f. See also Mae M. Ngai, *Impossible Subjects: Illegal Aliens and the Making of Modern America* (Princeton, N.J.: Princeton University Press, 2004). Historian Isabela Seong Leong Quintana has noted the difficulty in establishing an official start date for what is broadly known as the U.S. era of Chinese exclusion, and/or Asian exclusion during this nineteenth-century moment. Isabela Seong Leong Quintana, "Urban Borderlands: Neighborhood and Nation in Chinese and Mexican Los Angeles, 1870s-1930s," manuscript in preparation.

44. Pegler-Gordon, *In Sight of America,* 24.

45. See Mae M. Ngai's "From Colonial Subject to Undesirable Alien: Filipino Migration in the Invisible Empire," *Impossible Subjects: Illegal Aliens and the Making of Modern America* (Princeton, N.J.: Princeton University Press, 2004), 96–126. During World War II, recruited Filipino soldiers were yet again promised U.S. citizenship, which they often received without any recognition

and veteran benefits, however. See Buenavista and Gonzales, "DREAMs Deterred."

46. Cho, "A Double Bind," 125, emphasis added.

47. Revereza, "Stateless Cinema."

48. Revereza, "Stateless Cinema."

49. Miko Revereza, "Distancing," *Cine Droga,* https://cinedroga.com/distancing/distancing.html.

50. Hilderbrand, *Inherent Vice,* 6.

51. See, "Dis-integration," 23.

52. See, "Dis-integration," 22.

53. Revereza, "Stateless Cinema."

54. Fred Moten, *Stolen Life* (Durham, N.C.: Duke University Press, 2018), 131.

55. Tina Campt, *Image Matters: Archive, Photography, and the African Diaspora in Europe* (Durham, N.C.: Duke University Press, 2012), 87.

56. Cronk, "Interview: Miko Revereza."

57. Grisham, "Miko Revereza."

58. Revereza, "Stateless Cinema."

59. Shannon Mattern, "All Eyes on the Border," *Places Journal,* September 2018, https://placesjournal.org/article/all-eyes-on-the-border.

60. Huang, *Surface Relations,* 156.

61. Huang, *Surface Relations,* 157.

62. Huang, *Surface Relations, 160f.*

63. Cronk, "Interview: Miko Revereza."

64. Hiʻilei Julia Kawehipuaakahaopulani Hobart and Tamara Kneese, "Radical Care: Survival Strategies for Uncertain Times," *Social Text* 38, no. 1 (2020): 2, emphasis added.

65. Gayatri Gopinath, *Unruly Visions: The Aesthetic Practices of Queer Diaspora* (Durham, N.C., Duke University Press, 2018), 6.

66. See Jan Padios, "Exceptionalism as a Way of Life: U.S. Empire, Filipino Subjectivity, and the Global Call Center Industry," in *Ethnographies of U.S. Empire,* ed. Carole McGranahan and John F. Collins (Durham, N.C.: Duke University Press, 2018), 149–69.

67. See Roxanne Dunbar-Ortiz, *An Indigenous Peoples' History of the United States* (Boston: Beacon, 2014); Jeffrey S. Smith, "North America's Colonial European Roots, 1492 to 1867," in *North American Odyssey: Historical Geographies for the Twenty-first Century,* ed. C. Colten and G. Buckley, 27–48 (Lanham, Md.: Rowman & Littlefield, 2014).

68. Janne Lahti, *The American West and the World: Transnational and Comparative Perspectives* (New York: Routledge, 2019), 142.

69. See Gordon Chang and Shelley Fishkin, eds., *The Chinese and the Iron Road: Building the Transcontinental Railroad* (Stanford, Calif.: Stanford University Press, 2019); Manu Karuka, *Empire's Tracks: Indigenous Nations,*

Chinese Workers, and the Transcontinental Railroad (Oakland: University of California Press, 2019). For some insightful reads on coolie economies see also Lisa Lowe, *The Intimacies of Four Continents* (Durham, N.C.: Duke University Press, 2015); Lisa Yun, *The Coolie Speaks: Chinese Indentured Laborers and African Slaves in Cuba* (Philadelphia: Temple University Press, 2008); Moon-Ho Jung, *Coolies and Cane: Race, Labor, and Sugar in the Age of Emancipation* (Baltimore, Md.: Johns Hopkins University Press, 2006).

70. Manu Karuka, "Chinese Workers and the Transcontinental Railroad," *Boom California,* April 6, 2020, https://boomcalifornia.com/2020/04/06/chinese-workers-and-the-transcontinental-railroad/?fbclid=IwAR3edPCm HzRMaRY7L2MhFvxXChm31ZgeiMgYHOZch7eQ8g5krFUja703mwU. For an extended version, see Karuka, *Empire's Tracks.*

71. Iyko Day, "Settler Colonialism in Asian North American Representation," *Oxford Research Encyclopedia of Literature,* September 28, 2018, https://doi.org/10.1093/acrefore/9780190201098.013.795. See also Dean Itsuji Saranillio, *Unsustainable Empire: Alternative Histories of Hawai'i Statehood* (Durham, N.C.: Duke University Press, 2018).

72. Kim Tallbear, "Caretaking Relations, Not American Dreaming," *Kalfou: A Journal of Comparative and Relational Ethnic Studies* 6, no. 1 (2019): 24–41. Tallbear further writes, "While the foundation of Indigenous elimination is one of white supremacy, it is not only white people in power who work to eliminate or erase Indigenous peoples. Dreaming, even in inclusive and multicultural tones, of developing an ideal settler state implicitly supports the elimination of Indigenous peoples from this place." (24) See also Jodi Byrd's discussion of the term "arrivants . . . to signify those people forced into the Americas through the violence of European and Anglo-American colonialism and imperialism," including their descendants. Jodi Byrd, *Transit of Empire* (Durham, N.C.: Duke University Press, 2011), xix.

73. Tallbear, "Caretaking Relations," 36.

74. I find deep resonance here with Dean Itsuji Saranillio's critique of Asian settler colonialism and his related call "to situate these different histories in complex unity—not flattening difference and assuming they are always in solidarity or falling into the pitfalls of difference and framing these groups as always in opposition." Dean Itsuji Saranillio, "Why Asian Settler Colonialism Matters: A Thought Piece on Critiques, Debates, and Indigenous Difference," *Settler Colonial Studies* 3, no. 3–4 (2013): 282.

75. Tallbear, "Caretaking Relations," 25.

76. Cronk, "Interview: Miko Revereza."

77. Grisham, "Miko Revereza."

78. See Ruth Wilson Gilmore, *Golden Gulag: Prisons, Surplus, Crisis, and Opposition in Globalizing California* (Los Angeles: University of California Press, 2007).

79. Revereza, "Stateless Cinema."

172 | NOTES TO CHAPTER 4

4. Migrant Erotics

1. "Foreign Workers in Productive Industries and Social Welfare by Nationality," 公務統計報表程式, accessed July 4, 2022. https://statdb.mol.gov.tw/html/mon/c12030.htm.

2. See Hsiao-Chuan Hsia, "Foreign Brides, Multiple Citizenship and the Immigrant Movement in Taiwan," *Asian and Pacific Migration Journal* 18, no. 1 (2009): 17–46; Yen-Fen Tseng and Yukiko Komiya, "Classism in Immigration Control and Migrant Immigration," in *Politics of Difference in Taiwan,* ed. Tak-wing Ngo and Hong-zen Wang (Abingdon, U.K.: Routledge, 2011), 98–115.

3. For analyses of the visual economies in protest cultures, see Kathrin Fahlenbrach, Martin Klimke, and Joachim Scharloth, eds., *Protest Cultures. A Companion. Vol. 1* (New York: Berghahn, 2016); Kathrin Fahlenbrach, Erling Sivertsen, and Rolf Werenskjold, eds., *Media and Revolt. Strategies and Performances from the 1960s to the Present* (New York: Berghahn, 2014); and Nicole Doerr, Alice Mattoni, Simon Teune, eds., *Advances in the Visual Analysis of Social Movements* (Bingley, U.K.: Emerald, 2013).

4. Cf. Henry Jenkins, *Convergence Culture: Where Old and New Media Collide* (New York: New York University Press, 2008), and Henry Jenkins, Sam Ford, and Joshua Green, *Spreadable Media: Creating Value and Meaning in a Networked Culture* (New York: New York University Press, 2013).

5. I found the following writings also helpful to grapple with the global and local implications of specific identity terms: Antonia Chao, "Global Metaphors and Local Strategies in the Construction of Taiwan's Lesbian Identities," *Culture, Health & Sexuality: An International Journal for Research, Intervention and Care* 2, no. 4 (2000); Fran Martin, *Backward Glances: Contemporary Chinese Cultures and the Female Homoerotic Imaginary* (Durham, N.C.: Duke University Press, 2010); Susan Stryker and Aren Z. Aizura, "Introduction. Transgender Studies 2.0," in *The Transgender Studies Reader 2,* ed. Susan Stryker and Aren Z. Aizura (New York: Routledge, 2014), 1–12; Robert Diaz, Marissa Largo, and Fritz Pino, "Introduction: The 'Stuff' of Queer Horizons and Other Utopic Pursuits," in *Diasporic Intimacies: Queer Filipinos and Canadian Imaginaries,* ed. Robert Diaz, Marissa Largo, Fritz Pino (Evanston, Ill.: Northwestern University Press, 2018), xv–xxxvi; and Kevin Nadal's helpful Twitter breakdown of various identity labels around the Philippine diaspora, including Filipinx/a/o in Kevin Nadal (@kevinnadal), "#DearFilipinoAmericans Since FB & IG are down, let's have a conversation on Twitter. Many people have asked me if we should start using #Filipinx. I've shared my answer privately, but maybe we should talk about it publicly. Here's a thread of some initial thoughts. 1/17," Twitter, July 3, 2019, 12:34 p.m., https://twitter.com/kevinnadal/status/1146502369712254976.

6. See Gunter Schubert, "Das politische System Taiwans," in *Einführung in die politischen Systeme Ostasiens: VR China, Hongkong, Japan, Nordkorea, Südkorea, Taiwan,* ed. Claudia Derichs and Thomas Heberer (Opladen, Germany:

NOTES TO CHAPTER 4 | 173

Leske + Budrich, 2003); and Jieh-min Wu, "Taiwan after the Colonial Century. Bringing China into the Foreground," in *Comparatizing Taiwan*, ed. Shu-mei Shih and Ping-hui Liao (London: Routledge, 2015), 278–94.

7. The state recognizes sixteen Indigenous nationalities or nations that make up 2 percent of Taiwan's total population, i.e., 570,000. "Residence of Indigenous Peoples," Council of Indigenous Peoples, May 29, 2019. https://www.cip.gov.tw/en/news/data-list/200161A7D09A7FEC/2D9680BFE CBE80B6BB8A9BE96F98F55E-info.html.

8. Petrus Liu, *Queer Marxism in Two Chinas* (Durham, N.C.: Duke University Press, 2015), 158. See also Funie Hsu, Brian Hioe, and Wen Liu, "Collective Statement on Taiwan Independence: Building Global Solidarity and Rejecting U.S. Military Empire," *American Quarterly* 69, no. 3 (2017): 465–68.

9. Mark T. Berger, *The Battle for Asia: From Decolonization to Globalization* (London: Routledge, 2004), 228.

10. Sarah B. Snyder, "Human Rights and the Cold War," in *The Routledge Handbook of the Cold War*, ed. Craig Daigle and Artemy M. Kalinovsky (New York: Routledge, 2014), 237–48.

11. Amie Elizabeth Parry, "Exemplary Affect: Corruption and Transparency in Popular Cultures," *Wenshan Review of Literature and Culture* 9, no. 2 (2016): 46.

12. Kuan-hsing Chen, "The Imperialist Eye: The Cultural Imaginary of a Subempire and a Nation-State," *positions: asia critique* 8, no. 1 (2000): 60. See also Yun-han Chu and Pei-shan Lee, "Globalization and Economic Governance in Taiwan," in *Growth and Governance in Asia*, ed. Yoichiro Sato (Honolulu: Asia-Pacific Center for Security Studies, 2004), 49–58. Jin-kyung Lee offers a related discussion in the context of South Korea's almost concurrently unfolding subimperialism in Southeast Asia. Jin-kyung Lee, *Service Economies: Militarism, Sex Work, and Migrant Labor in South Korea* (Minneapolis: University of Minnesota Press, 2010).

13. See Inderpal Grewal, *Transnational America: Feminisms, Diasporas, Neoliberalisms* (Durham, N.C.: Duke University Press, 2005); Josephine Ho, "Is Global Governance Bad for East Asian Queers?" *GLQ: A Journal of Lesbian and Gay Studies* 14, no. 4 (2008): 457–79 and "Queer Existence under Global Governance: A Taiwan Exemplar," *positions: asia critique* 18, no. 2 (2010): 537–54; and Snyder, "Human Rights and The Cold War."

14. This labor emigration system has become a major foothold in the Philippine economy. Built on a U.S. colonial model of targeted skill training, it has also made available a large migrant labor force for low-pay service sectors worldwide. See Robyn Magalit Rodriguez, "Toward a Critical Filipino Studies Approach to Philippine Migration," in *Filipino Studies: Palimpsests of Nation and Diaspora*, ed. Martin F. Manalansan and Augusto F. Espiritu (New York: New York University Press, 2016), 33–55. As of 2020, an estimated 2.2 million Filipino citizens work legally abroad. See Philippine Statistics Authority,

174 | NOTES TO CHAPTER 4

"Total Number of OFWs Estimated at 2.2 Million," June 4, 2020, https://psa .gov.ph/statistics/survey/labor-and-employment/survey-overseas-filipinos.

15. See Rhacel Salazar Parreñas, *Servants of Globalization: Migration and Domestic Work* (Stanford, Calif.: Stanford University Press, 2015) and *The Force of Domesticity: Filipina Migrants and Globalization* (New York: New York University Press, 2008); and Pei-Chia Lan, *Global Cinderellas: Migrant Domestics and Newly Rich Employers in Taiwan* (Durham, N.C.: Duke University Press, 2006).

16. Jane M. Gaines, "Documentary Radicality," *Canadian Journal of Film Studies* 16, no. 1 (2007): 19.

17. See also Howard Chiang and Alvin K. Wong, "Queering the Transnational Turn: Regionalism and Queer Asias," *Gender, Place & Culture* 23, no. 11 (2016): 1643–56; and Audrey Yue, "Trans-Singapore: Some Notes towards Queer Asia as Method," *Inter-Asia Cultural Studies* 18, no. 1 (2017): 10–24.

18. *Rainbow Popcorn* was entirely financed with private funds, including donations from friends and a grant from the Lipman-Miliband Trust, a British charity supporting social justice projects.

19. *Lesbian Factory*'s voice-over speaks in Mandarin, and the worker interviews are in English. Quotes are taken from English dialogue or English subtitles.

20. To highlight another instance of migrant and queer video proximity: *Hospital Wing 8 East*'s director Huang Hui-chen made the award-winning *Small Talk* (2016), a documentary about her long-term closeted lesbian mother.

21. Kuei-fen Chiu and Yingjin Zhang, *New Chinese-Language Documentaries: Ethics, Subject and Place* (Oxon, U.K.: Routledge, 2015), 43.

22. See Jun Okada, *Making Asian American Film and Video: History, Institutions, Movements* (New Brunswick, N.J.: Rutgers University Press, 2015), which I discuss in chapter 2.

23. Cited from Article 11 of the Public Television Act in Taiwan. The Article further elaborates the following mission of public service broadcasting, "1. Furnish complete information, fairly serve the public, and not serve profit-making objectives 2. Provide the public proper access to PTS, and especially *protect the rights and interests of disadvantaged groups* 3. Offer or sponsor the production and presentation of various folk arts, literature, and arts, in order to promote balanced cultural development 4. Introduce new information and concepts 5. Produce and broadcast programs that safeguard human dignity; meet the fundamental constitutional spirit of freedom, democracy, and rule of law; and maintain diversity, objectivity, fairness, and balance of different ethnic groups." Taiwanese Ministry of Culture, "Public Television Act," *Laws & Regulations Database of The Republic of China,* December 30, 2009, https://law.moj.gov .tw/ENG/LawClass/LawAll.aspx?pcode=P0050025.

24. Taiwanese Ministry of Culture, "Public Television Act."

25. Gary D. Rawnsley and Ming-Yeh Rawnsley, "Public Television and Empowerment in Taiwan," *Public Affairs* 78, no. 1 (2005): 24.

26. See Taiwanese Ministry of Foreign Affairs, "Broadcast Media Report," *Infotaiwan,* May 25, 2013, http://www.taiwan.gov.tw/ct.asp?xItem=105381&ctNode=3563&mp=1. See also Jinna Tay, "Television in Chinese Geo-Linguistic Markets: Deregulation, Reregulation and Market Forces in the Post-Broadcast Era," in *Television Studies After TV: Understanding Television in the Post-Broadcast Era,* ed. Graeme Turner, Jinna Tay (New York: Routledge, 2009), 105–114.

27. "PTS Taiwan: Vision for a Better Future," PTS World Taiwan, accessed July 4, 2022, https://about.pts.org.tw/en/; "An Intro of Taiwan Public Television Service (PTS) 2011," accessed July 4, 2022. https://vimeo.com/26102450. See Chun-wei Daniel Lin, "Against the Grain: The Battle for Public Service Broadcasting in Taiwan," in *Routledge Handbook of Chinese Media,* ed. Gary D. Rawnsley and Ming-yeh T. Rawnsley (London: Routledge, 2015), 281–97; and Ming-Yeh T. Rawnsley and Chien-san Feng, "Anti-Media Monopoly Policies and Further Democratisation in Taiwan," *Journal of Current Chinese Affairs* 3 (2014): 105–28.

28. Conservative politicians and Christian parties in particular make every effort to keep public space "proper"—reminiscent of the attempted banning of foreign workers' leisurely hangout at Central Station—not shying away from raiding gay bars, saunas, and even private parties to screen for "obscenity." See Ho, "Is Global Governance Bad" and Liu, *Queer Marxism.* This has not prevented the government from claiming the Taiwan Pride parade as a major tourist attraction in Taipei and political accomplishment of Taiwan—and thus the state—more broadly. Initially state subsidized, the parade is East Asia's largest LGBTQ event.

29. Roderick A. Ferguson, *The Reorder of Things: The University and Its Pedagogies of Minority Difference* (Minneapolis: University of Minnesota Press, 2012), 214. See also my discussion in chapter 2.

30. See Psyche Cho, "Selected Documentaries from 2010 TIDF Set for Free Screening Tour," *Culture.tw,* June 17, 2011, http://www.culture.tw/index.php?option=com_content&task=view&id=2093&Itemid=235. The film screened primarily at LGBTQ and social justice-themed festivals, including in China, Hong Kong, India, Korea, Canada, Belgium, France, Germany, and Sweden. See also Tzu-hui Celina Hung's discussion of what she calls the "new immigrant documentary" in Taiwan: Tzu-hui Celina Hung, "Documenting 'Immigrant Brides' in Multicultural Taiwan," in *Asian Video Cultures: In the Penumbra of the Global,* ed. Joshua Neves and Bhaskar Sarkar (Durham, N.C.: Duke University Press, 2017): 158–76.

31. For Taiwan, see Sylvia Li-chin Lin, "Engendering Victimhood: Women in Literature of Atrocity," *positions* 17, no. 2 (2009): 411–34; Li-hsin Kuo, "Sentimentalism and De-politicization: Some Problems of Documentary Culture in Contemporary Taiwan," *Documentary Box* 25 (2005), http://www.yidff.jp/docbox/25/box25-2-e.html; Hans Tao-Ming Huang, *Queer Politics and Sexual Modernity in Taiwan* (Hong Kong: Hong Kong University Press, 2011); and

176 | NOTES TO CHAPTER 4

Liu, *Queer Marxism*. Similarly, multiple scholars have written on the use of sentimental discourse by the Philippine state, its colonial legacy, and liberal appropriation. Among these scholars are Vicente L. Rafael, *White Love and Other Events in Filipino History* (Durham, N.C.: Duke University Press, 2000); Denise Cruz, *Transpacific Femininities: The Making of the Modern Filipina* (Durham, N.C.: Duke University Press, 2012); and Julius Bautista, "Export-Quality Martyrs: Roman Catholicism and Transnational Labor in the Philippines," *Cultural Anthropology* 30, no. 3 (2015): 424–47. I elaborate in more detail on some of this scholarship below.

32. Elizabeth Cowie, *Recording Reality, Desiring the Real* (Minneapolis: University of Minnesota Press, 2011), 2.

33. Thomas Waugh, *The Right to Play Oneself: Looking Back on Documentary Film* (Minneapolis: University of Minnesota Press, 2011), 1. See also Jane M. Gaines, "The Melos in Marxist Theory," in *Cinema and the Question of Class,* ed. David E. James and Rick Berg (Minneapolis: University of Minnesota Press, 1996), 56–71, and "Documentary Radicality"; Paula Rabinowitz, "Sentimental Contracts: Dreams and Documents of American Labor," in *Feminism and Documentary,* ed. Diane Waldman and Janet Walker (Minneapolis: University of Minnesota Press, 1999), 43–63; Wendy S. Hesford, *Spectacular Rhetorics: Human Rights Visions, Recognitions, Feminisms* (Durham, N.C.: Duke University Press, 2011); Leshu Torchin, *Creating the Witness: Documenting Genocide on Film, Video, and the Internet* (Minneapolis: University of Minnesota Press, 2012); Pooja Rangan, *Immediations: The Humanitarian Impulse in Documentary* (Durham, N.C.: Duke University Press, 2017). For a broader outlining of sentimentality in American cultural politics see Jennifer A. Williamson, "Introduction: American Sentimentalism from the Nineteenth Century to the Present," *From the Sentimental Mode: Essays in Literature, Film and Television,* ed. Jennifer A. Williamson, Jennifer Larson, and Ashley Reed (Jefferson, N.C.: McFarland, 2014), 3–13.

34. Lauren Berlant and Earl McCabe, "Depressive Realism. An Interview with Lauren Berlant," *Hypocrite Reader* issue 5, 2011, https://hypocritereader .com/5/depressive-realism. See also Rey Chow, *Sentimental Fabulations, Contemporary Chinese Films: Attachment in the Age of Global Visibility* (New York: Columbia University Press, 2007), 15.

35. Lauren Berlant, "Love, a Queer Feeling," in *Homosexuality & Psychoanalysis,* ed. Tim Dean and Christopher Lane (Chicago: University of Chicago Press, 2001), 432–51.

36. Neferti Tadiar, *Things Fall Away: Philippine Historical Experience and the Makings of Globalization* (Durham, N.C.: Duke University Press, 2009), 123.

37. Vicente Rafael, " 'Your Grief Is Our Gossip': Overseas Filipinos and Other Spectral Presences," *Public Culture* 9, no. 2 (1997): 276.

38. Elizabeth Freeman, *Time Binds: Queer Temporalities, Queer Histories* (Durham, N.C.: Duke University Press, 2010), 3.

39. Freeman, *Time Binds,* 3.

40. Arlie Russell Hochschild, "Love and Gold," in *Global Woman: Nannies, Maids, and Sex Workers in the New Economy,* ed. Barbara Ehrenreich and Arlie Russell Hochschild (New York: Metropolitan Books, 2004), 26.

41. Yu-Fang Cho, "Nuclear Diffusion: Notes toward Reimagining Reproductive Justice in a Militarized Asia Pacific," *Amerasia Journal* 41, no. 3 (2015): 13.

42. Freeman, *Time Binds,* 3.

43. Freeman, *Time Binds,* 3.

44. Freeman, *Time Binds,* 4.

45. Freeman, *Time Binds,* 3.

46. Amie Elizabeth Parry, "Inter-Asian Migratory Roads: The Gamble of Time in Our Stories," *Inter-Asia Cultural Studies* 13, no. 2 (2012): 176–88. Bliss Lim shared with me that the theme of conditional romance abroad is a popular trope in OFW melodrama, too.

47. On documentary reflexivity see for example Bill Nichols, *Introduction to Documentary* (Bloomington: Indiana University Press, 2001), 128.

48. Freeman, *Time Binds,* 3.

49. A further topic to explore is the role of religion and, specifically, the Catholic church in the Filipinas' (self-)representation. Both films show the protagonists attending mass and reflecting on their position as loyal Catholics and desiring lesbians, which they see as neither mutually exclusive nor contradicting.

50. Neferti Tadiar, "Decolonization, 'Race,' and Remaindered Life under Empire," *Qui Parle* 23, no. 2 (2015): 152.

51. Rabinowitz, "Sentimental Contracts," 844.

52. Rabinowitz, "Sentimental Contracts," 838.

53. Rangan, *Immediations,* 6.

54. Ho, "Is Global Governance Bad" and "Queer Existence"; Jen-peng Liu and Naifei Ding, "Reticent Poetics, Queer Politics," *Inter-Asia Cultural Studies* 6, no. 1 (2005): 30–55; Huang, *Queer Politics*; Liu, *Queer Marxism.* Tsung-yi Michelle Huang and Chi-she Li target specifically the sentimental representation of migrant women in Taiwan's broadcasting. "Like a Family, but Not Quite. Emotional Labor and Cinematic Politics of Intimacy," in *The Global and the Intimate: Feminism in Our Times,* ed. Geraldine Pratt and Victoria Rosner (New York: Columbia University Press, 2010), 211–31.

5. *Me llamo Peng*

1. Me llamo Peng (film blog), "Me Llamo Peng: Equipo/Team," accessed July 3, 2022, http://mellamopeng.blogspot.com/p/equipo.html; "Jahel Guerra: Photography Artist," accessed July 3, 2022, https://www.jahel-guerra .com.

2. Ann Cvetkovich, *Depression: A Public Feeling* (Durham, N.C.: Duke University Press, 2012), 21.

3. Victoria Molina de Carranza, "La cámara amiga." *Alegría, Que son dos*

178 | NOTES TO CHAPTER 5

días (blog), May 21, 2012, http://alegriaquesondosdias.blogspot.com/2012/05/la-camara-amiga.html.

4. Sasha Costanza-Chock, *Out of the Shadows, Into the Streets! Transmedia Organizing and the Immigrant Rights Movement* (Cambridge, Mass.: MIT Press, 2014), 187.

5. "Behind Peng," press kit, n.d.

6. The directors' backgrounds also speak to various forms of migration. Guerra left her home country, Venezuela, in 2002 at the height of the country's political crisis. She moved to the United States to study, then to France, and eventually to Spain. Perhaps unsurprisingly, identity and mobility have been central to her artwork. Molina de Carranza spent time abroad in the Netherlands and Taiwan to study.

7. Email to the author, August 5, 2020.

8. "Behind Peng."

9. "Behind Peng."

10. "Me Llamo Peng: Conociendo a Peng," *Me llamo Peng* (film blog), accessed July 3, 2022, http://mellamopeng.blogspot.com/p/personaje.html. The film's opening captions offer a slightly different timeline: "Peng Ruan arrived in Europe in 2002 and started filming everything. In total, he shot 60 hours of footage, showing his life over a period of six years."

11. Rosalind Gill and Andy Pratt, "In the Social Factory?: Immaterial Labour, Precariousness and Cultural Work," *Theory, Culture & Society* 25, no. 7–8 (2008): 19.

12. Winnie Wong, *Van Gogh on Demand: China and the Readymade* (Chicago: University of Chicago Press, 2014), 45. Wong revises how discourses on creativity and individuality have historically centered on Western subjects and foreclosed Chinese subjects from the claim of original creation—as she calls it, "the historical legacies of the Chinese copyist and the Western originalist" (43). Eng, Ruskola, and Shen similarly maintain that "whether in the form of political rights and citizenship, capitalism and the free market, or individual reason and subjectivity . . . China has played a central role as Europe's civilizational other." David L. Eng, Teemu Ruskola, and Shuang Shen, "Introduction: China and the Human," *Social Text* 29, no. 4 (2011): 4.

13. Lauren Berlant, *Cruel Optimism* (Durham, N.C.: Duke University Press, 2011), 1, emphasis added. There is a close relation between Berlant's cruel optimism and discourses on the self-entrepreneurial subject as helpfully discussed in Pheng Cheah, "Capitalizing Humanity: The Global Disposition of People and Things," in *Accumulating Insecurity: Violence and Dispossession in the Making of Everyday Life,* ed. Shelley Feldman, Charles Geisler, and Gayatri A. Menon (Athens: University of Georgia Press, 2011), 298–318. Berlant is particularly helpful in her focus on affect and self-management.

14. "Cifras de Población (CP) a 1 de julio de 2020. Estadística de Migraciones (EM). Primer semestre de 2020." Instituto Nacional de Estadística, January 28, 2021, https://www.ine.es/prensa/cp_j2020_p.pdf.; Gladys Nieto

writes: "Following Spain's economic boom in the 1980s, the demand for household services (including for middle-income households) and care providers for the elderly rose sharply. It is here, together with agriculture and construction, all characterized by low wages, insecurity, and poor working conditions, where non-EU migrants can be found." Gladys Nieto, "The Chinese in Spain," *International Migration* 41, no. 3 (2003): 219. See also Minghuan Li, "New Chinese Immigrants in Spain: The Migration Process, Demographic Characteristics and Adaptation Strategies," in *Contemporary Chinese Diasporas,* ed. Min Zhou (Singapore: Springer/Palgrave Macmillan, 2017), 285–307. For a different portrayal of a rising generation of successful Chinese Spanish entrepreneurs see Luis Gómez, "The New Chinese," *El País,* August 27, 2012, http://elpais.com/elpais/2012/08/27/inenglish/1346069596_299391.html.

15. Wayne A. Cornelius. "Spain: The Uneasy Transition from Labor Exporter to Labor Importer," in *Controlling Immigration: A Global Perspective.* 2nd ed., ed. Wayne A. Cornelius, Takeyuki Tsuda, Philip L. Martin, and James F. Hollifield (Stanford, Calif: Stanford University Press, 2004), 398.

16. Cornelius, "Spain," 399.

17. Kate Hooper, *Spain's Labour Migration Policies in the Aftermath of Economic Crisis* (Brussels: Migration Policy Institute Europe, 2019), 1, https://www.migrationpolicy.org/sites/default/files/publications/MPIE-Spain MigrationPathways-Final.pdf. Chinese Spanish middle-class entrepreneurs became known for thriving through the long-lasting recession, attracting both public praise and resentment as exemplary workers. The media reasoned such exemplary success was a result of Chinese "thriftiness and a capacity for hard work," promoting quotes like the following from the community itself: "In China, we believe that the key issue is not whether you lose money or not, but whether you manage to hold on. So the Chinese have developed a great ability to withstand a crisis. You have to endure." Tobias Buck, "China's Migrants Thrive in Spain's Financial Crisis," *Financial Times,* October 9, 2014, https://www.ft.com/content/f8d02554-3e93-11e4-a620-00144feabdc0. See also Dan Bilefski, "Spain's Chinese Immigrants Thrive in Tough Economy," *New York Times,* January 5, 2013, https://www.nytimes.com/2013/01/03/world/europe/spains-chinese-immigrants-thrive-in-tough-economy.html. *Me llamo Peng* likewise features the image of Asian exemplarity, which is to say, the ability to withstand and endure. As most of *Me llamo Peng* takes place in Catalonia, it would be interesting to think further about Spain's border and immigration politics in relation to Catalonia's striving for independence. See, for instance, Gunther Dietz and Belén Agrela, "Commentary," in *Controlling Immigration: A Global Perspective,* ed. Wayne A. Cornelius, Takeyuki Tsuda, Philip L. Martin, and James F. Hollifield (Stanford, Calif.: Stanford University Press, 2004).

18. Lisa Marie Cacho, *Social Death: Racialized Rightlessness and the Criminalization of the Unprotected* (New York: New York University Press, 2012), 6.

19. Helen Meekosha, "Decolonising Disability: Thinking and Acting Globally," *Disability & Society* 26, no. 6 (2011): 668.

180 | NOTES TO CHAPTER 5

20. Peng's disposable body resembles what Grace Hong describes as a neoliberal rendering of certain populations as "existentially surplus," as "not necessary to capital as potential sources of labor, but instead [as] useful for their intrinsic lack of value." Grace Kyungwon Hong, "Existentially Surplus: Women of Color Feminism and the New Crises of Capitalism," *GLQ: A Journal of Lesbian and Gay Studies* 18, no. 1 (2011): 92. Peng's labor continues to be demanded, however, exemplifying the simultaneity of varying modes of value extraction under contemporary capitalism.

21. While the subtitles read "But there is nothing wrong. I don't think it's contagious," Peng's Chinese may also be translated into the rhetorical question "There shouldn't be any danger of contagion, should there?"

22. "Behind Peng."

23. "Behind Peng."

24. Directors' email to the author, August 1, 2020. For a nuanced reading of participatory filmmaking see Angela J. Aguayo, *Documentary Resistance: Social Change and Participatory Media* (New York: Oxford University Press, 2019).

25. Email to the author, August 2, 2020.

26. Sara Ahmed, "Selfcare as Warfare," *feministkilljoys,* August 25, 2014, http://feministkilljoys.com/2014/08/25/selfcare-as-warfare. See also Audre Lorde, "A Burst of Light: Living with Cancer," in *A Burst of Light: Essays by Audre Lorde* (Ithaca, N.Y.: Firebrand Books, 1988).

27. Iyko Day, *Alien Capital: Asian Racialization and the Logic of Settler Colonial Capitalism* (Durham, N.C.: Duke University Press, 2016), 16. Day defines romantic anticapitalism as the liberal fantasy of authentic human agency and an unmediated relation to the material work versus capital's alienation, exploitation, and abstraction, summarized "as an opposition between a concrete natural world and a destructively abstract, value-driven one."

Index

Abstract (2012), 37, 44–45
Ahmed, Sara, 14, 67, 134
AIDS activism, 7
America, "browning of," 75
Andrijasevic, Rutvica, 8
Angst Essen / Eat Fear (2008), 30–35
Arab Germans, 27. *See also* Turkish
Germans
Arvin, Maile, 160n18
Asian American film and video: as
category, 61–62, 108; representa-
tional demands of, 53, 62, 66
Asian American Pacific Islanders, as
category, 51, 58
Asian Americans, as need-free, 54, 57,
63, 66
Asian American women, mental
health statistics on, 48, 56–58
Asian Century, 13, 26, 125, 140n51
Asian exclusion in the United States,
81–82, 93–94, 169n43; of Chinese,
81, 169n43; of Filipinos, 82, 169n45
Asian Germans, 18, 22, 27–30; as
category, 27; celebration of
Vietnamese and Korean student
performance and, 26. *See also*
Germany
"Asian Prussians," 26
Asian racialization, 4–5, 27, 57,
148n38, 150n58; DREAMer
(il)legalization and, 82; as form
of mediation, 4–5, 11; in Germany
(*see* Germany: Asian racialization
in); subimperial economies and,

100–101, 104–5; as understood
in the United States, 58. *See also*
racialization
Asians on Demand: aspirational
subjecthood of, 16; as caretakers, 52, 120; expectations of
biographical accuracy and, 18,
23; as (inter)media(ries), 10–11;
as media(ting) function, 4, 12,
15; neoliberal logic of, 3–4, 6, 11,
13–16; as privileged elites, 13–14; as
representational function ascribed
to Asians and Asianness, 4, 9, 13,
26, 40, 64; representational labor
of, 4, 9, 13, 26, 40, 64; rhetoric of
exemplarity and, 4, 13, 26, 105
Asian women: representational labor
of, 40; sexualization of, 17, 27, 40,
53, 151. *See also* bondage
Asiatische Deutsche. See Asian
Germans
Aufderheide, Patricia, 79
Auntie Sewing Squad, 49–50
Auslander, Philip, 59

Banerjee, Mita, 29
Bao, Weihong, 148n37
Berlant, Lauren, 128, 178n13
Bernards, Brian, 10
bondage, 40–43

Cacho, Lisa Marie, 130
caihong bale (rainbow guava,
彩虹芭樂), 116

182 | INDEX

Campt, Tina, 85
care, 20, 90, 94, 103, 129, 133–34; caretaking relations and, 94; in *No Data Plan,* 90; queer collective, 123; of Taiwanese citizens by Southeast Asian contract workers, 101. *See also* self-care
Chang, Iris, 64
cheer, 52, 63, 65, 68
Chen, Julie Yujie, 9
Chen Kuan-hsing, 10
Chen, Mel Y., 57, 168n29
Chen, Tina, 53–54
Cheng, Anne Anlin, 143n8, 165n75
China, dispute over sovereignty between Taiwan and, 100, 103–4
Chinese Exclusion Act of 1882, 81
Chinese exclusion in the United States. *See* Asian exclusion in the United States
Chinese indentured workers. *See* coolies
Chiu, Kuei-fen, 108
Cho, Michelle, 59
Cho, Yu-Fang, 114
Choi, Sun-ju, 153n13, 155n28
Chow, Rey, 16, 24
Chun, Wendy Hui Kyong, 4
cinematic perception, 5
coolies, 10, 93, 148n38
Costanza-Chock, Sasha, 126, 146n21
cruel optimism, 20, 128, 134
Curtis, Robin, 21
Cvetkovich, Ann, 162n38

DACA (Deferred Action for Childhood Arrivals), 70, 74–75. *See also* DREAMers
Day, Iyko, 11, 94
Demos, T. J., 36
Ding, Naifei, 121, 177
Disintegration (2017), 18, 22, 24–25, 70
Distancing (2019), 16, 19, 69–75, 82, 98
documentary, 36, 79–80, 106, 112;

affect and, 88, 121; ethics, 80; humanitarian, 121; human rights-based, 112; labor, 121; radicality, 106; Miko Revereza on, 80; Taiwanese activist, 103, 108
dorm sex, 115–16
DREAM Act (Development, Relief, and Education for Alien Minors Act), 77, 82
DREAMers, 76–79, 82, 84; Miko Revereza on, 78–79, 84; use of media outlets by, 77; Jose Antonio Vargas on, 78. *See also* Asian racialization: DREAMer (il)legalization and

Elsaesser, Thomas, 36, 40
El-Tayeb, Fatima, 23–24
Eng, David L., 178n12, 165–66n75
Erdem, Esra, 27
essay film, 23, 38, 40–41
estrangement, 15–16, 24
Eurozone crisis of 2008, 130, 133
exclusion. *See* Asian exclusion in the United States

Fassbinder, Rainer Werner, 21–22, 24–25, 31–33; *Ali: Fear Eats the Soul* (1974), 31–33; *The Bitter Tears of Petra von Kant* (1972), 21–25
Fenner, Angelica, 21
Ferguson, Roderick A., 61, 109
Figge, Maja, 155n27
Freeman, Elizabeth, 113, 116
fugitivism, 75, 82, 85

Gastarbeiter. See Germany: guest worker programs of East and West
Gates, Racquel, 157–58n49
Germany, 17–18, 21, 25–27, 29, 31–32, 34–35; anti-Muslim and anti-Turkish racism in, 18, 24, 27, 32; Asian racialization in, 25–29; celebration of Vietnamese German

and Korean German students by, 26; claims of racelessness in, 3, 16, 18, 23–28, 30; ethnic studies, American studies, and Asian German studies in, 29; guest worker programs of East and West, 18, 29; guest worker studies in, 29; Middle Eastern residents in, 28; migrant history of, 28–29; promotions of Asian exemplarity by, 25–28; racialized masculinities in, 34; South and Southeast Asians residents in, 28; South Korean workers in postwar West, 29; Vietnamese migrant workers in postwar East, 29. *See also* Asian Germans

Gitelman, Lisa, 9
Goldberg, David Theo, 23
Gopinath, Gayatri, 91, 151n64
Gregg, Melissa, 9
Guerra Roa, Jahel, 20, 125–28, 132–33, 178n6

Ha, Kien Nghi, 28, 152n2, 153n13, 155n26
Haritaworn, Jin, 152n8, 158n50
Harris, Laura, 75
Hegde, Radha, 76–78
Heidenreich, Nanna, 154n24, 155n30
Hilderbrand, Lucas, 7–8, 70, 83, 145n16
Ho, Josephine, 110, 121, 175n28
Hobart, Hiʻilei Julia Kawehipuaakahaopulani, 170n64
Hong, Grace Kyungwon, 3, 5, 11, 13, 180n20
Horsfield, Kate, 7
Huang, Hans Tao-Ming, 121
Huang, Vivian L., 37, 52, 88, 90

impersonation: *Angst Essen / Eat Fear* and Ming Wong's use of, 33; Asian American, 53–54; Kristina Wong's use of, 19, 53–54
Instagram Stories, 95–97

JIT (Just in Time) production, 9, 147
Juhasz, Alexandra, 7, 79
Jun, Helen Heran, 3, 52

Karuka, Manu, 93–94
Keeling, Kara, 5, 14, 16, 145n15, 151n60
Kember, Sarah, 10
Kim, Jihoon, 36
Kim, Suk-Young, 59
King, Homay, 3, 4, 25, 33, 150n57
Kitanaka, Junko, 161n88
Kneese, Tamara, 90
Krämer, Sybille, 10–12

Lebow, Alisa, 79
Lee, James Kyung-Jin, 58
Lee, Jin-kyung, 10, 173n12
Lee, Rachel, 63
Lerne Deutsch mit Petra von Kant / Learn German with Petra von Kant (2007), 21, 23–25, 152n7, 151n1, 156n35
Lesbian Factory (2010), 19–20, 99–100, 102–3, 105–23, 174n19
Liu, Petrus, 104, 110, 121, 175n28
liveness, 49, 61, 65. *See also* Wong, Kristina: demands for liveness from
Lovely Andrea (2007), 37–46; bondage photography in, 38, 42; circulation of images of women in, 38; essay form in, 40 (*see also* essay film); Kurdish–Turkish conflict in, 43–46
Lye, Colleen, 3

Ma, Ming-Yuen S., 6
mediation, 4, 9–12, 59, 147–48n35. *See also* Asians on Demand: as media(ting) function
Meekosha, Helen, 130
Melamed, Jodi, 14
Mercer, Kobena, 34, 50
messenger, 12, 16, 36

184 | INDEX

Metzl, Jonathan, 57
Michaelsen, Anja Sunhyun, 155n27, 155–56n30
migrant erotics, 20, 115–16, 120
migrant workers: in Dubai, 118; in Germany (*see* Germany: migrant history of); in Spain, 130
migrant workers in Taiwan, 99–101, 105, 108, 110; from Philippines, 101, 105, 113, 118, 122; public opinion about, 101; targeted management of, 105; from Vietnam, 101
Molina de Carranza, Victoria, 125
Moten, Fred, 63–64, 68, 85
Muñoz, José Esteban, 16, 25, 60, 65

neoliberalism, 11, 14–15
Neves, Joshua, 6
New German Cinema, 18, 35
Ngai, Sianne, 57
Nguyen, Hoang Tan, 152n10
No Data Plan (2019), 19, 69–71, 85–98
November (2004), 45

OECD (Organisation for Economic Co-operation and Development), 26
OFT (only for Taiwan), 115–17
OFWs (Overseas Filipino Workers), in Taiwan, 101, 105, 113, 118, 122
Oishi, Eve, 1
Okada, Jun, 61–62, 66–67, 174n22
Ong, Aihwa, 3

Pacific Islanders and Hawaiians, as category. *See* Asian American Pacific Islanders, as category
Parreñas Shimizu, Celine, 37, 40, 47, 54
Parry, Amie Elizabeth, 105, 116
Pegler-Gordon, Anna, 81
photographic state documentation in the United States, 81–82

Phruksachart, Melissa, 13
PISA (Programme for International Student Assessment), 26
poor images, 36–37, 41
PRC (People's Republic of China). *See* China, dispute over sovereignty between Taiwan and
Prussia, 26
PTS (Public Television Service of Taiwan), 106, 108–9
public television network, of Barcelona, 133
Public Television Service (of Taiwan). *See* PTS

queer activism, 109
queer Filipinas. *See* OFT (only for Taiwan)
queer intimate attachments, 116
Quintana, Isabela Seong Leong, 169n43

Rabinowitz, Paula, 121
racelessness, 23–24; European claims of, 23–25, 37; German claims of, 3, 16, 18, 23–28, 30
racialization, 4, 16–17. *See also* Asian racialization
Rafael, Vicente L., 112
Rainbow Popcorn (2012), 19–20, 100, 102–3, 105–6, 116–20, 122–23, 174n18
Rangan, Pooja, 79, 121, 176n33
Rasse, 28
Rassismus, 28
representational demands, of Asian American film and video, 53, 62, 66
representational demands/labor, 9
Revereza, Miko, 69; *Biometrics* (2019), 75; *Disintegration* (2017), 18, 22, 24–25, 70; *Distancing* (2019), 19, 69–75, 82, 98; on docu-

mentation, 69, 80; on DREAMers, 78–79, 84; *No Data Plan* (2019), 19, 69–75, 82, 85–98; "Towards a Stateless Cinema" (2019), 69–70, 74–75, 80, 83–85; and undocumented storytelling (*see* undocument); use of Instagram Story and selfies by, 71, 95–98
ROC (Republic of China). *See* Taiwan
Ruskola, Teemu, 178n12

Santa Ana, Jeffrey, 52
Sarkar, Bhaskar, 6
Schreiber, Rebecca M., 77
See, Sarita Echavez, 70, 83
self-care, 20, 48, 65, 125, 129, 134; Peng's camera as tool of, 20; Kristina Wong and, 55, 65–68
selfies. *See* Revereza, Miko: use of Instagram Story and selfies by
sentimental activism, 20, 101, 103, 105, 112, 120–21
sentimentality, 112, 121
sentimental storytelling, 20, 101, 103, 105, 112, 120–21
settler colonialism, 93–94, 98
Shah, Nishant, 14
Sharma, Preeti, 49, 52
Shen, Shuang, 178n12
Shimakawa, Karen, 63
slow cinema, 19, 86
statelessness, 80, 82–84. *See also* Revereza, Miko: "Towards a Stateless Cinema" (2019)
Steinberg, Marc, 9, 147n29
Steinmann, Catherine A., 23
Steyerl, Hito, 1–2, 15, 17–18, 22; *Abstract* (2012), 37, 44–45; on confessional discourse, 21, 37, 40–41; *Die Leere Mitte* (The empty center, 1998), 35; *November* (2004), 37; *Spricht die Subalterne deutsch?* (Does the subaltern speak German?), 35; *Strike* (2010), 1, 16, 35; *Strike II* (2012), 1–2, 15–16, 35–36
Sturken, Marita, 145n16
Suda, Kimiko, 153n13
Suderburg, Erika, 6

Tadiar, Neferti, 11–12, 113, 120
Taiwan: commitments to multiculturalism by, 19, 108; disinvestment from citizen care by, 105; as exemplary Asian state, 4, 104; public opinion on migrant workers in, 101; public television in (*see* PTS); state feminism of, 121; support for Southeast Asian workers by, 108
Tallbear, Kim, 94, 17n72
Tauqir, Tamsila, 27
Teves, Stephanie Nohelani, 160n18
TIWA (Taiwan International Workers' Association), 19–20, 99
TIWA-organized protest of 2015, 99–102
Tiwary, Ishita, 146n19
Torres, Sasha, 14, 60–61
"Towards a Stateless Cinema" (2019), 74–75, 80, 83–85
T-Po (*t-po gong chang,* T婆工廠), 103
Turkey, 45
Turkish Germans, 18, 24, 26–29

undocument, 74–75, 85
Undocumented (2013), 78
Uyehara, Denise, 59

van Doorn, Niels, 9
Vargas, Jose Antonio, 77–78, 82
Vertragsarbeiter. See Germany: guest worker programs of East and West
video: activism, 7, 121; analog versus digital, 5–6, 77, 109, 144–45n15; art and activist spheres of, 7; on-demand expectations for, 8–9;

186 | INDEX

progressive potential of, 7; user accessibility of, 6–8, 77

will to institutionality, 61, 109
Wong Flew Over the Cuckoo's Nest (2006–2013), 18, 47–48; as concert video (2011/2013), 49, 59, 61. *See also* Wong, Kristina
Wong, Kristina, 47–49, 68; blurring of reality and fiction by, 19, 47, 54–55, 57, 62, 65; California genealogy of, 49; demands of liveness from, 49, 53, 59, 61–62, 64–65, 68; use of cheer by, 52, 63, 65, 68; use of humor by, 47, 52–53, 63
Wong, Lily, 37
Wong, Ming, 30–31; *Angst Essen / Eat Fear* (2008), 30–34; *Angst Essen /*

Eat Fear (2008), impersonation in, 33; exploitations of whiteness by, 153n11; *Lerne Deutsch mit Petra von Kant / Learn German with Petra von Kant* (2007), 21, 23–25, 151n1, 156n35; on top-down multiculturalism, 30–31
Wong, Winnie, 128, 178n12
Wongsurawat, Wasana, 10

Yapp, Hentyle, 151n60
Yoon, Hyoejin, 52
Yue, Genevieve, 37

Zhang, Yingjin, 108
Zhang, Zhen, 7, 146n20
Zuo, Mila, 37
Zylinska, Joanna, 10

Feng-Mei Heberer is assistant professor of cinema studies at New York University.

Milton Keynes UK
Ingram Content Group UK Ltd.
UKHW021206240424
441647UK00010B/346